CASSELL STUDIES IN PASTORAL CARE AND PERSON
AND SOCIAL EDUCATION

CARING FOR CHILDREN

CASSELL STUDIES IN PASTORAL CARE AND PERSONAL
AND SOCIAL EDUCATION

CARING FOR CHILDREN

International Perspectives on Pastoral Care and PSE

Peter Lang, Ron Best and
Anna Lichtenberg (Editors)

CASSELL

Cassell
Villiers House,
41/47 Strand,
London WC2N 5JE

387 Park Avenue South,
New York,
NY 10016–8810

First published 1994

British Library Cataloguing-in-Publication Data
A catalogue record for this book is available from the British Library.

ISBN 0-304-32754-9 (hardback)
     0-304-32752-2 (paperback)

Typeset by Colset Pte Ltd, Singapore

Printed and bound in Great Britain by
Biddles Limited, Guildford and King's Lynn

Contents

Series editors' foreword

In 1988, we were invited to participate in the biennial conference of the Singapore Educational Administration Society, which took as its theme 'The Pupil's Growth – Our Major Concern'. This conference brought together teachers, academics and educational administrators who, within their designated roles in the organization, resourcing and management of educational provision, recognized that, in the final analysis, their work was of little consequence if the needs of the child were not at its centre.

Among those presenting papers on that occasion was Dr Norm Hyde of the (then) Western Australian College of Advanced Education (now Edith Cowan University). It was no accident that, two years later, what we believe was the first international conference on pastoral care in education was held in Perth under the auspices of the International Institute for Policy and Administrative Studies (IIPAS) of that institution. This attracted delegates from Australia, New Zealand and South East Asia, with keynote speakers from Canada and the UK.

Another two years on, we found ourselves among those delivering papers and running workshops at yet another conference 'down under', this time at Bond University in Queensland. Here the chosen theme for the conference was 'Towards Effective Participation in Working Life'.

Throughout this period, we continued to edit *Pastoral Care in Education*, the journal of the National Association for Pastoral Care in Education. We found ourselves receiving a small but growing trickle of articles submitted for publication by teachers and researchers from many countries around the world. Like the Singapore, Perth and Bond conferences, these articles showed a considerable and growing international interest in the role of pastoral care and personal, social and moral education in the development of the whole person. The precise words used to describe this interest were, of course, different from culture to culture. Each country had its own distinctive perspective, but the common theme of concern for children as more than empty buckets to be filled with knowledge was clear enough.

A selection of the papers from the Perth conference presented a ready-made basis for a book which would provide comparative perspectives on pastoral care and affective education. Anna Lichtenberg, a key member of the team that organized the Perth conference, joined us in editing, revising and developing the best of the papers, while we commissioned a number of additional papers from countries that had not been represented.

We do not pretend that this collection represents more than a sample of the many and diverse approaches to personal and social education adopted around the world, but it is not an insignificant sample. In bringing together the work of practitioners, researchers and theoreticians from many countries, we believe it meets a growing demand from teachers and educationalists for opportunities to improve their provision by learning from their colleagues in other places.

We believe this is the first book to adopt a comparative international perspective to this important topic. We are proud to include it in the series.

Ron Best
Peter Lang

PART I

Perspectives

CHAPTER 1

Care and education

The comparative perspective

RON BEST AND PETER LANG

Introduction

Generalizations are always dangerous; generalizations across cultures and national boundaries are particularly so. Even within one nation, subcultural differences between class, status, ethnic and religious groups make categorical statements questionable.

Such cultural diversity is both a blessing and a curse. On the one hand, its connections with problems of social inequality, racial tension, religious bigotry, discrimination and, all too often, violence are obvious, though to attribute such conflict exclusively to cultural diversity is simplistic. More often than not, it is economic structures and processes and the unequal distribution of economic, social and political power between particular social groups, rather than the cultural differences between those groups *per se*, that generate tensions. But given the interpenetration of beliefs, values, lifestyles and economic activity, to see cultural difference as a cause rather than correlative factor is natural enough.

On the other hand, cultural diversity is enriching. It has the potential to open to us an altogether wider range of experiences in all departments of our lives than is true of a monocultural society. We need think only of the vivid aesthetic experiences provided by music, drama and dance from all over the world and the variety added to life in any society by sports imported from elsewhere to see that this is so.

The potential for our intellectual lives also to be enhanced by cross-cultural experience is just as great but, it seems, less easy to accept. In particular, the difficulties of successfully integrating fundamentally different philosophies are considerable. The concepts of 'truth', 'causation' and 'history' which are taken for granted in Western empiricism are difficult to reconcile with those of Eastern mysticism or, for that matter, with the 'dreaming' of the Australian aborigines. This difficulty should not surprise us. Whereas, in regard to (say) sport, taste in fashion or music, we should expect our natural ethnocentrism to be broken down by our growing familiarity with other cultures, in intellectual matters it is not so simple. If the very way we *think* is (apparently) so different, it is not a matter of merely accommodating a new activity. Distancing ourselves from those habits of thought which are second nature to us, and rebuilding our conceptual world on radically different foundations is both an enormous intellectual task and highly threatening to our security.

The relationship between philosophical systems and political ideologies is a significant factor. Part of the reluctance to accommodate to modes of thought which are substantially different from our own is that these modes of thought may entail – or at any rate are associated with – moral imperatives which pose a challenge to our own value systems and thus, inevitably, to social order. The legitimacy of the power and privilege enjoyed by significant members of our social groups is itself brought into question.

The scale of the perceived threat may be recognized in the degree to which a society's education system is open to ideas from other cultures. Under the threat of cultural imperialism, where the fundamental values validating economic arrangements are being questioned, central control of the curriculum is predictable. Curricula will be strongly 'framed' (Bernstein, 1971), and established religious beliefs, moral values, ethnocentric histories and the explicit promotion of patriotism and loyalty to existing systems will be features of the prescribed content. While it is easy to read these signs in *other* societies, especially those which are our traditional enemies, we need to see them as a natural consequence of the political function of the education system in any society (Musgrave, 1965).

Widening horizons

It is now something of a cliché that we live in a 'global village'. We can no longer sensibly consider societies as isolated entities, untouched by their neighbours. With multinational corporations, worldwide mass media and instantaneous communications possible around the globe, it is arguable that we are *all* neighbours. We need to recognize our mutual economic and ecological dependence and, therefore, interdependence.

Interdependence entails both common understandings and functional differentiation: a shared destiny may mean the recognition of individual differences within a common commitment to such fundamantal values as the sanctity of human life and the stewardship of the environment. Within this scheme of things, peoples need to be willing to share their ideas, to respect differences, and to learn from one another.

The value of comparative and international studies in education has recently been restated. Crossley and Broadfoot (1992, p. 106) identify four purposes for such studies: first, that in studying the systems of other countries we shall better understand our own; second, to assist 'in the solution of identified problems and/or in the future development of educational policy and practice'; third, 'to better understand the nature of the relationships between education and the broader social, political and economic sectors of society'; fourth, to promote 'improved international understanding, co-operation and goodwill'.

It is a basic premise of this book that the study of the commonalities and the differences between the way education is perceived, defined and given substance in institutions and practice in different cultures is important for promoting the appreciation of both cultural difference and common destiny. Moreover, an understanding of how other systems and other cultures address similar problems can enrich the approach used in any particular system. To look outwards for ideas and inspiration is as important as the consolidation of past achievements. This is particularly so in regard to personal and social education, for to grow as a person capable of participating effectively in a particular social environment, where that environment is daily more global and less insular, requires an unprecedented openness of mind and heart.

Holistic education

One generalization at least is permissible: that education is concerned with something more than the purely cognitive. The fact that for many citizens in many societies 'education' is identified exclusively with 'what you learn at school', and that what you learn at school is often seen as restricted to a body of knowledge to be memorized and reproduced as required in examinations, does not alter this fact. As the radical critics of the 1960s and 1970s pointed out, education may be identified with schooling, but that does not make it the same thing (Bowles and Gintis, 1976; Illich, 1973).

Any reasonable analysis of the concept of education, and, indeed, any sustained study of systems of schooling in diverse cultures, will quickly show that education is concerned with the affective, the moral and the political as much as with the cognitive. Our attitudes to our country, our fellow humans, our selves, our future lives and so on are integral to what we learn at school, whether this is part of an explicit, overt curriculum or part of the 'hidden curriculum' manifest in the structures, relationships and routines of the institution.

Moreover, the premise that education is an essential aspect of our preparation for future life raises issues which go far beyond merely learning in the conventional sense. Our attention is focused upon promoting propensities for certain kinds of behaviour – the attitudes and inclinations appropriate to the 'world of work' – and on the personal and social skills necessary to cope with the demands of any vocation. Nowadays our thoughts must turn more frequently to the capacity of the individual to cope *without* work. An important aspect of education is the idea that it should be equipping the individual to negotiate a path through life, whether or not full-time paid employment lies along that path. What is being articulated here is an altogether broader aim for education than that of the transmission of culture or the acquisition of knowledge.

Such holistic notions of personal growth and social development are underpinned by a commitment to some concept of the welfare or well-being of the individual as a person, as something more than 'an empty bucket to be filled with knowledge' (Haigh, 1975). Such a concept was as central to the doctrines of the 'great educators' – Locke, Rousseau, Dewey, Pestalozzi, Montessori, Froebel – as it was to the radical critics of the 1960s and 1970s: Illich, Goodman, Freire, John Holt, Postman and Weingartner and so on. For those educationalists of the 1970s and 1980s whose concern has been explicitly with counselling (e.g. Rogers, 1983), pastoral care (e.g. Marland, 1974; Hamblin, 1978; McGuiness, 1982) or personal and social education (e.g. Pring, 1984; Lang, 1988), education and the growth of the 'whole person' are synonymous.

In Britain this broad commitment to the all-round well-being of the child is most often described as 'pastoral care'. This concept received one of its most comprehensive definitions in a report (DES, 1989, p. 3) by Her Majesty's Inspectorate:

> In detail, pastoral care is concerned with promoting pupils' personal and social development and fostering positive attitudes: through the quality of teaching and learning; through the nature of relationships amongst pupils, teachers and adults other than teachers; through arrangements for monitoring pupils' overall progress, academic, personal and social; through specific pastoral structures and support systems; and through extracurricular activities and the school ethos. Pastoral care, accordingly, should help a school to articulate its values, involve all teachers and help pupils to achieve success. In such a context it offers support for the learning, behaviour and welfare of all pupils, and addresses the particular difficulties some individual children may be experiencing. It seeks to help ensure that all pupils, and particularly girls and members of ethnic minorities, are enabled to benefit from the full range of educational opportunities which the school has available.

Allied to the notion of pastoral care is that of personal and social education (PSE), which is frequently seen as the translation of pastoral care into a curriculum component.

Such concepts, though differently named, are well-accepted in many countries, and, indeed, it is difficult to see what education would mean in any culture if they were not. As Pring (in Lang, 1988) has argued, personal and social education is presumed by the notion of education itself. If education is concerned with changing an individual through promoting growth within a social context, the proposition that education is personal and social is tautological.

There are differences in emphasis, of course, and it is by no means the case that this truth is equally obvious nor given the same force in different cultures, nor even in the same culture at different times. Nor does it follow that because there is a recognition that what we want to happen must be institutionalized (Marland, 1974) and not left to chance, the structures, content and procedures by which this growth is promoted will be the same always and everywhere.

What 'personal and social development' might mean will clearly depend upon the relative emphasis given to the 'personal' and the 'social'. As Pring (1989), Fiehn (1989) and others have pointed out, this is partly a matter of the necessary tension between the individual and the collectivity. If PSE is to promote individual autonomy, this means equipping young people with a propensity to criticize and subvert the (social) status quo, and to experiment with alternative arrangements. On the other hand, if PSE is to raise social awareness and promote functional integration, this may be to emphasize social conformity at the expense of the freedom of the individual. This tension is something which has had to be faced in each of the countries represented in this book.

This is more than simply a conceptual matter. It is intensely political and must be seen in the context of those related tensions and contradictions which characterize the political sphere.

Crossley and Broadfoot (1992) remind us that in the planning and provision of education, there are deep-running themes and dogmas which generate their own tensions and make comparative and international studies particularly informative. At the same time they pose problems for researchers precisely because they touch upon sensitive issues to do with moral values and political ideologies (Crossley and Broadfoot, 1992, pp. 106–7). In the UK and elsewhere, the assertion of the powerful ideology of radical individualism of the 'New Right', with its emphases on consumerism, competition, the free market and the 'enterprise culture' has generated a 'discourse of derision' (Ball, 1990) which systematically discredits the 'progressivism' of the 1960s and 1970s. This discourse is not entirely consistent, however, for individualism is constrained here by a growing central and downward determination of the curriculum, and is clearly to be kept within the limits of a particular notion of autonomy as freedom in the marketplace.

In British politics at least – and this seems broadly true in other Western democracies – the post-war consensus made much more of the concepts of community and collective responsibility (epitomized by the concept of the welfare state) than is generally acceptable in the prevailing discourse of today. In the UK, Mrs Thatcher's famous assertion that 'there is no such thing as society' might be seen as the ultimate rejection of such a collectivism, less traumatic (and less bloody) perhaps than its rejection at the turn of the decade in Romania, Germany and the USSR, but no less final. The way that teachers' pastoral work is viewed, and the provision which is made for it in any system, needs to be related to such political movements, and thus seen as much as a political and historical matter as a cross-cultural one (Best and Decker, 1985).

Common ground

As the contributors to this book make clear, many countries give expression to the need for schools to promote the well-being of their pupils as individual persons and as members of society. This commitment may be perceived in the way teachers are expected to respond to cases of individual need, as in times of personal anxiety, financial hardship, social pressure or emotional crisis. They may be expected also to provide support for youngsters where there is domestic tension or family instability, and to mediate and conciliate when there are relationship problems between students and between students and teachers in the school context. This commitment may be visible also where school curricula include programmes designed to enhance children's skills for coping with such problems when and as they arise, to anticipate 'critical incidents' (Hamblin, 1978) in children's lives and thus prevent their escalation to crisis point. And it is manifest in the provision of curriculum subjects (or cross-curricular themes, projects or programmes) which are specifically designed to promote personal and social development and thus enhance the quality of life of the pupil and, as a natural consequence, the lives of other citizens with whom he or she comes into contact.

The common ground between countries is sometimes obscured by differences in organization, approach and vocabulary. For instance, there are differences in the degree to which it is considered that this provision can be made by teachers and the degree to which it is thought to require participation from those with specialist training. In some countries (e.g. the USA, Canada), reactive support with personal or relationship problems, or with life-choices, may be held to require the services of specialist counsellors, or at least of teachers who have chosen to specialize in this work. In others (notably the UK), 'every teacher is a pastoral teacher' is the claim if not the reality. There are contrasts also between the stages of schooling. For example, in France *les écoles maternelles* have an explicitly caring ('mothering') ethos which is by no means as obvious in *les écoles primaires*. In the UK, generalist primary teachers are widely held to provide pastoral care automatically as part of their role, whereas in secondary schools there is a division of labour in varying degree between 'academic' and 'pastoral' teachers.

Labels vary too. Confusion is likely as much because the same words are used to describe different things as because different words are used to describe the same thing. For instance, whereas in England 'guidance' is a fairly precise word for working with individuals faced with specific choices (as in 'vocational guidance' or 'careers guidance'), in Scotland 'guidance' has a much wider meaning and is roughly synonymous with the English concept of 'pastoral care'. 'Pastoral care' has been adopted in Singapore, where the Ministry of Education has, since 1986, embarked upon a policy of institutionalizing pastoral work along English lines, and is also an accepted phrase in Australia, though not without ambiguity in the (largely Catholic) church sector.

'Guidance' may also refer to curriculum programmes, as in Canada and Western Australia, whereas in England and Wales the preferred label is 'personal and social education' (PSE) or some variant of it; for example, 'personal, social and health education' (PSHE). Such programmes may include education for citizenship and aspects of moral education roughly equivalent to 'civics' in the USA and 'social studies' in Japan (Hashisako, 1990). In parts of Australia, 'career education', emphasizing the broad concept of a career as a 'life path', appears to do the same job. The term 'pastoral curriculum', however, seems to be restricted to England and

Wales. Specific programmes delivered by the class teacher ('form tutor' in the UK, 'home-room teacher' in the USA) are also variously known as 'tutorial programmes' (in the UK), 'guidance tutoring' (in Queensland), or sometimes named after commercially available packs of materials (e.g. 'Skills for Adolescence'; see Chapter 13) and 'Active Tutorial Work' (Baldwin and Wells, 1979–83).

What is more important than the words we use to describe something is what we actually *do* under those labels. In this regard we must not be misled by what are superficial differences. Study visits to observe leadership programmes in schools in Minneapolis, Illinois, Ohio, Kentucky and Missouri in the USA, and pastoral care/PSE programmes in Essex and Suffolk in the UK led one Australian to observe:

> It seems that the route taken, the baggage carried can differ widely, but the end result of leadership programmes, PSE or pastoral care programmes is the formation of the personal identity of the adolescent. This identity is expressed in a realization of the balance of work, leisure, concern for others, commitment to the community and a sense of identity within that community. Such an identity encapsulates the concept of duties and rights in a working partnership, bringing a sense of balance and well-being. (Sexton, 1991, p. 12)

Yet there are clearly differences, and there is no doubt that schools in each of the countries Sexton visited could benefit from a careful and critical scrutiny of the way the others go about it. Unfortunately, educational policy – whether at the level of the individual school, the local education authority, the state, provincial or national government – is rarely made on the basis of long and careful research, even within the local context, let alone on the basis of international comparisons.

Towards a firmer foundation

Decisions about educational provision are frequently taken on the basis of impressions rather than evidence, by convention rather than analysis. All too often, underlying prejudices close our eyes to some possibilities (for example, the British suspicion of anything American); or else they make us unduly receptive to other possibilities, with logically indefensible results, as, for example, when the economic success of a country (Japan is the obvious example) is the basis for advocating that country's approach to education. In fact, where personal/social/moral/health education are concerned, the Japanese experience is interesting, not least as a study of American influence in the post-war transition from the chauvinistic 'Shushin' to a Westernized 'social studies' (Hashisako, 1990). But that is hardly a justification for simplistic extrapolations.

There is much to be gained from cross-cultural, international comparisons, but they need to be placed on a much firmer footing than has generally been the case. There are a number of ways in which this might be achieved.

First, there need to be wider networks for the communication of news, the reporting of initiatives, the sharing of good practice and the cross-fertilization of ideas.

Second, the research base of comparative studies needs to be deepened and systematized: valid (and useful) comparisons must be based upon a sound body of empirical data, carefully amassed and rigorously analysed. Such research needs to focus upon policies, structures and practices within their historical and social contexts.

Third, this aspect of teachers' work needs to be taken more seriously at government (national, regional, local) levels. Wider networking and sound research are necessary if politicians are to accord personal and social education the importance it deserves.

Developments in the last decade or so have been encouraging in a number of ways. The foundation in 1982 of the National Association for Pastoral Care in Education (NAPCE) in the UK has been one important development. It boasts members in Singapore, Hong Kong, Saudi Arabia, St Helena, Papua New Guinea and Australia, and its journal, *Pastoral Care in Education*, has carried articles from or about events in Australia, Singapore, New Zealand and Israel, as well as the UK. Its articles include theoretical papers, research reports, ideas for improving professional practice and book reviews. The founding of an Australian Association for Pastoral Care in Education in 1990 is evidence of comparable developments in the southern hemisphere.

Another development has been the spate of international conferences and seminars on pastoral care and related issues in recent years. These include the third biennial seminar of the Singapore Educational Administration Society in 1988, entitled 'The Child's Growth: Our Major Concern', an international conference in Perth (Western Australia) in 1990 entitled 'Pastoral Care: A Whole School Responsibility', from which several papers in this volume originate, and in April 1992 a conference in Queensland entitled 'Towards Effective Participation in Working Life', which attracted some 400 practitioners in pastoral care, personal and social education, careers guidance and educational counselling from Australia, New Zealand, the UK, the USA, Hong Kong and Singapore.

One by-product of these events has been the launching of a major programme of international comparative research. Originating in Western Australia, the 'Teachers as Active Carers' programme has loosely related research projects under way in a number of countries, with data already in hand from Australia, New Zealand, Canada, the UK, Nigeria and Singapore.

Conclusion

A concern for the development of the whole person is common to the educational philosophies and systems of many countries. The labels may not be the same and the structures and practices by which commitment is converted into practice may be different, but the underlying values have much in common.

It is clear that much can be done to deepen and widen our understanding, and therefore to better inform and so improve the service we provide to our pupils, by an open-minded consideration of such different approaches. The developments described in the preceding section have made major contributions to the knowledge base of international comparisons upon which such improvements may be founded. This book aims to contribute further to this trend.

References

Baldwin, J. and Wells, H. (1979–83) *Active Tutorial Work*. Oxford: Blackwell/Lancashire County Council.

Ball, S. (1990) *Politics and Policy Making in Education*. London: Routledge.

Bernstein, B. (1971) On the classification and framing of educational knowledge. In Young, M.F.D. (ed.) *Knowledge and Control*. London: Collier-Macmillan.

Best, R. and Decker, S. (1985) Pastoral care and welfare: some underlying issues. In Ribbins, P. (ed.) *Schooling and Welfare*. Lewes: Falmer.

Best, R., Maher, P., Baderman, G., Kirby, K., Osborne, A. and Rabbett, P. (eds) (1989) *Whole School, Whole Person*. Harlow: Longman/SCDC.

Bowles, S. and Gintis, H. (1976) *Schooling in Capitalist America: Educational Reform and the Contradictions of Economic Life*. London: Heinemann.

Crossley, M. and Broadfoot, P. (1992) Comparative and international research in education: scope, problems and potential. *British Educational Research Journal*, 18(2), 99–112.

DES (1989) *Pastoral Care in Secondary Schools: An Inspection of Some Aspects of Pastoral Care in 1987–88*. London: Department of Education and Science.

Fiehn, J. (1989) The place of personal and social education in the curriculum. In Best, R. *et al.* (1989) *Whole School, Whole Person*. Harlow: Longman/SCDC.

Haigh, G. (1975) *Pastoral Care*. London: Pitman.

Hamblin, D.H. (1978) *The Teacher and Pastoral Care*. Oxford: Blackwell.

Hashisako, K. (1990) Personal and social education in Japan: recent curriculum changes in Japan. *Compare*, 20(2), 163–78.

Illich, I. (1973) *Deschooling Society*. Harmondsworth: Penguin.

Lang, P. (ed.) (1988) *Thinking About ... Personal and Social Education in the Primary School*. Oxford: Blackwell.

McGuiness, J.B. (1982) *Planned Pastoral Care*. Maidenhead: McGraw-Hill.

Marland, M. (1974) *Pastoral Care*. London: Heinemann.

Musgrave, P.W. (1965) *The Sociology of Education*. London: Methuen.

Pring, R.A. (1984) *Personal and Social Education in the Curriculum*. Sevenoaks: Hodder & Stoughton.

Pring, R. (1989) Developing personal and social education in schools. In Best, R. *et al.* (eds) *Whole School, Whole Person.* Harlow: Longman.

Rogers, C. (1983) *Freedom to Learn for the '80s.* London: Charles E. Merrill.

Sexton, J. (1991) The varied masks of pastoral care. *Pastoral Care in Education*, 9(1), 9-12.

CHAPTER 2

Care, control and community

RON BEST

Setting the scene

I was invited recently to participate in a staff development day at
a mixed secondary school somewhere in the south-east of England.
I agreed to attend a planning meeting with the headteacher and the
deputy head (pastoral) to explore the contribution I might make. This
meeting turned out to be very revealing.

The stimulus for the training day was a growing dissatisfaction with
the system of sanctions operating in the school. This was only the
'presenting problem', of course. The subtext was, as always, rather more
complex. In a recent staffing reshuffle, a teacher had been promoted to
the (pastoral) post of head of lower school, where he quickly found
himself inundated with youngsters referred to him for misbehaviour.
With the 'ultimate deterrent' of corporal punishment now illegal, he
felt powerless to deal adequately with some referrals. This, in turn,
had led teachers to by-pass him and refer miscreants directly to the
deputy heads and, on occasions, even to the head. For his part, the head
found himself under increasing pressure to exercise powers of exclusion
which, although used fairly frequently as a short-term measure, he was
unwilling to apply more frequently or for longer periods.

The head of lower school contended that there was a growing incidence
of confrontation between teachers and pupils, and that this was because
the system of sanctions was not effective. The deputy head (pastoral)
considered that it was the failure of the staff to use the sanctions effectively (rather than the sanctions themselves) which was at fault. The
head countered that 'the kids are no more difficult now than they have
been at any time in the school's history', although he considered some
behavioural problems to be a result of the decline of the 'controlled
atmosphere' of formal, traditional methods and the anarchic vacuum
created by ill-considered 'progressive' approaches to classroom management. Moreover, he thought 'confrontation' to be a relative matter and,
like 'bad behaviour', one which would be defined in different ways by
different teachers. In all likelihood, he thought, the problem was being

exaggerated. But he was bowing to pressure. What was wanted, he concluded, was a training day to review the range of sanctions available and to allow staff to be informed by some 'expert' about alternative sanctions which were known to 'work'.

Some features of control in schools

I suspect this situation is by no means atypical. It has certain features which exemplify some of the tensions and fallacies which surround the question of order and control in schools.

First, there is a measure of *displacement* going on here. What begins as a problem for an individual class teacher is off-loaded onto the shoulders of middle management. When this is ineffective, the teacher does not question the wisdom of referral, but again displaces the problem by moving it one (or more) steps further up the line.

Second, the issue is being *depersonalized*. What begins in supposed confrontation between two persons ends up as a malfunction in the system. The system of sanctions as a set of institutional procedures becomes the scapegoat for individuals' failure to solve what is essentially an *interpersonal* matter.

Third, the incident is being *decontextualized*. As the problem is passed from pillar to post, it is further divorced from the social (group) context of its origins and redefined as an institutional hiccough.

Fourth, there is a clash here between two opposed views of the nature of social reality and of behaviour which is considered disruptive (Young, 1971). On the one hand there is the *absolutist* view of those who see the vast majority of people as agreeing as to what is correct behaviour and what is reprehensible: 'good' and 'bad', 'right' and 'wrong' are absolutes determined by social consensus. Behaviour which violates this consensus is held to be pathological and dysfunctional to the society. On the other hand, there is the *relativist* view which holds that what is 'normal' and what is 'deviant' is not something that can be judged in an absolute way; for what is 'normal' for one group is 'deviant' for another and vice versa. One can only judge the rightness or wrongness of an act relatively against the norms and values of the particular subculture one chooses as one's reference group. In this view, what is defined as 'bad behaviour' and, indeed, 'confrontation' will depend upon the yardstick assumed by the teacher who is doing the defining and that, in turn, is in some measure contingent upon the culture of each classroom.

Fifth, there is an emphasis here on teachers' *management* roles to the exclusion of their *pastoral* roles. The discussion was dominated by the need for teachers to manage the classroom environment better, and for middle and senior management to perform their routine functions in maintaining an orderly institutional framework for social life. None of the contributors to the planning meeting talked about the role of the teacher as counsellor, confidante, mentor or source of moral support. No one spoke of the need to provide a sympathetic hearing to the pupil with personal, social or emotional problems. No one spoke of home–school liaison, the co-operation of supporting agencies or the potential of the welfare network.

Sixth, for all that, this was seen as a *pastoral* problem. It was a pastoral middle manager who demanded action; it was the deputy head (pastoral) who set up the meeting; and it was a supposed pastoral 'expert' who was approached for the necessary expertise.

What are we to make of this?

An old problem

There is nothing new in thinking of problems of discipline and control as somehow the province of pastoral care. It was a major feature of the critique of the late 1970s (e.g. Best *et al.*, 1977; Lang, 1977) that the rhetoric of concern for children's personal, social and emotional well-being concealed a less palatable reality. In fact, what teachers in posts of 'pastoral' responsibility provided more than anything else was a hierarchy of progressively more powerful (and fearsome) authority figures to whom deviants might be referred for correction. This was most eloquently put in Williamson's classic formulation of pastoral care as really 'pastoralization' (Williamson, 1980).

An unfortunate consequence of this critique was a growing feeling among some teachers that concepts such as 'discipline', 'control', 'sanctions' and 'punishment' had no place in the vocabulary of caring people. Moreover, the growth of a pastoral curriculum – including personal, social and moral education (PSME), health education and programmes of tutorial work – gave pastoral staff a proactive and developmental role which seemed to make involvement in overtly disciplinary activities even less appropriate.

I have argued elsewhere (Best, 1988) that this is a misconception if we understand control properly to be an essential feature of an orderly social institution, and that what is crucial is how, why, by whom and under what circumstances control is exercised. What was worrying about the planning meeting described above was its very restricted notion of control as depersonalized, hierarchical and routine.

Except for the head's sweeping generalization about the informal, child-centred teaching styles of 'progressive education', little thought was given to the context and circumstances within which the offending behaviour was occurring. To focus on sanctions is to concentrate on appropriate responses to occasions when order has been deemed already to have broken down, rather than to analyse the features and causes of the disorder itself. It is to adopt the absolutist perspective in which a consensus about right and wrong is assumed, and in which the possibility that indiscipline is more a matter of labelling or circumstance than of a generic form of behaviour is not countenanced. The possibility of a reasoned, moral and independent decision to engage in (say) civil disobedience is denied. As Young (1971) argues, the absolutist position comprises a denial of personal integrity. This is clearly at odds with the ideal of the moral autonomy of the whole person which pastoral care and PSME embrace as fundamental.

The person at the centre

There is a fairly obvious form of control which is suggested by such an ideal, and that is *self*-control. As teachers, we are quick to describe our curricular aims for PSME in terms of self-development, self-awareness, and the like. When involved in guidance or counselling we emphasize the importance of self-image, self-esteem and a positive self-concept. The problem is that we are far from clear what we mean by the 'self' or, for that matter, the 'person'. This point has been cogently argued by Hibberd (1984, p. 175), who observes that:

> a great deal of the literature of pastoral care, at least on this side of the Atlantic, has been content to leave the view of self deeply embedded within practice and has not attempted to unearth the implicit assumptions it makes about the human self.

He goes on (p. 176) to suggest three facts about selves. First, that:

> There is no synonym for 'self' ... no other term which catches at one and the same time the uniqueness, the depth and the privacy of selfhood.

Second, that:

> There is no demonstrable proof that I am the self I take myself to be, nor can there be!

For which reason the development of 'self' is fraught with the perils of self-doubt, self-judgement, self-consciousness and so on. Third (p. 177), that:

> There's no such thing as self-development in isolation from other selves!

The self is fundamentally a social product.

The implications of these facts for teaching are considerable. They remind us that the object of our labours as educators is the *person*, the *individual*, that 'self' which is unique, deep and intensely private. In its very uniqueness lies its pricelessness. In its ultimate inscrutability lie its mystery and its fragility. In its social genesis lie its dependence on others and its vulnerability. When we hold the destiny of another self in our hands, we are charged with the greatest responsibility anyone could have. We may nurture it or cherish it. But we may also wound it, distort it or deny it. For Hibberd, there are two important consequences following from all this. First (p. 177), that:

> We shall have to abandon the rather loose talk of autonomy which has developed in the discourse of pastoral care.... We must not attempt to make the case for pastoral care by shortcircuiting the need for a view of self by an appeal to an unexamined notion of autonomy.

Second (pp. 176–7), we must take on board the implications of the social context for self-development in its fullest sense:

> We must have a concern with school as a moral community.... The teacher/pupil relationship will need to be seen, in some respects at

least, as a model relationship defining for the pupil what human relationships can be and what they may become.

Our earlier unease with a preoccupation with sanctions now seems vindicated. *For to depersonalize, institutionalize and routinize control without a consideration of the impact of this upon those selves whose development we are charged with is beyond defence.*

An interactionist perspective

The decontextualization of behaviour in the institutional response to indiscipline is counter-productive. A consideration of the social context within which selves are produced, expressed, sustained and so on, provides a useful starting point for a more constructive approach. This has been fruitfully demonstrated by Chris Watkins and Patsy Wagner (1987a, b). Watkins and Wagner criticize the prevailing attitude which thinks of indiscipline as primarily a problem which is 'inside the pupil, and often generally outside of the school (for example, in the over-used notion of pupils' home background)' (Watkins and Wagner, 1987b, p. 3). They argue that to take such a view is to 'dis-empower' teachers because it accepts that the cause lies beyond their sphere of influence. It also depersonalizes the pupils by 'shovel[ling] them off to have their person-hood processed by counsellors or whoever ...' unless other features of the event are given serious consideration. And that means recognizing the classroom as a social arena with patterns of behaviour, a dynamic of interpersonal relationships and group processes, and a more or less strong, more or less fragile subculture of its own.

Underpinning this approach is the symbolic interactionist theory of social psychology, which originated with G.H. Mead (1934) and was developed in respect of education by, among others, D.H. Hargreaves (1972, 1975), Woods (1979) and Hammersley and Woods (1984). In this theory, classroom interaction is to be understood in terms of the perspectives of the actors, the definitions they make of the situation, the presence and expected attitudes of 'significant others', and the more or less shared meanings of significant gestures and significant symbols. Within such a context, deviance is to be seen as a relative matter:

> Whether a pupil's action is seen as a 'breach of discipline' will depend on who does it, where, when, why, to whom, in front of whom, and so on. (Watkins and Wagner, 1987a, p. 9)

Moreover, a full understanding of deviance will need to take account of its perception and definition by more than one of the participants, and of a wide range of influences, including personal aspects relating to the lives of the pupils, institutional aspects relating to the school as an organization with a structure of roles and a set of procedures, and wider cultural issues such as class, ethnicity and gender (p. 31). Schools are not particularly good at undertaking such analysis, it seems, and least of all in respect to punishment:

> For over fifty years studies have demonstrated that praise is a much more powerful influence on behaviour than punishment. Punishment

serves mainly to repress particular behaviour rather than to educate into new ones.

Commonly, the process of punishment in schools is carried out with little reference to an understanding of the social context in which the disruptive behaviour took place. (Watkins and Wagner, 1987a, p. 33)

Watkins and Wagner go on to demonstrate the need for schools to confront the issue of discipline in a much more analytical and reflective way than is commonly the case. With an emphasis on the identification of patterns of behaviour which vary in scope and frequency, they show how a whole-school approach can engage the conditions which are likely to accommodate disruptive or disturbing behaviour. 'Triggers' which are likely to set off such behaviour may be identified and (not least) the significance of certain features of both context and incident may be revealed in the perspectives of the children and the teachers affected by it.

The role for the pastoral system in all this is considerable. It is the pastoral team who are in the best position to lead the analysis of behavioural patterns across time and space. It is they, after all, who are charged with an overview of the individual pupil's educational, personal and social progress. To reduce the pastoral system merely to a hierarchy of referral points in the way suggested at the planning meeting is clearly not on. Nor, in the light of Watkins and Wagner's analysis, is a preoccupation with sanctions. *To reduce pastoral care to a routine managerial or corrective reaction to unanalysed and decontextualized 'incidents' is neither to diagnose their causes nor to produce a developmental, proactive or preventative environment.*

The school as a moral community

Both Hibberd (1984) and Watkins and Wagner (1987a, b) direct our attention to the effect which the school as a social collectivity may have on the behaviour and developing 'selves' of the pupils. It is clear from a variety of research findings that schools do make a difference, that the 'ethos' or climate of the school is significant for the successful achievement of its goals (Watkins and Wagner, 1987b, pp. 37–9). It seems to me that the features of the successful school include those which make the school a community: a sense of belonging, a mutual concern for the well-being of fellow members, a value in the group for its own sake and so on.

This is a concept which has long been a feature of the rhetoric – if less often of the reality – of pastoral care in schools. The form or tutor group as a 'small, caring community' was seen as a necessary precondition for tutorial programmes like *Group Tutoring for the Form Tutor* (Button, 1982) and *Active Tutorial Work* (Baldwin and Wells, 1979–81). Such programmes inevitably deal with questions of discipline, rule-keeping, self-control and so on, but there are logical extensions of the community idea which are frequently ignored.

One such extension is the concept of the child as a *citizen* in the community that is the school. Citizenship offers certain rights or privileges but it also entails certain obligations and requires that certain duties be performed.

What are the rights of the citizen? To what is the citizen of a community entitled? I suggest that any list (and this one is by no means exhaustive) would include:

- opportunities to participate in corporate activities, including decision-making;
- opportunities to feel a sense of belonging, pride and a common destiny;
- the right to be treated with respect and valued for oneself;
- the right to have one's liberty protected from the excessive behaviour of others (this will entail a set of rules and a system of sanctions);
- the right to be treated impartially and justly within the rules of the community.

Where pastoral care is most broadly conceived as encompassing a pastoral curriculum of PSME and the like as well as responsive casework with individuals, it can be seen to be making a positive contribution to the provision of these entitlements. But it is sometimes more narrowly conceived as a sympathetic (and sometimes emotional) response to individuals in need or distress. Where this is the case, there is a danger that the 'prevailing fantasy' of 'tender-mindedness' (Cowell and Wilson, 1984, p. 7) takes over. The school becomes something *less* than a community because it ignores the importance of structures, rituals and shared tasks which give real communities their potency and their members a genuine sense of identity and security.

The fourth and fifth in my list of citizens' rights are an important corrective. They remind us that there is a *moral* dimension to the community. It is expressed in its rules and sanctions, for it is here that the fundamental values of the group are translated into prescriptions for action. One would hope that it is here that the rights of individual liberty and the integrity of the person are celebrated and defended.

So schools *should* have rules. And in order to protect the individual members, a system of sanctions to ensure they are kept as far as possible, is justified. But this becomes distorted if we make our rules and sanctions ends in themselves. When this occurs, individual liberty suffers. This is admirably expressed in John Stuart Mill's classic statement:

> the sole end for which mankind are warranted, individually or collectively, in interfering with the liberty of action of any of their number, is self-protection. That the only purpose for which power can be rightfully exercised over any member of a civilized community, against his will, is to prevent harm to others. (Mill, 1964, pp. 72–3)

Moreover, if we see only the requirement that citizens perform their duties – and punish the 'criminals' who don't – we lose sight of their *rights*, and of the fact that the vast majority of children *are* obeying the rules for most of the time. This is a point well made by Watkins and Wagner (1987b, p. 43) in their suggestion of a 'rules review'.

If we reflect once more on the planning meeting with which this paper began, the importance of these points should be clear. Pastoral care has a tremendous role to play in the promotion and strengthening of the school as a community. In permeating the relationships between teachers, pupils, parents and ancillary staff, a pastoral perspective may develop the feelings of community membership, involvement and responsibility. In focusing parts of the curriculum on the distinctively personal and social development of the child, a pastoral perspective may help develop skills for community participation and appreciation of rules, rights and obligations. In responding to the personal, social and emotional needs of individuals experiencing 'critical incidents' of one kind or another (Hamblin, 1978), pastoral casework can demonstrate collective commitment to the individual as both citizen and unique 'self'.

Pastoral care must be seen as promoting order by its humanistic regard for the 'whole person' as a citizen in the community of the school. It must not be restricted to 'emotional first aid' nor be exclusively a control mechanism.

The way things are going

There is reason to speculate that the planning meeting with which I began was an example not so much of an anachronism, as of a straw in the wind, an indicator of a shift in social priorities and cultural norms. There may be interesting parallels here between the Australian and UK experience.

In an interesting article in *Pastoral Care in Education*, John Merchant of St Andrew's Cathedral School, Sydney, argues that pastoral care systems in Australian schools may be degenerating into systems of 'surveillance and behaviour control' (Merchant, 1988, p. 11). Using the criminology of Louis Cohen and Michel Foucault's historical sociology of ideas, Merchant interprets such developments as 'Active Tutorial Work', 'laddering', the increasing sophistication of records and the emergence of a ' "professional" group as technicians of behaviour' (*op. cit.*, p. 13) as homologous to the processes of law enforcement and, significantly, to the emergence of the *prison* in Western society. Ultimately, these processes have to do with the relationship between social classes, knowledge and power.

More immediately, the processes of *depersonalization, displacement, decontexualization* and *routinization* in the *management* of disorder, identified in the planning meeting, bear a striking equivalence to some of the themes which Merchant identifies. In particular, he sees four main dangers (*op. cit.*, p. 13):

- a growing concentration of coercive technologies of behaviour management and manipulation under the pastoral care umbrella;
- the growth in a 'professional' group as technicians of behaviour,

i.e. specialized pastoral staff whose prime role becomes one of behaviour control;

- a growing power of normalization as bodies of knowledge are gathered through surveillance of individuals so that *departures from the norm* become the focus of attention, over and above offences against, and attacks on, the common interest; and
- the potential in schools for 'iatrogenic feedback loops', i.e. the mopping up of casualties within social institutions created by their own operations.

In my view, these dangers are masked by the use of the fashionable category of *management*. This is a key concept in Watkins and Wagner's approach, where, despite the recognition of personal, social and cultural issues, the burden of the argument is about enhancing the teacher's effectiveness as a manager. Thus, in a succinct summary (1987b, pp. 6–7, 8–9) they focus on those skills of the teacher which involve:

- managing the physical setting (layout, seating, resources, etc.);
- managing the social structure (groupings, working patterns);
- managing activities and the psychological setting of the classroom; and
- managing a group meeting of teachers.

This may be interpreted as a welcome vote of confidence in teachers' capacity to achieve valued objectives by a rational–objectivist approach. But an unsophisticated reading might lead to the reduction of the child to an object in the classroom or, worse, to a purely administrative category: 'that which has to be managed'.

This is a likely consequence also of the influential Elton Report, *Discipline in Schools* (DES/Welsh Office, 1989). There is much in the report which is to be welcomed, of course. Our pastoral-care hearts beat a little faster when, for example, we read paragraphs 14 and 15 of the summary (p. 13).

14. We stress the importance of personal and social education as a means of promoting the values of mutual respect, self-discipline and social responsibility which underlie good behaviour, and we recommend that personal and social education should be strengthened both inside and outside the National Curriculum.

15. We emphasise the importance of the pastoral role of class teachers and form tutors, and the need for schools to maintain regular contact with the education welfare service and other support agencies rather than calling on them as a last resort.

But our immediate delight must be tempered when we take in an earlier paragraph (p. 12, my emphasis):

7. We conclude that the *central problem of disruption* could be significantly reduced by helping teachers to become *more effective classroom managers*. We see the roles of initial and inservice training

as crucial to this process. This leads us to make two key recommendations. The first is that all initial teacher training courses should include specific *practical training in ways of motivating and managing groups of pupils, and of dealing with those who challenge authority*. The second is that *similar inservice training should be provided through school-based groups*. These groups should aim not only to refine classroom management skills, but also to develop patterns of *mutual support among colleagues*.

Here the tone is both confrontational and redolent of a behaviour modification approach to discipline which is quite inimical to a person-centred approach to education. The dangers of this have been well stated by Hanko (1989, p. 140) in respect particularly of children with special educational needs:

> such training in management skills, while effective in setting necessary limits to objectively unacceptable behaviour, may not always also be geared to:
>
> > sharpening teachers' understanding of what needs this behaviour may express, and thus to responding to it more appropriately;
> >
> > dealing with what the display of such needs may do to them as teachers (nothing is more conducive to reacting inappropriately than anxiety about not being able to handle disruption and about losing control);
> >
> > developing the kind of continuing school-based inservice provision needed to enable teachers at all levels to teach even their disrupting or otherwise disturbing pupils successfully.

She goes on to observe that:

> unless behaviour management is based on deeper understanding of anxiety-generating disruption it easily constitutes mere reaction to surface behaviour or turns into *control by repression*. Either way this may well ensure surface managerial success but may do nothing to deal with the underlying needs. It may even increase these needs and exacerbate pupils' sense of isolation, disaffection and alienation.

And, further, that:

> Inservice training focusing mainly on management skills may also do little to help teachers resist the tendency *defensively to condemn such pupils rather than to assess their needs non-judgementally*. Instead it may encourage teachers to see segregation as a 'solution' for pupils who, unlike the severely disturbed and violent, could be better helped while integrated.

However that may be, my experience of recent developments in UK teacher training indicates that it is paragraph 7 rather than paragraphs 14 and 15 of the report which are receiving most attention.

To larger issues

The British experience also encourages speculation about homologies between what is happening in education and the exercise of power-coercive management strategies at national level.

Some years ago, I collaborated with Steve Decker in an article (Best and Decker, 1985) which attempted to draw some parallels between pastoral care in schools and the welfare state in Britain since the war. We suggested that pastoral care systems stood in roughly the same relationship to the (academic) curriculum as the various social services – state education, unemployment benefits, the National Health Service and so on – stood to the mainstream business world of the private sector. We inferred that it would be possible to identify distinct perspectives on pastoral care in education which would parallel established political attitudes to the welfare state. These have been attributed by George and Wilding (1976) to the 'Marxists', the 'Fabian Socialists', the 'reluctant collectivists', and the 'anti-collectivists'. There would be those who saw pastoral care as distracting attention from an unsatisfactory curriculum, those who saw it as contributing positively to making schools more humane communities, those who conceded it as necessary for the 'no-copers', and those who saw it as encouraging the 'no-hopers'.

If we make the further inference that changes in the relative influence of these perspectives on the welfare state will be paralleled by changes in the popularity of distinctive attitudes to pastoral care in schools, what we wrote in the early 1980s now seems strangely prophetic. For what has happened in Britain since then has been an unremitting hardening of the Conservative government's stance on issues of welfare, which, latterly, has been paralleled by a hardening of its attitudes on education. In society at large, major public utilities have been privatized and sold off to speculators while the welfare services – non-profitable by definition – have been starved of funds and subjected to public degradation. More official tears are shed over the possibility that some beneficiaries of these services escape paying for them than over those who need them but can no longer afford them, or who are denied them because the state no longer invests sufficient capital to maintain the level of provision. The anti-collectivists have all but carried the day.

In schooling, the continued protection of the independent sector, the provision of opportunities for state schools to 'opt out' and become independent, and the promotion of free enterprise competition through the reform of governing bodies, the extension of parental choice and the delegation of financial responsibility to individual schools, are a natural counterpoint to these wider political developments. The advent of a National Curriculum and its related schemes of statutory assessment seem likely to so occupy teachers' time and energy as to leave little space for pastoral care. The marginalization of personal, social and moral education as a 'cross-curricular theme' is, in itself, a significant restriction of the sphere of influence of pastoral care.

For those schools that have moved from a narrow preoccupation with correction and 'emotional first-aid' to a proactive role for pastoral teachers, the tide may well be turning. If it is, pastoral care will be reduced to its former role in servicing or facilitating the 'real' work of the school. For others (represented perhaps by the school with which this chapter began) this may require little change. However that may be, I believe we need to press for an altogether more imaginative, more proactive, more analytical and more *pastoral* approach to discipline and order in schools wherever they may be and whatever their stage of development.

References

Baldwin, J. and Wells, H. (1979–81) *Active Tutorial Work.* Oxford: Lancashire County Council/Blackwell.

Best, R. (1988) Care and Control – are we getting it right? *Pastoral Care in Education*, 6(2), 2–9.

Best, R. and Decker, S. (1985) Pastoral care and welfare: some underlying issues. In Ribbins, P. (ed.), *Schooling and Welfare.* Lewes: Falmer.

Best, R. *et al.* (1977) Pastoral care: concept and process. *British Journal of Educational Studies*, 25(2), 124–35.

Best, R. *et al.* (1980) *Perspectives on Pastoral Care.* London: Heinemann.

Button, L. (1982) *Group Tutoring for the Form Teacher.* London: Hodder & Stoughton.

Cowell, B. and Wilson, J. (1984) Pastoral care: some prevailing fantasies. *Pastoral Care in Education*, 2(2), 147–51.

DES/Welsh Office (1989) *Discipline in Schools* (the Elton Report) London: HMSO.

George, V. and Wilding, H. (1976) *Ideology and Social Welfare.* London: Routledge.

Hamblin, D. (1978) *The Teacher and Pastoral Care.* Oxford: Blackwell.

Hammersley, M. and Woods, P. (eds) (1984) *Life in Schools: The Sociology of Pupil Culture.* Milton Keynes: Open University Press.

Hanko, G. (1989) After Elton. How to 'manage' disruption? *British Journal of Special Education*, 16(4), 140–3.

Hargreaves, D.H. (1972) *Interpersonal Relations and Education.* London: Routledge.

Hargreaves, D.H. *et al.* (1975) *Deviance in Classrooms.* London: Routledge.

Hibberd, F. (1984) Does pastoral care need a theory of self? *Pastoral Care in Education*, 2(3), 174–81.

Lang, P. (1977) It's easier to punish us in small groups. *Times Educational Supplement*, 6 May.

Mead, G.H. (1934) *Mind, Self and Society: From the Standpoint of a Social Behaviorist.* Chicago: University of Chicago Press.

Merchant, J. (1988) The pastoral care/discipline conjunction and its relation to social control. *Pastoral Care in Education*, 6(2), 9–14.

Mills, J.S. (1964) *Utilitarianism; Liberty; Representative Government* (Everyman edition). London: Dent. (First published 1861).
Ribbins, P. (ed.) (1985) *Schooling and Welfare*. Lewes: Falmer.
Watkins, C. and Wagner, P. (1987a) *School Discipline: A Whole School Approach*. Oxford: Blackwell.
Watkins, C. and Wagner, P. (1987b) Care and control: the group management perspective. *Pastoral Care in Education*, 6(3).
Williamson, D. (1980) 'Pastoral care' or 'pastoralization'? In Best, R. *et al.* (1980) *Perspectives on Pastoral Care*. London: Heinemann.
Woods, P. (1979) *The Divided School*. London: Routledge.
Young, J. (1971) *The Drugtakers: The Social Meaning of Drug Use*. London: MacGibbon & Kee/Paladin.

CHAPTER 3

Trying, but could do better

A review of pastoral care in England and elsewhere

PETER LANG

Introduction

This chapter aims to provide an overview of pastoral care in the UK and a number of other countries, employing an issues- and critique-led approach. It represents a personal interpretation of the problems and issues which characterize pastoral care in England and a number of other countries.

My main argument is that though there has been positive develop-ment in the formulation and practice of pastoral care, many problems and issues, often the ones identified a few years ago, remain. In addition there are some new ones. I am not suggesting that no effective pastoral care exists: no caring teachers, no thoughtfully and efficiently developed systems. But such individual examples have always existed. Rather I am questioning the assumption that there has been some form of *general* movement towards more effective pastoral care systems. There is still much work to be done to improve pastoral care practices in school.

I shall discuss these issues using the four key areas identified in my earlier work (Lang and Hyde, 1987):

(a)   What do we mean by 'pastoral care'?
(b)   Is pastoral care becoming more effective?
(c)   How might the progress of pastoral care be described?
(d)   What are the key developments?

I shall consider each in the light of some current examples and commen-taries, concluding with some ideas on the way things might be moved forward. It must be said that my views and arguments would not be shared by all those involved in pastoral care in England, and that they are presented partly in the belief that the situation is likely to be improved only by some form of radical shake-up rather than by further doses of gradualism. What I say is based on generally supportive data from a number of different countries. For example, Jacques-André Tschoumy, a Swiss author writing for a European audience, on human rights education (something that falls within the province of pastoral care) has expressed the following concern:

> Human rights education covers a number of underlying issues which are rarely if ever made explicit, and . . . these issues stand in the way of such education, which is characterised at present by its theoretical content and the limited extent to which it is practised in our school. (Tschoumy, 1989)

There are parallels between this and my arguments. Moreover, the title of Tschoumy's paper – 'Saying and doing: why the gap? – seemed particularly apt because in this chapter I shall be asking: have practitioners got better at saying but not at doing?

A starting point

Some years ago Lang and Hyde (1987), in discussing questions (a) to (d) listed above, noted:

- an absence of both theoretical construct and accepted definition;
- a critical perspective based mainly upon critical commentaries and research;
- an evolutionary model that illustrates the developmental stages through which pastoral care has progressed;
- the persistence of the problems supposedly addressed by pastoral care.

I shall consider each of these issues in turn in the light of some current evidence and commentary.

(a) What do we mean by pastoral care?

> [There are] 'fundamental problems concerned with the absence both of theoretical construct and an accepted definition of the term pastoral care. (Lang and Hyde, 1987, p. 1)

We seem further now than ever, both in Britain and internationally, from a theoretical construct and an accepted definition of pastoral care, and so the fundamental problems remain. Perhaps in the UK the development of personal and social education (PSE) and its relatively high profile in the emerging National Curriculum guidelines has contributed to this, because one critical factor for the effectiveness of pastoral care and personal and social education, where they co-exist, is the clarity and precision with which their relationship is articulated – something which partly depends on conceptual clarity and adequate definition. That is not a new problem (Watkins, 1985), but in a situation where most national policy statements refer to 'personal and social education' and not 'pastoral care' it is now a critical issue.

For example, the Education Reform Act of 1988 requires maintained schools to provide 'a balanced and broadly based curriculum that (a) promotes the spiritual, moral, cultural, mental and physical development of pupils at the school and of society; and (b) prepares such pupils for the opportunities, responsibilities and experiences of adult life'. Guidelines produced by the National Curriculum Council have so far suggested that these demands can mainly be met through personal and social education and have made no mention of pastoral care (NCC, 1989). In fact, the situation has been further complicated by the use of the terms 'personal and social development' and 'personal and social education' without making adequate and clear distinction between the two. More recently still, the emphasis has moved to 'spiritual, moral and social development'.

It is crucial that there should be clarity at school level about the meanings of both 'personal and social education' and 'pastoral care'. However, at school as well as at policy level, statements about both have tended to remain warm, general and undeveloped. The following paragraph (HMI, 1989), dealing with the relationship between pastoral care and personal and social education, is typical:

> Personal and social development can be promoted through sound pastoral care. This ensures that each boy and girl can relate personally to an individual class teacher or tutor who is also responsible for overseeing his or her overall progress. Guidance should be given as necessary on personal, educational and, in secondary school, vocational matters. Such help needs to be supported by a coherent record system, readily accessible to teachers and open to parents. Some individual pupils will also, from time to time or more continuously, have particular problems to cope with. Partly to help to deal with such cases, it is helpful if those teachers concerned with pastoral care have counselling skills, or are at least aware of the sort of support which may be available from trained counsellors. For numbers of pupils the effectiveness of pastoral care will be influenced by how well a school uses the expertise of outside agencies. However, a major aim of pastoral care should be to develop ways of encouraging the personal and social development of all pupils, not simply to react to the difficulties faced or caused by some.

Current policy documents and guidelines abound in such statements. Everything said is important, and indeed an advance on the sort of statements made in the past; however, the nature of the relationship between pastoral care and personal and social education is apparently assumed to be unproblematic, as is also the meaning of the two terms.

Yet elsewhere the theoretical underpinning and definition of pastoral care is not ignored. In a recent issue of the journal *Pastoral Care in Education* several papers (e.g. Ribbins, 1989; Best, 1989) dealt with it and with closely related issues. Indeed, Peter Ribbins listed in his footnotes a range of attempts to define or describe pastoral care. The problem continues to be that what writers say appears to have a limited effect on what bureaucrats and teachers understand and do.

In support of this point take the following extract from a research report on British secondary schools by Taylor (1989):

> Another key issue – also a difficulty for the research – was the fact that both structurally and operationally there was often an uneasy

and unclear relationship between the pastoral and PSE systems and personnel. Some staff experienced difficulty in judging the relative importance of the two systems and which was the school's main approach to the affective curriculum. Even where there was a PSE co-ordinator a proper evaluation and resolution of the role and of the pastoral and curriculum co-ordination of the two systems had not necessarily occurred. Yet staff needed to be clear about lines of responsibility and management. Financing of PC and/or PSE was almost always relatively low compared with other subject departmental budgets. In some case it was minimal and seemed to operate on the 'beg, borrow or steal' approach. When funds were available staff were often unclear about allocation procedures. Accommodation, like finance, in practice tended to indicate whether the school's main priority was PC or PSE.

It would seem that at a practical level effective definitions of and conceptual clarity on pastoral care (and, indeed, personal and social education) are still lacking. The extract also demonstrates the increasing tension between the two areas in the UK context. Thus if the schools which provided the data for this research are typical, and there is no reason to suppose that they are not, it seems possible that the situation is now actually less clear than in 1987. Although analysis has been undertaken, it has not been done either by policy-makers or those in schools, and has had little impact at the practical level.

I suggested that not only are the problems and issues observed in 1987 still in evidence, but that there are some new ones. One of these relates to the problem of making valid international comparisons as awareness of the international dimensions of pastoral care increases and, indeed, as it spreads to countries previously not involved. I have suggested (Lang, 1989) that there could be benefits, but also significant difficulties, from making such comparisons:

> One of the values of trying to make comparisons with the terms and practices of other countries is that it compels one to address some of the issues. What is it that one is going to compare the term for? Its usage or the practice associated with it? Thus if one is seeking pastoral care beyond these shores should one look only where the term is actually used or are there other criteria that can be applied?

I suggested also that though pastoral care had a number of unique qualities it was, in fact, one manifestation of a broader educational concern: a concern often to be found in countries where the term itself is not used. Indeed, I believe that a too rigid adherence to the term can be quite counter-productive and limiting to educational vision. I became particularly conscious of this in my role as consultant to the Singapore Ministry of Education on introducing pastoral care into selected secondary schools. In Singapore there already existed traditions of guidance, counselling and pupil welfare. In the early stages of the project there was considerable stress on the term 'pastoral care' rather than on the qualities it embraces. In my view this led some of those concerned with the existing traditions to assume either that 'pastoral care' was just another name for what they were already doing, or that is described something totally different; most found it hard to see it as part of a broader tradition.

In Lang (1989) I described a range of international examples of this difficulty. However, as my more recent concern has been with Europe, I would like to take a new example, which I find particularly striking. The author of the extract refers to a project involving primary schools in Austria, Cyprus, Denmark, Finland, Greece, Italy, the Netherlands, Norway, Sweden, Switzerland, the UK and West Germany.

> Quite a lot of contact schools ascertain that there is an increasing lack of satisfying social relations between children and adults. That is why they think it an explicit task for the school to provide the children, for the sake of the development of their personality, with certain models by way of the adults working there, with whom they can iden-tify themselves: somebody whom you care for, who is interested in you (not only your new jumper), who is open about him/herself, who has an identity of his/her own. This places teachers in the situation of having to enter into individual relationships with individual children (instead of a collective relation with a group). And that requires an organization of a group in which there is time for 'one-to-one contacts'.
>
> At some schools this principle has led to explicit educational activities in the field of 'learning to work together' and 'self-control/learning to be myself' for the older children. It also asks for open contacts with parents about the child as a person. A task which teachers also bring in is: associating with adults. At many schools both the necessity and the difficulty have been ascertained. (Kopmels, 1988)

What is this describing if not some of the essentials of effective pastoral care, and possibly also personal and social education? It illustrates my point in the most graphic terms; for if we only seek pastoral care where it is known by that name we would ignore this. We would ignore it, first, because in most of the countries where these schools are situated the term in never used, and, second, because it refers to primary schools: a stage of education not normally using the term even in countries where it is used at secondary level.

(b) Is pastoral care becoming more effective?

> Critical perspectives [are] based mainly upon critical commentaries and research about the problems and inadequacies that can be iden-tified in the development and current practices of pastoral care in both countries. (Lang and Hyde, 1987)

To what extent does the practice of pastoral care continue to fall short of the ideal? Or perhaps to what extent does pastoral care still tend to serve other needs than those explicitly stated? I shall now present a number of observations and examples which suggest that the shortfall of practice in relation to what is officially claimed is still considerable. Take the following example from a paper by an Australian practitioner, reflecting on time spent observing pastoral care in England:

> Neither in Britain nor Australia is there much evidence to suggest that schools actually employ some basic, philosophical stance to underpin their policy making, whether or not we make the pastoral/ academic distinction. Policy statements often appear to be drawn up according to expediency, to alleviate symptoms, or because 'we should have one'. School philosophy statements are seldom developed by a whole school community, and, even when they are, are then relegated to their school prospectus and rarely referred to again.
>
> Is a pastoral care/person centred approach possible when the school hasn't actually defined what that might be? How can a total staff be committed to an ideal that they have not arrived at together, let alone act on it? When schools omit the process, Pastoral Care continues to be seen as an allocation of time, rather than as a total school educational ideal capable of creating optimal learning conditions for each individual student – as a luxury rather than a necessity. When schools attempt to take a major concept on board without working it through (and isn't process often more important than outcome?) the result is similar to playing a game without knowing the rules, or the object of the game. (Hellwig, 1989)

This passage actually relates back to the previous section in its observations on schools' inability to grapple with the actual nature and meaning of pastoral care. However, it is also about the unsatisfactory nature of practice, which is my concern now. (It also underlines my earlier suggestion that these issues are as relevant to Australia as the UK.)

Hellwig is of course basing her arguments on general impressions, but where detailed investigations have been made the results appear to support her. In 1989 a report on just such an investigation appeared in the UK when Her Majesty's Inspectors reported on pastoral care in 27 secondary schools in England. These schools were chosen at random, so again it can be assumed that the main findings (given below, with my comments) have fairly general application.

Two-thirds of the schools' aims and objectives made inadequate reference to pastoral care. This gives support to both the points made above about uncertainty about the nature and meaning of pastoral care, and also to Hellwig's observations.

The extent of contact between tutors and pupils varied very considerably from school to school. In 23 of the schools a critical evaluation of the amount of time devoted to tutorial activity was urgently required. Without adequate time it is hard to see how practice can be effective.

In a considerable majority of the tutorial sessions seen, quality of activity was unsatisfactory in various respects. Later I shall suggest that one of the central reasons for the static situation of pastoral care is the overall inability to develop an appropriate and effective pedagogy. HMI observations add weight to my argument.

Guidance and counselling: there were fairly satisfactory arrangements for responding to pupils in difficulty. As I have said, perhaps this has always been the case. Later I shall also stress that pastoral care has tended to be too reactive. This observation by HMI could be seen as supporting that view.

Two-thirds had a formal system of rewards but in general clear criteria for giving rewards had not been established. Later I shall argue that one of the reasons for the problems under discussion is schools' inability to really engage with practice. HMI's point here is just one of many examples of this.

In about two-thirds of the schools there was a carefully documented approach to dealing with misbehaviour, with an appropriate range of sanctions available. This would be expected if my point about over-emphasis on reaction is correct.

In the great majority of schools more attention was paid to promoting good behaviour through a range of sanctions than through the use of rewards and privileges. Again, what would be expected in a system too concerned with reaction.

None of the schools attempted any formal monitoring or evaluation of their procedures relating to rewards and sanctions. This is another example of the general failure of schools to engage directly with practice.

In almost all the schools the great majority of pupils showed positive attitudes and appeared well motivated. Was this because of the schools' pastoral care or in spite of it?

The role of the form tutor was usually seen as important; however, tutors seldom received adequate support for the performance of their duties. This seems a good example of the mismatch between ideal and reality.

Very few schools had clearly thought-out policies which ensured that pastoral and academic approaches reinforced and supported each other effectively. Therein the key to the failure of pastoral care to progress.

Generally, schools were seen as effective at caring, less so at co-ordinated, coherent strategies to promote sense of well-being and positive outlook. This reinforces the picture of schools being fairly good, as ever, in terms of reacting, but failing to adopt innovatory ideas, policies or practices.

These broad findings by HMI are supported by some more recent and specific research, undertaken by David Morphy under my supervision.

Table 3.1. Number of events recorded under each category

	A1	109	B1	186	C1	21
	A2	23	B2	55	C2	30
	A3	29	B3	45	C3	48
	A4	91	B4	55	C4	106
Total		252		341		205

See text for explanation of A1, B1, etc.

What is described forms only a small part of a much broader investigation but there are two particular strengths to the study. The sample represents a very typical selection of average schools, representative of the general UK situation, and the approach used in this specific example is an explicit attempt to engage with practice.

Forty-two staff (14 female, 28 male) holding posts for pastoral responsibilities in seven high schools were selected to provide a representative sample of one local education authority. The selected staff kept a diary on one day in January 1990.

In the analysis of the reports (1) only events relevant to their pastoral posts were numbered for transferring to a grid (Table 3.1); (2) a total of 798 events were numbered; and (3) the number of recorded events ranged from 10 to 62.

A framework for categorization was developed from an analysis of the data.

A. *Contacts with pupils*
    A1   regarding misbehaviour
    A2   regarding attendance
    A3   responding to their request
    A4   regarding school regulations, e.g. uniform, exit permits

B. *Contacts with adults*
    B1   other colleagues
    B2   parents
    B3   external personal
    B4   senior colleagues

C. *Administration*
    C1   writing references, reports (not subject)
    C2   checking registers, compiling attendance figures
    C3   preparation and planning future events, including meetings, pastoral curriculum
    C4   catch-all category for a range of activities, including taking home sick pupils, taking assembly, putting out chairs, arranging medicals

Thus the average day for a year head would include 20 events (other than teaching); three pupils would be dealt with for misbehaviour and a further one for truancy. One pupil would come with a request and two would be seen regarding school regulations. There would be four conversations with colleagues mostly about problem pupils and two with senior colleagues. One parent would be seen or spoken to on the telephone as would one outside agency. One report or reference would be written and one consultation with registers made. One future event would be considered, planned or prepared for and three other tasks completed, at least one involving assembly. There were considerable consistencies between individuals and schools. In fact any head of year or house transferring to another school would find him or herself doing very much the same job.

Only 5 per cent of contacts were at the request of pupils to answer a need. Only 6 per cent of time was given to future planning. Staff could be seen as reactive agents responding to events, rather than working in a proactive style. However, the school with the highest number of planning events also had one of the lowest numbers of pupils seen for misbehaviour.

Only four out of 798 events showed staff engaged in activating work for a pastoral curriculum. These were two activities in two schools; only one was long-term planning.

Best (1989) outlined a model of the school's pastoral work and suggested a fourfold categorization:

1. Casework dealing with individual needs of a child
2. Curriculum based on the pupils
3. Control
4. Management based on needs of staff

Using this categorization, events could be allocated as shown in Table 3.2. If we remember that only C3 is future planning and most of B1 and B4 are conversations about 'problem children' management can be seen to be largely reactive.

A further piece of particularly significant data regarding these seven schools was in relation to active pedagogy. In six out of the seven, the Active Tutorial Work (ATW) programme (Baldwin and Wells, 1980) had been started but was no longer in operation. In four out of the seven schools it is possible to record the life cycle of ATW as its birth, short

Table 3.2

Casework	Control	Management
A3 29	A1 109	B1 186
C1 21	A2 23	B2 55
	A4 91	B3 45
	C2 30	B4 55
		C3 48
		C4 106
50	253	495

life and lingering death. Yet all seven schools are actively engaged in developing Personal and Social Education programmes; in some the process is very recently started, in others it is some two to three years old. None of this is recorded in the diaries.

Thus this detailed snapshot of a day in the life of the pastoral middle manager suggests that the reactive and 'problem-focused' emphasis remains, and that such managers spend little if any time on constructive forward planning. Things do not appear to be changing very much. This reactive orientation is not something special to inadequate pastoral care. Such an emphasis can be found in other, related approaches. An example of this can be seen in recent developments in Hong Kong, where guidance is being developed as a response to behavioural problems in schools and thus the policies and approaches being encouraged have a strong orientation toward this (Education Department Hong Kong, 1986)

This situation is not, then, unique to the UK; it is certainly reflected in some other systems. However, to what extent? And how often are they equally static? I have already written on the situation in Canada and the USA (Lang, 1989). I now propose to consider what can be learnt from the situation in Europe and Singapore.

European comparisons

As I have already suggested, it is not easy to make comparisons with countries where the term 'pastoral care' is not used. It is also clear that the state of development of some and teacher attitudes in other European education systems make the existence of anything remotely equating to pastoral care either in practice or attitude extremely unlikely, though perhaps not impossible. Equally, recent changes in the political situation of eastern European countries raise new issues. For example, I feel that developments in eastern Germany should mean that the schools there would benefit from the development of pastoral care and personal and social education. However, when I discussed this with a senior educational administrator from (West) Berlin, he argued that there were more vital priorities.

There are, however, a number of clues to found in some European systems which suggest that a dialogue would be possible. In both Denmark and Germany there are class teachers and the role appears to have some significance. In Denmark the National Curriculum prescribes an hour's discussion time a week for all classes at every level to be held with their class teacher. In Germany many schools have *Vertrauenslehrer* ('teachers you can trust') to whom pupils may go with problems; they also have political education conducted through Socratic discussion methods. Portugal is in the process of introducing personal and social education, though it seems it will be of fairly low status. Most recently, I have been consulted about the introduction of pastorally orientated tutorial work in Spain, though the exact nature of this is not yet clear.

One of the most significant recent insights comes from the *Pedagogical Bulletin of the European Schools*. The European schools are nine schools run by the European Commission and situated in a number of member states. The work concerned was a series of papers written by a German teacher, Peer Schmidt-Walter, working at the school at Karlsruhe in Germany. In one paper Schmidt-Walter (1989a) discusses the idea of the development of class rules by the pupils themselves. He argues for the need for pupils to be involved in a real sense so that they feel some responsibility towards what is happening. The rules that are listed are in a number of cases clear examples of a proactive and positive developmental approach. Examples are:

- All pupils, boy and girls, are equal; as is the teacher.
- Pupils and teacher must treat each other in such a way that none is afraid of another. No one should hit, insult or compromise another.
- Pupils and teacher have the right, without interruption or interference, to voice their opinions.

If Peer Schmidt-Walter and his pupils have turned these ideals into reality in his classroom he will have attained a rare level of true pastoral care, though of course he will not call it that.

In a second paper, Schmidt-Walter (1989b) considers the issue of homework, where he argues that a caring school is one that has a clear policy on homework, which teachers follow – a policy which encourages pupils and leaves them some time for other activities rather than making unrealistic and counter-productive demands on them. Again, he is dealing with the type of issue, and the sensitive treatment it needs, that is central to a proactive approach to pastoral care. Is this German teacher an isolated visionary? Or does he represent a view that many concerned and committed European teachers might adopt? The answer probably lies somewhere between these two extremes, but again it does suggest the real possibility of a productive dialogue.

Equally, though, there are indications that parallel problems exist to those I have described in connection with pastoral care. Human rights education has been a significant theme in European education for nearly a decade. However, the paper quoted in my introduction (Tschoumy, 1989) suggested a wide divergence between policy and practice. This is again reflected in a Europe-wide report concerned with skills that could as easily be seen as elements of pastoral care.

> Human rights education does not necessarily include work on problem-solving in the immediate environment. Teaching the skills of interpersonal conflict resolution and co-operation can be regarded as a very narrow field since it only rarely arises as an educational issue in its own right. On the other hand many of those we spoke to regarded it as 'just a part of good teaching' – something which is learned through practice and example rather than the acquisition of a definable set of knowledge, attitudes and skills. Most education authorities seemed to assume that, because they are educating children for life in a democratic society, they will automatically learn to co-operate with and be considerate of one another. Hence there is no need to familiarize children specifically with the idea and practice of constructive conflict resolution.

Although statements of purpose are undoubtedly a necessary prerequisite for the establishment of a democratic system of education, in our view they are not sufficient. Many of the educators interviewed seemed to be unaware that they were not communicating the essentials of non-violent behaviour to the schools. As a result they were usually more optimistic as to the practical success of these educational goals than those responsible for implementing them. (Walker, 1989)

Broad educational concern, of which pastoral care is one manifestation, certainly exists in other European countries but the precise nature and full extent of this remains to be researched.

Singapore

In many ways the development of pastoral care in Singapore is too recent an event to allow conclusions. Even in the first 17 schools to be involved in the pilot project it has only officially existed for about two and a half years. Nevertheless it has illustrated a number of important points. Pastoral care appears to be culturally transferable, though, as with counselling, there are many cross-cultural issues and questions that have yet to be dealt with. The problems of pastoral care also appear to be transferable: many of the problems encountered by the schools in Singapore are very similar to those encountered in schools in the UK. What is most significant, however, is the way that a number of schools have managed in a very short space of time to create a pastoral system and related practice which I found to be as good as or better than that in many equivalent English schools, where the development had taken four or five times as long. What now remains to be seen is whether, having reached a stage where they are on a par with English schools, the Singaporean schools will become equally bogged down, or will find ways of moving forward.

(c) How might the progress of pastoral care be described?

An evolutionary model that illustrates the developmental stages through which pastoral care has progressed in England over the past two decades. (Lang and Hyde, 1987, p. 6)

The 'evolutionary model' to which we made reference proposed four stages of development:

1. Late 1950s and early 1960s: 'The management and control of students of primary interest to schools. Emphasis ... placed on administrative and organizational structures.

2. Late 1960s to the mid-1970s: 'Increasing awareness that a significant number of students faced severe learning and personal problems. Increased support was provided in schools for personal, vocational and educational counselling.'

3. Late 1970s and early 1980s: 'Emergence of "pastoral curricula"

focused on personal, social and moral development and the acquisition of personal and interpersonal skills.'

4. Mid- to late 1980s: 'Changes in curriculum and pedagogy together with emphases on school-level change and collective decision-making.'

In relation to the model of which the above is part the writers cautioned: 'It is clear that not all schools, either in England or Western Australia, will have passed through each of the four phases illustrated in the model; it is clear that, developmentally, a significant number are still situated in phase one of the model' (p. 7). However, in spite of this caution, the model was presented as a developmental one and, though this was not stated, could be seen as suggesting at an implicit level that schools might be expected to move through to stage 4.

> Changes in the curriculum and pedagogy that have become explicit in this fourth phase appear to be much more fundamental and far-reaching in scope. In a most important way, current thinkng about pastoral care has shown a pressing need for the curriculum and its attendant pedagogic practices to be drastically reshaped in order to reflect a changing society and the changing needs of students. (Lang and Hyde, 1987, p. 7)

In terms of the rhetoric of pastoral care I would suggest that this statement is typical of those made about the positive way in which pastoral care is developing. Indeed, the power of this rhetorical perspective leads me to reinvoke a concept which I developed some years ago: that of 'pastoral fantasy' or 'incantation'. I described this (Lang, 1984, p. 228) as follows:

> Pastoral incantation or fantasy is dialogue which is heavily interspersed with words or concepts which have strong favourable and warm connotative meanings for the speaker, and usually for at least some of those with whom they are engaged in discussion.

The point about pastoral incantation is that it lets you off the hook: talking in itself becomes sufficient. I would suggest that statements about the positive development of pastoral care are in danger of becoming pastoral fantasy on a grand scale. They are also, I would argue, another symptom of the inability to engage with actual practice. Consider the following statement form the HMI report (1989), already referred to:

> In general this survey confirmed what has been a consistent HMI finding, that schools experience considerable difficulties when they attempt to link or integrate pastoral and academic approaches. In some schools there were underlying tensions between the academic and pastoral systems, in others they operated to a large extent independently of one another. It was uncommon to find formal links such as regular timetabled meetings between heads of department and heads of year. Very few schools had clearly thought out policies which ensured that pastoral and academic approaches reinforced and

supported each other effectively. Instead of the pastoral system being mainly intended to help promote the effective learning for all pupils, there was a tendency for the main focus of its activities to be those pupils who had already started to fail. (HMI, 1989)

If these comments are coupled to David Morphy's findings that pastoral middle managers spend almost no time on planning, the promise of the Lang and Hyde developmental model appears to fall rather flat.

Though a number of recent books have stressed the need for pastoral and academic integration – the need for pastoral care to be reflected in the curriculum (Hamblin, 1989; McGuiness, 1989; Galloway, 1990) – little seems to be changing in schools. The answer to my original question appears to be that we are indeed getting better at saying but are still unable to improve the doing.

(d) What are the key developments?

The final section of Lang and Hyde (1987) identified a number of positive developments in the situation at that time. I would not wish to suggest that the situation in the UK or internationally is completely gloomy; however, it is clear that the problems remain and to some extent have increased. It is vital that this is recognized if real rather than 'fantasy' progress is to be made. Certainly the continuing development and influence of the National Association of Pastoral Care in Education (NAPCE) is still a positive sign in the UK. Again, rather more attention at a policy level is being given to pastoral care than used to be the case. However, what has been perhaps the single most significant development – Records of Achievement – may now lose momentum in the UK owing to the government's half-hearted support. Records of Achievement involve a number of processes and ideas which are at the very heart of good pastoral care. They are designed to record and celebrate student achievement over the full spectrum of their activities and life, not just the academic and school-orientated; they involve a process of formative assessment in which the student is involved in discussing and negotiating with teachers to produce something which they both support; and the record is the property of the student. Where properly resourced and developed such records can have a significant effect on schools, and particularly on the quality of their pastoral care. This is particularly because the teacher–pupil negotiation offers the opportunity to engage with practice and ultimately to affect the curriculum.

Conclusion

I have attempted to provide a critical and personal review of the current situation of pastoral care in the UK and elsewhere; my concern has not been to provide a complete and coherent picture but to raise awareness.

The message so far as I am concerned is as follows: in the UK, Australia and elsewhere we must learn to start from process and role. Once we understand and can convey what pastoral care in the classroom actually looks and feels like, we have something to build one. Once we have identified that part of every teacher's role to which pastoral care belongs we have our starting point. The mistake seems to be that we have started on the outside rather than starting from the inside and building on this.

Ultimately we have to find ways of engaging with practice and developing a far more rigorous and tougher approach to evaluation. Until pastoral care is recognizable in the curriculum and in the practice of the majority of classrooms there will be no quantum leap forward, we shall simply continue to rearrange the deckchairs, if not on the *Titanic* at least on the deck of a liner that ran aground some time ago.

References

Baldwin, J. and Wells, H. (1980) *Active Tutorial Work Books 1-6.* Oxford: Blackwell.

Best, R. (1989) Pastoral care: some reflections and a restatement. *Pastoral Care in Education*, 7(4), 7-13.

DES (1989) *Personal and Social Education 5 to 16.* London: HMSO.

Education Department Hong Kong (1986) *Guidance Work in Secondary Schools: A Suggested Guide for Principals and Teachers.* Hong Kong: Education Department.

Galloway, D. (1990) *Pupil Welfare and Counselling: An Approach to Personal and Social Education across the Curriculum.* Harlow: Longman.

Hamblin, D. (1989) *Staff Development for Pastoral Care.* Oxford: Blackwell.

Hellwig, E. (1989) Pastoral Care for the 1990s and beyond: a visitor viewpoint. *Pastoral Care in Education*, 7(1), 6-12.

HMI (1989) *Pastoral Care in Secondary Schools: An Inspection of Some Aspects of Pastoral Care in 1987-88.* London: HMSO.

Kopmels, D. (1988) *The Contact School Plan*: Project No. 8 of Innovation in primary education. Strasbourg: Council of Europe.

Lang, P. (1984) Pastoral care: concern or contradiction? Unpublished MA thesis, University of Warwick.

Lang, P. (1989) What's so special about pastoral care? *Pastoral Care in Education*, 7(4), 21-7.

Lang, P. and Hyde, N. (1987) Pastoral care: not making the same mistakes twice. *Curriculum Perspectives, Australian Curriculum Studies Association*, 7(2), 9-17.

McGuiness, J. (1989) *A Whole School Approach to Pastoral Care.* London: Kogan Page.

National Curriculum Council (1989) *The National Curriculum and Whole Curriculum Planning: Preliminary Guidelines.* York: NCC.

Ribbins, P. (1989) Pastoral care: in praise of diversity. *Pastoral Care in Education*, 7(4), 28-36.

Schmidt-Walter, P. (1989a) Wir mussen uns Gesetze geben. *Pedagogical Bulletin of the European Schools*, VII(104), 8-16.

Schmidt-Walter, P. (1989b) The whys and wherefores of homework. *Pedagogical Bulletin of the European Schools*, VII(104), 8–16.

Taylor, M.J. (1989) *A Good Education for All: An Investigation of Issues in Implementing Policies in Pastoral Care and Personal and Social Education in Secondary Schools*. End of award report. Slough: National Foundation for Educational Research.

Tschoumy, J.-A. (1989) Saying and doing: why the gap? Paper presented at Colloquy of Directors of Educational Research Institutions, Ericeira (Portugal). Strasbourg: Council of Europe.

Walker, J. (1989) *Violence and conflict resolution in schools: a study of the teaching of interpersonal problem-solving skills in primary and secondary schools in Europe*. Strasbourg: Quaker Council for European Affairs, Council for Cultural Co-operation.

Watkins, C. (1985) Does pastoral care equal personal and social education? *Pastoral Care in Education*, 3(3), 179–83.

CHAPTER 4

A systems perspective on whole-school guidance/pastoral care programmes

RICHARD A. YOUNG

The school as a caring community, the personal and social development of students, and careers education are but three issues familiar to school personnel in both the UK and Canada. The efforts of schools to address these and other issues through whole-school programmes is the subject of this chapter. The terms 'guidance' and 'pastoral care' are used in the UK to refer to programmes that address these and other issues. In Canada, 'guidance' and, more particularly, 'guidance and counselling' subsume much of what elsewhere is referred to as pastoral care. In this chapter, I will use a systems perspective to describe and critique the Canadian experience in school guidance and counselling programmes, with particular reference to the responsibility of the whole school for offering these programmes.

The Canadian experience in school guidance and counselling is long and varied, beginning with recognizable efforts immediately after World War II (Herman, 1981). At its inception, it was almost entirely influenced by practices in the USA. And although there is a great deal of commonality across the country, each province, which has jurisdiction over education in the Canadian federation, tailors specific programmes to its own needs and systems. I will need to make generalizations about the Canadian experience that may or may not hold for particular provinces or local boards of education.

I will begin by providing a brief overview of the secondary school guidance and counselling programmes in Canada. Subsequently, I will use a human systems approach to critique these programmes. This framework will enable the reader to understand the strengths and weaknesses of the programmes as they relate to the objectives of the school and the needs of the students. The reader will also be able to use this human systems framework to understand similar programmes, such as pastoral care, in other jurisdictions as well as in specific schools.

Guidance and counselling programmes in Canadian schools

Traditionally, the primary goal of school guidance and counselling programmes has been to facilitate development in three areas of the student's life: educational, vocational, and personal–social. Specifically, these programmes were intended to help students adapt to school and the educational process, assist them in determining and implementing vocational goals and plans after secondary school, and ameliorate their personal–social concerns as they arise. More recently, counsellors have used the terms *developmental, preventive* and *remedial* to further differentiate the goals of school guidance and counselling programmes. In practice, the emphasis of the counsellor's work has been in the remedial domain. However, the rationale that underlies these programmes is based on a developmental perspective (e.g. Tennyson *et al.*, 1989; Van Hesteren and Pawlovich, 1989). Recently, teachers and counsellors have had to respond to increased demands and expectations from schools and society such that there is an increased use of the curriculum, small-group programmes and other means to offer guidance and counselling. But in terms of the whole school being responsible for the development or delivery of guidance and counselling programmes, there is, in the Canadian experience, a tension between what is espoused as philosophy (which is developmental) and what is in fact implemented as practice (which is frequently remedial). This situation is not unlike the gap that exists in many realms between intentions and actions.

The developmental orientation is well represented in the list of needs for adolescents that comprise part of a recent position paper on guidance and counselling services in Canada (Van Hesteren and Pawlovich, 1989). These range from a 'need to grow in self-understanding in the direction of developing a positive sense of personal identity' to a 'need ... to understand how social, economic, political, and technological processes have an impact on the consciousness and lives of individuals and groups' (pp. 188–9).

Secondary schools in Canada are likely to have counsellors whose role is sufficiently different from the teacher's role to require separate and specialized training. Counsellors offer and direct the school guidance and counselling programme. Although counsellors have been able to define a distinct role for themselves in schools, a tension continues to exist between the extent to which their role definition meets the needs of the whole school or of only a few of its students through highly individualized approaches.

It should be recognized that the programmes exist at both ideal and real levels. A number of organizations, including those representing professional counsellors as well as universities involved in counsellor education have developed elaborate models of school guidance programmes that are quite consistent in many respects with the pastoral care approach. This recent effort is to make the counsellor a proactive agent in the school in terms of the developmental goals of the curriculum. Provincial ministries of education and local school districts vary in the implementation of these approaches.

We are now able to examine these programmes in more detail using a framework that is particularly useful to programmes in which human services are provided.

Human system perspective on school programmes

Egan (1985) identified four components of systems related to programmes, institutions and agencies: a receiving system, a performance system, a human resources system, and a group of contextual factors in which these systems operate (see Figure 4.1). For our purposes, the receiving system refers to the needs of students, parents and, to some extent, teachers, and to society in general. The performance system refers to the efforts of the school to meet the needs of the receiving system. It includes the school's mission, philosophy, major aims, specific objectives and the programme tasks that the school uses to implement its objectives. Human resources refers to the people that are required to make the system work, most specifically teachers, counsellors and administrators, as well as students. Finally, the contextual system refers to factors specific to the context of the programme which affect its operation; for example, school climate or the attitude of teachers to educational change. This critique will address the human resources, the performance system and the contextual factors in detail.

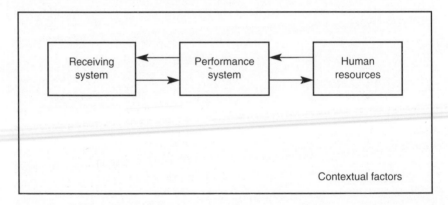

Figure 4.1 Components of human systems approach (adapted from Egan, 1985).

Human resources

The human resource dimension of a system is not usually the first to be considered in the development of a programme. Programme development begins with the needs of the receiving system. However, it is important to begin our analysis with the human resource dimension because it immediately brings into focus what is a critical factor to the success of these programmes in Canada, and what contributes most to their weaknesses when it is not considered.

What stands out in the approach to school guidance and counselling just described is the human resource dimension. Stated more specifically, people are the most important factor in the development and implementation of human service programmes. This principle is as true of pastoral care programmes as it is of the Canadian programmes, but for different reasons, as I will point out. The importance of the human resource dimension has arisen because of the particular history of the programmes in Canada. Over the past thirty years, counsellors have been able to 'carve out' a place for themselves in Canadian schools.

The Canadian system of guidance and counselling programmes is built around specialist counsellors who offer and direct these programmes in schools. Counsellors provide direct service to students and help others implement aspects of the programme. These specialists have distinct roles within the school organization. They are usually trained specifically for their positions, although the practice of appointing non-trained personnel still exists.

Some of the specific merits in the human resource domain of the specialist approach to guidance and counselling are as follows:

1. Counsellors have a working knowledge of their school, and of schools in general, usually based on a range of experiences in the school.

2. There is a highly uniform model of counsellor training in Canada focused on the interpersonal or helping skills and a developmental perspective (Egan, 1990). Counsellors are expected to have a high degree of competence in the skills that serve in relationship building, problem identification and action. The specific skills central to this approach are: active listening, accurate empathic responding, probing, information-giving, summarizing, advanced empathy, challenging and confrontation, and immediacy.

Since the late 1960s, there has been a movement in North America that has promoted the giving away of psychology, a basic tenet of which is that virtually anyone can learn the skills just listed (e.g. Larson, 1984). This movement has been very influential in the growth and orientation of guidance and counselling programmes. Recently, a note of caution has been heard (e.g. Martin, 1990), for the skills, that form the basis of counsellor practice need to be accompanied by a sophisticated level of understanding of the interaction between the counsellor and the student, and of the helping process. The Canadian approach fails to achieve its full strength when untrained counsellors are appointed.

3. The specialized approach has the advantage of clear division of roles and responsibilities. As the helping process is basic to the function of the counsellor, role conflict is avoided. Role conflict may arise in systems and approaches that do not have designated role differentiation. Ideally, role conflict should not occur in a school where objectives and values are compatible. But in reality, since the objectives of schooling are broad and varied and the means of implementing them diverse, role conflict does occur. This is particularly problematic when that experience is within the teacher (intrapersonal role conflict) and results in difficulty in program implementation. Role conflict is engendered by a range of different expectations by the people with whom the teacher or counsellor comes in contact within the school situation.

Role clarity is enhanced through job descriptions. The present-day school is a complex organization. Society's expectations of what the school should do have broadened in Canada. In recent years, the schools in Vancouver, for example, have become concerned with feeding children who come to school without breakfast. Schools are also required to teach students about safe sexual behaviour and practices to decrease their chances of contracting AIDS (e.g. British Columbia Ministry of Education, 1987; Fineberg, 1988). Schools are expected to integrate individuals from many cultures into the mainstream of a multicultural society. These new expectations are, of course, in addition to the usual mission of the school to provide teaching in a number of subject areas to prepare young people to participate fully in their society. The variety of demands on the school requires that it consider the diversification of roles among the personnel it employs to deliver its programmes.

4. The fourth advantage of the specialist approach is that it enables counsellors to be effective leaders in schools: a clear professional identity qualifies one to provide leadership and expertise to others. As well, the level of personal investment in the programme is likely to increase with the increase of the professional training of the personnel offering the programme.

From a human resource perspective, the liabilities of the approach I have described are as follows:

1. The appointment of counsellors can occur for administrative expediency without relation to skills, training or role. The practice has a domino effect on the implementation of effective guidance and counselling programmes in schools.

2. In systems that become entrenched with specialized personnel, the danger arises that human resources, rather than the needs of the users, may drive the programme. Counsellors and teachers may offer parallel programmes in which there is little integration. A whole-school pastoral care system may avoid this limitation by involving the majority of the teachers not only in the development of the programme but in its implementation.

3. The specialist approach can be implemented in a rigid manner that does not allow for teachers to reconceptualize and broaden their roles in the classroom as facilitator, listener, convenor, counsellor, etc.

4. A final concern is that at present there are few formal guidelines or evaluation procedures in place for the evaluation of counsellors.

Performance system

The aspects of the guidance and counselling or pastoral care programme that comprise the performance system and are of concern to this discussion are mission of the school, broad aims, specific outcome goals, and programme tasks.

The performance system is perhaps what is the concern of most people working in guidance and counselling or pastoral care because it represents what the school is about. Schools try to effect change. At one level we can consider the broad philosophy, or mission of a school; at another level, we need to focus on the programme tasks that carry the programme to the students and other stakeholders in the system. Perhaps our aim should be to change the mission of schools by proposing that pastoral care be a whole-school responsibility. The theme not only asks that the pastoral care programme be delivered by all the teachers and administrators in the school, but it implies that the school incorporate the goals of pastoral care as part of its mission.

Professional counsellors offering a guidance and counselling programme in a school are particularly good at the programme task level; that is, carrying out specific programmes with students. In this, counsellors frequently see themselves as line workers. Given a defined role within the school and possessing appropriate skills, they go about carrying out their job. One of the current challenges in Canadian school systems is that counsellors are being asked to implement more diversified programmes using a variety of methods. But the downside of the specialist approach, which schools have encountered in various ways, is that programmes can become isolated from the whole school. In terms of the performance system, the approach I have described has its greatest difficulty addressing the mission and broad aims of the school in a proactive manner.

The Canadian approach has specific merits in terms of the performance system:

1. Counsellors see themselves as line workers. They are particularly good at programme task dimensions of the performance system. Because of their specialized training, programmes can be focused and delivered appropriately.

2. The strength of the performance system at programme task level can be extended to programmes involving the whole school. I would like to provide two examples of programme tasks in which the special expertise of counsellors is evident and involve the whole school:

Peer counselling Peer counselling is a programme in which senior students are trained and supervised to act in a counselling and tutoring role to younger students. Begun in the 1970s in the United States, it has gained popularity in Canada in the past decade (see, for example, the whole issue of the *Canadian Journal of Counselling*, 23(1) 1989; see also Blair and Brusko (1985); Carr and Saunders (1979); Downe *et al.* (1986); Frisz (1986); and Myrick and Erney (1979). Not the least of the factors that have influenced its development is the responsibility that students themselves can take for the implementation of a caring and helping perspective in the school. It is truly an example of a whole-school approach. Peer counselling is also popular because students can provide a bridge between the adult subculture and the adolescent subculture and serve as positive role models to all students (Gougeon, 1989). In some cases, academic credit is given to students involved in the programme, but more frequently it is a volunteer programme. In most schools, participation as a peer counsellor is sought after by many students, and the programmes are usually unable to accommodate all the students who wish to participate.

The counsellor has a very specific role and function in this type of programme, that of training and supervision. The students in the programme are asked to use the same helping skills model that the counsellors themselves employ, and which has formed the basis of their training. Central to the training programme are the helping skills identified earlier (Egan, 1990), but these skills and the programme itself can fail if the person responsible for the training and supervision does not assume a facilitative rather than a teaching role. To shift roles from teacher to facilitator is not easy for many school personnel, who have become accustomed to the former. This role differentiation, as mentioned earlier, is one of the tensions of the specialist versus generalist model.

Family life education programme   Another example of the role of the counsellor in whole-school programmes can be derived from the recent introduction of a mandatory family life education programme for all students in grades 7–11 by the Government of British Columbia (British Columbia Ministry of Education, 1987). The programmme, which consists of about 10–12 hours of instruction each year, was initiated as a result of the government's concern with the AIDS epidemic. Although the provincial Ministry of Education prepared the curriculum and offered teachers a limited amount of inservice training, schools have the responsibility for implementing the programme and assigning teachers to it. As one would expect, schools took a variety of approaches, assigning teachers to the course who had difficulty in teaching it. Among the problems encountered were the discomfort of discussing sex and sexual behaviour with adolescents, their own knowledge and expertise in the field, and the expectations they placed on themselves about being experts in the field (Friesen *et al.*, 1988).

The question I want to address is: What is the role of the well-trained counsellor in such a programme? This type of programme involves values, communication, personal development and sensitivities, as well as inherent differences in the purpose of the curriculum (e.g. Fineberg, 1988). It is in these areas that counsellors can be particularly helpful. In an ideal approach to this programme, the counsellor would not necessarily be the classroom teacher but would be able to offer to teachers specific training and support during the course in areas that have been identified: communication skills, relationships, values, and adolescent development.

3. At the level of remedial programmes there is an opportunity to provide specialized and intensive assistance to students. It should be recognized that, from the mental health perspective, adolescents spend a good deal of time in school. Thus, it is an institution which can support and extend mental health interventions for particular students. While there is some movement away from individual counselling to group and curriculum interventions, individual counselling continues to have a definite place in Canadian guidance and counselling programmes. If anything, the expectation is for counsellors more expertly trained in mental health rather than simply a demand for more counsellors. Counsellors are asked to deal with issues such as child abuse, family problems and particularly drug and alcohol abuse.

The performance system based on the specialist approach may incur the following liabilities:

1. The performance system may suffer from tension among its various stakeholders and from, in most cases, not having used any needs assessment to arrive at the components of its performance system. There are likely to be inconsistencies between the formal mission of the school and/or school board and the needs of the students. The guidance and counselling programme may attempt to address these needs informally, again often without any hard data. But in doing so, the programme and the counsellors may be acting on their own without school board approval and without involving the whole school in meeting the objectives. The pastoral care or guidance and counselling programme must co-ordinate its activities with the overall system.

2. Deliberate psychological education refers to the use of the school curriculum to attain psychological growth for its students. It has had a history of about twenty years in North America (e.g. Sprinthall and Mosher, 1970). There is probably more verbal support of psychological education than there are actual in-class programmes in this area. School counsellors have also used the term 'curriculum infusion' to refer to the use of the regular curriculum areas for teaching of career, decision-making, and other aspects of psychological development. Counsellors have not been notable in their initiation of curriculum infusion or psychological education although the curriculum has changed in subtle ways to reflect the extent to which psychological frameworks and understandings are in common usage and much more in the purview of teachers from a variety of disciplines.

A more recent phenomenon is the use of published programmes for classroom use that are intended to promote psychological skills and development. One such programme, *Skills for Adolescence* (Quest International, 1988), is apparently in use in over 25,000 classrooms in Canada, the USA and the UK (Peters, 1988). It involves approximately 60 hours of classroom activities that address skills in decision-making and problem-solving, coping with stress and feelings, communication and social relationships, and developing personal competencies and feelings of self-confidence. In addition to extensive teacher training, it offers parent activities and community involvement by students. These initiatives represent whole-school approaches that can operate independently of specialist guidance and counselling services, but are enhanced through leadership and support from counsellors.

3. Similarly, counsellors have not been particularly active in curriculum development in 'affective education', although most counsellors are able and willing to support such movements. However, counsellors have worked in this area independently of classroom teachers, as is evident from the report on guidance and counselling services in the Edmonton public schools: '[t]he trend was for objectives related to the affective development of students to be perceived as being achieved to the greatest extent in all three school levels [elementary, junior and senior high school]' (Edmonton School District No. 7, 1986, p. ii). There is an increasing perception that affective development of students is the

proper domain for the work of counsellors. Such a perception, however, may be mistakenly interpreted by classroom teachers as implying that they should not be involved in the affective dimensions of schooling.

4. Perhaps because guidance and counselling programmes are already in place, counsellors have not taken the responsibility to work at other levels of the performance system. For example, counsellors are typically not involved in the development of the mission of the school. They do not assist in the enunciation of the broad aims of the school. As a result, through their professional training, they can get 'hooked' on various programmes which they carry to the school without sufficient understanding of their relation to the aims of the whole-school programme. At the same time, the human relations or caring philosophy does not reach the level of the administration nor is it incorporated into the mission of the school. Published programmes which involve the inservice training of school personnel, such as *Youth Empowering Systems* (National Training Associates, 1989), represent recent efforts to address the whole-school mission or philosophy. This particular programme is intended to foster a pervasive caring climate in the school.

Figure 4.2 may serve to highlight and summarize one of the main differences between the guidance and counselling system that has evolved in North America and a whole-school approach to pastoral care from a performance system perspective. In North America, specialist counsellors can be highly competent in the implementation of programmes but,as has been pointed out, these programmes may not be directed to the needs of most students nor do they necessarily represent the mission of the school. As specialists who implement specific programmes, counsellors may be removed from having a critical influence on the school's policy, major aims as well as the central programmes of the school (the curriculum). In contrast, a whole-school approach to pastoral care may experience more difficulty as it moves down the series of factors in Figure 4.2. Without specialized training, specific role descrip-

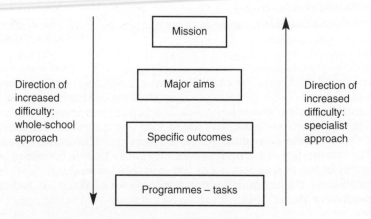

Figure 4.2 Direction of increase of difficulty in performance system: specialist versus whole-school approach.

tions and time allocation for programme implementation, the pastoral care system may remain at the level of mission or major aims, or when implemented, it is sporadic and uneven.

Contextual factors

The performance and human resource systems operate within a broader context comprised of a host of factors that need to be considered. Among the important contextual factors of a whole-school approach to pastoral care or guidance and counselling are school climate, the reward system and the attitude of teachers to educational change. There are, of course, others which will not be discussed here, not the least of which is politics.

School climate The implementation of pastoral care and similar programmes is a function of the school climate. The question that needs to be addressed is who within the school has expertise in the field of school climate. Thomas (1989) suggested that in contrast to the hard data of effectiveness such as test scores, achievement, drop-outs ratios, and expenditure per pupil, the culture of the school is made up of several elements: purpose, quality, affection, collegiality, teamwork, recognition and character. These elements can be encouraged through the work of the counsellor, if the counsellor has training in these areas, but they need to be supported by a school philosophy or mission that includes such elements.

Thomas (1989, p. 250) suggested the following means to enhance the school climate:

1. Support the position that success for every student is the basic purpose of schools.
2. Expect the best from everyone.
3. Express affection for students and help others do the same.
4. Promote collegiality and teamwork within the school.
5. Initiate a comprehensive recognition programme for staff members and students.
6. Promote ethical practices.

The promotion of a positive school climate is not necessarily the counsellor's job, but it does represent skills in human development, communication, group process and human relationship that counsellors typically have. This type of involvement in the school also provides the counsellor with a definite role and place in the school – it delineates a proactive role. The counsellor in the Canadian system has been peripherally involved in some of these issues; for example, attendance, drop-outs, social problems, and attitudes toward school. All of these can be framed more positively.

The reward system Do teachers, administrators and the students themselves have the incentives to work toward and achieve their goals?

One major tension in this area is the use of punishment. Unfortunately, punishment has been traditionally associated with schools as a means to extinguish inappropriate and/or unwanted behaviour. The Canadian specialist approach to guidance and counselling has allowed counsellors to remove themselves from roles associated with school punishment. The challenge of pastoral care as a whole-school responsibility is to foster a climate in which students are rewarded rather than punished. Perhaps the most challenging part of the pastoral care system, particularly as it is envisaged as the responsibility of the whole school, is to create an environment in which there is a shift from a punishment-orientated atmosphere to a reward-orientated one.

In addition to a context that rewards students, staff members also need to be rewarded for improvements to the operation of the school and when objectives are attained. This, of course, applies particularly in the case of the implementation of the pastoral care programme. The questions of 'Who is rewarded?' 'Why are they rewarded?' and 'How are they rewarded?' need to be addressed.

Attitudes toward change   A third important contextual factor that may influence the operation of whole-school pastoral care or guidance and counselling programmes is the attitude of teachers to educational change. Educational change occurs at many levels, such as at the level of the mission of the school, in the specific programmes that the school offers, in the training of the personnel who offer the programmes. In Canada, there has been recent evidence of the resistance of teachers to educational change that is imposed from without. The difficulty in implementing change is increased in environments in which there is a seemingly continuous expectation for change. Whatever the focus of proposed change in the school because of the pastoral care programme, one can expect that the attitude of teachers to change will be a contextual factor that will need to be addressed.

In a traditional, and fairly well-established, approach, such as the guidance and counselling programmes in place in many parts of Canada, the extent of change is minimal. Thus, the attitude to change is less important to the successful operation of the programme. However, if the pastoral care or guidance and counselling programme represents a change in existing policy or practice, its implementation may be complex and unpredictable.

Fullan (1982, 1983) identified four factors that affect the implementation of educational change: (1) characteristics of the innovation; (2) characteristics of the school district; (3) characteristics of the school, and (4) factors external to the local school district. Space does not permit a full review of these characteristics, but it is important to note that each needs to be considered in detail if one expects to implement a new programme, or a new approach to an old programme, successfully.

I have the following suggestions to assist in developing and implementing developmentally oriented curricula: Use the political process. Have an identifiable expertise. Recognize what is positive about the current curriculum and practices. Build on aspects that are helpful to teachers in their work. Be specific about the outcomes of programmes and interventions.

Conclusion

In the area of whole-school approaches to guidance and counselling or pastoral care, there is evidence of substantial progress. The shift of responsibility for these programmes to the whole school requires strategies that take into account the specific history of these kinds of programmes in political jurisdictions as well as in particular schools. The systems approach to human service programmes provides a means to understand the history and the issues involved in programme development and implementation.

References

Blair, G.H. and Brusko, M. (1985) Starting a peer counseling programme in high school. *Journal of School Health*, 55, 116–18.

British Columbia Ministry of Education (1987) *Family Life Education 7–12: Curriculum Guide 7–12*. Victoria, BC: British Columbia Ministry of Education.

Carr, R. and Saunders, G. (1979) *The Peer Counselling Starter Kit*. Victoria, BC: The Peer Counselling Project, University of Victoria.

Downe, A.J. *et al.* (1986) Peer counseling: more on an emerging strategy. *School Counselor*, 33, 355–64.

Edmonton School District No. 7 (1986) *Guidance and Counselling Program Review: 1985–86 Summary Report*. Edmonton, Alberta: Edmonton School District No. 7.

Egan, G. (1985) *Change Agent Skills in Helping and Human Service Settings*. Monterey, CA: Brooks/Cole.

Egan, G. (1990) *The Skilled Helper* (4th edn). Monterey, CA: Brooks/Cole.

Fineberg, H.V. (1988) Education to prevent AIDS: prospects and obstacles. *Science*, 239, 592–6.

Friesen, J.D., Arcus, M.E., Fisher, D., Thomas, J., and Young, R.A. (1988) *A Field-Based Investigation of the British Columbia Family Life Education Programme*. Victoria, BC: Ministry of Education, Government of British Columbia.

Frisz, R.H. (1986) Peer counseling: establishing a network of training and supervision. *Journal of Counseling and Development*, 64, 457–9.

Fullan, M. (1982) *The Meaning of Educational Change*. Toronto: OISE Press.

Fullan, M. (1983) Evaluating programme implementation: what can be learned from Follow Through. *Curriculum Inquiry*, 13(2), 215–27.

Gougeon, C. (1989) Guidelines for special issues training sessions in secondary school peer counselling programmes. *Canadian Journal of Counselling*, 23, 120–26.

Herman, A. (1981) *Guidance in Canadian Schools*. Calgary, Alberta: Detselig Entreprises.

Larson, D. (ed.) (1984) *Teaching Psychological Skills: Models for Giving Psychology Away*. Monterey, CA: Brooks/Cole.

Martin, J. (1990) Confusions in psychological skills training. *Journal of Counseling and Development*, 68, 402–07.

Myrick, R.D. and Erney, T. (1979) *Youth Helping Youth: A Handbook for Training Peer Facilitators*. Minneapolis, MN: Educational Media Corp.

National Training Associates (1989) *Youth Empowering Systems*. Sebastopol, CA: National Training Associates.

Peters, R.D. (1988) Mental health promotion in children and adolescents. *Canadian Journal of Behavioural Science*, 20, 389–401.

Quest International (1988) *Skills for adolescence*. Granville, OH: Quest International.

Sprinthall, N. and Mosher, R. (1970) Psychological education in secondary schools: a programme to promote individual and human development. *American Psychologist*, 25, 911–24.

Tennyson, W.W., Miller, G.D., Skovholt, T.G. and Williams, R.C. (1989) Secondary school counselors: What do they do? What is important? *School Counselor*, 36, 253–9.

Thomas, M.D. (1989) The counselor in effective schools. *School Counselor*, 36, 247–52.

Van Hesteren, F. and Pawlovich, W. (1989) A Canadian Guidance and Counselling Association position paper for the provision of counselling services. *Canadian Journal of Counselling*, 23, 184–93.

CHAPTER 5

Developmental counselling and guidance programmes in the schools

Developments in the USA

NORMAN C. GYSBERS

The history of organized counselling and guidance in the USA can be divided into three distinct but overlapping time periods. The first period began around the turn of the century and continued into the 1920s. It was characterized by an emphasis on the transition from school to work: the choice of an occupation, appropriate preparation for it, and the attainment of success in it (Parsons, 1909). The second period emerged in the 1920s as distinct changes began to occur in the theory and practice of guidance. Beginning in the 1920s, guidance theory and practice became more clinically orientated. Increasingly, emphasis was placed on counselling, counselling for personal adjustment. This emphasis continued to dominate the field until the late 1960s. Today, counselling and guidance in the USA has entered a new era. The focus is on comprehensive, developmental counselling and guidance programmes organized systematically around person-centred outcomes – programmes that have both preventive and responsive components. This chapter briefly reviews this evolution and then presents in more detail the nature and structure of comprehensive, developmental counselling and guidance programmes in the USA today.

The early years 1900–1920: counselling and guidance for selection and placement

Modern guidance and counselling in the USA was born during the early 1900s at the height of the Progressive Movement as 'but one manifestation of the broader movement of progressive reform which occurred in this country in the late nineteenth and early twentieth centuries' (Stephens, 1970, p. 5). Individuals such as Frank Parsons, Meyer Bloomfield, Jessie Davis, Anna Reed, Eli Weaver and David Hill, working through a number of organizations and movements, such as the settlement house movement, the National Society for Promotion of Industrial Education (NSPIE) and schools in Grand Rapids, Seattle, New York and New Orleans, were instrumental in formulating and implementing early conceptions of counselling and guidance in the United States.

A major emphasis of counselling and guidance between 1900 and 1920 was the transition from school to work. The term 'vocational guidance' was used for the first time by Frank Parsons in 1908 to define and describe organized guidance activities which assisted individuals in this transition process (Davis, 1969). Parsons' formulation of vocational guidance indicates he viewed it as a series of contacts with a counsellor in which individuals would come to an understanding of self and the work world. Self-study was an important part of this process. The anticipated outcomes of these activities were that individuals would choose appropriate occupations and then prepare and progress in them.

Changes in theory and practice, 1920–1970: counselling and guidance for adjustment

Parsons' formulation plus those of other early leaders had, by 1920, spread across the United States. During the early 1920s however, a number of visible shifts began to occur in these early approaches. Gradually, traditional vocational concerns began to be overshadowed by the educational and psychological problems of personal adjustment (Johnson, 1972). Vocational guidance began to take on a more personal, diagnostic, clinical orientation. As a result, a new model began to emerge, one that was clinical in nature. Counselling rather than guidance became more popular.

While the personal adjustment theme continued to play a dominant role in counselling and guidance theory and practice from the 1930s to 1960s, the earlier conception of guidance as vocational continued to show strength too. Evidence of this was apparent in the efforts of such organizations as the National Vocational Guidance Association (now the National Career Development Association) and the federal government as they both worked to develop and improve occupational information and vocational guidance practices during the 1930s (the Depression years) and the 1940s (the war years and returning veterans). It was apparent too, in federal legislation, including the George–Barden Act of 1946, the Vocational Educational Act of 1963 and the Amendments to that Act in 1968.

A new focus, 1970 and beyond: counselling and guidance for development

Although the personal adjustment theme for counselling and guidance continued to play a dominant role in theory and practice through the 1960s, it was clear that substantial changes were already under way by that time. The call for change in the focus and practice of counselling and guidance in the United States in the 1960s came from diverse sources: writers who were interested in career guidance and career development (Ashcroft, 1966; Hoyt, 1974; Tennyson *et al.*, 1965); individuals who were concerned about the efficacy of the prevailing model of guidance in the schools (Borow, 1966; Aubrey, 1969); writers who were concerned about programme evaluation (Wellman and Twiford, 1961; Wellman, 1968); and individuals who advocated a developmental approach to guidance in the schools (Mathewson, 1962; Zaccaria, 1966). The call for change was reinforced by the accountability movement in education in the USA which had begun during the 1960s. As education was being called to be accountable for its outcomes, so too was counselling and guidance.

In the early 1970s the accountability movement intensified. It was joined by increasing interests in career development theory, research, and practice and their educational manifestations, career guidance and career education. Other educational movements such as psychological education, moral education and process education also were under way. In addition, interest in the development of comprehensive, systematic approaches to guidance programme development and management continued to increase. The convergence of these movements in the 1970s served as a stimulus to continue the task of defining guidance developmentally in measurable individual outcome terms – as a programme in its own right with a content base rather than as process-orientated services, ancillary to the other programmes in the schools.

The work of putting comprehensive, developmental counselling and guidance programmes into place in the schools of the USA continued in the 1980s and early 1990s. Many states published state guides to assist local school district counsellors and administrators to remodel and revitalize their local programmes. How the states of Missouri, Alaska and New Hampshire as well as several school districts across the country undertook the planning, designing, implementing and evaluating phases of installing their comprehensive developmental programmes was documented by Gysbers (1990) in an ERIC/CAPS publication, *Comprehensive Guidance Programs That Work*.

Thus, what began at the turn of the century in US schools under the term 'vocational guidance' with a selection and placement focus, and then shifted in the 1920s, 1930s, 1940s and 1950s to a focus on personal adjustment, organized around a counsellor–clinical-services model, has now assumed a developmental focus, organized around the framework of a comprehensive programme. Selection, placement and adjustment remain, but are included in the concept of development. Organizationally the framework of a comprehensive programme has incorporated the vocational guidance, counsellor–clinical-services models, and, in the 1990s, has become the major way of organizing and managing counselling and guidance in the schools. The position orientations of the past have been transformed into developmental, comprehensive counselling and guidance programmes.

Basic premises undergirding comprehensive developmental counselling and guidance programmes

Just as we need to understand how counselling and guidance in US schools evolved into a programme, so too do we need to understand the basic premises which undergird the comprehensive, developmental programme concept. An understanding of these basic premises is important because they are serving as the philosophical foundation for the organization and management of counselling and guidance in the schools of the United States in the 1990s and beyond.

Counselling and guidance is a programme.
As a programme counselling and guidance has characteristics similar to other programmes in education, including:

1. Student outcomes (student competencies);
2. Activities and processes to assist students in achieving these outcomes;
3. Professionally recognized personnel; and
4. Materials and resources.

Guidance programmes are developmental and comprehensive.
Developmental, comprehensive counselling and guidance programmes are developmental in that counselling and guidance activities are conducted on a regular, planned and systematic basis to assist students to achieve specified competencies. Although the immediate and crisis needs of students are to be met, a major focus of comprehensive, developmental programmes is to provide all students with experiences to help them grow and develop. Guidance programmes are comprehensive in that a full range of activities and services such as assessment, information, consultation, counselling, and referral, placement, follow-up and follow-through are provided.

Comprehensive, development counselling and guidance programmes feature a team approach.
A comprehensive, developmental programme of counselling and guidance is based on the assumption that all school staff are involved. At the same time, it is understood that professionally certified school counsellors are central to the programme. School counsellors provide direct services to students as well as work in consultative and collaborative relations with other members of the guidance team, including teachers, administrators, parents and members of the community.

Comprehensive, developmental guidance programme elements

The structure for comprehensive, developmental counselling and guidance programmes presented in this chapter was developed by Gysbers and Henderson (1988) based on earlier work by Gysbers and Moore (1981). It has been adopted and/or adapted by many states and local school districts in the United States as a way to organize and manage their counselling and guidance responsibilities. The structure has three elements: content; organizational framework, sample activities, time; and resources.

Content

One of the assumptions upon which comprehensive, developmental counselling and guidance programmes are based is that there is guidance content that all students should learn in a sequential, systematic way. A major feature of comprehensive, developmental counselling and guidance is a focus on student outcomes (competencies), the achievement of which are the responsibility of the programme. Knowledge and skills to be learned by students as a result of the programme are variously gouped under such categories as (1) personal, social, career and educational; (2) knowledge of self and others, career planning and exploration, and educational and vocational development; or (3) learning, personal/ social, and career/vocational. These categories serve to identify domain or content areas of human growth and development from which student competencies are drawn.

Organizational framework, activities, time

The organizational framework element contains three structural components and four programme components along with example programme activities and counsellor time distributions across the four programme components.

Structural components The first structural component is *definition*. The definition of the programme identifies the centrality of counselling and guidance within the educational process and delineates, in broad outcome terms, the competencies students will possess as a result of their participation in the programme. The second structural component is *rationale*. It focuses on reasons why students need to acquire counselling and guidance competencies and have access to the assistance that comprehensive developmental counselling and guidance programmes provide. The final structural component is *assumptions*. Assumptions identify and describe the premises on which comprehensive, developmental counselling and guidance programmes rest. They give the programme shape and direction.

To illustrate what one of these components looks like in more detail, the following is the rationale used by Northside Independent School District, San Antonio, Texas.

NORTHSIDE COMPREHENSIVE GUIDANCE PROGRAM RATIONALE

The ever-increasing needs of children and the expectations of today's society impose growing demands on our educational system and its resources. Educators are challenged to educate students with diverse backgrounds at an ever-higher level of literacy to meet the demands of an internationally competitive, technological marketplace. At the same time, societal and other factors cause some of our children to attend school ill-equipped emotionally, physically, and/or socially to learn. Schools must respond by providing support for all students to learn effectively.

Community influences and societal changes generate identifiable student needs which may not be met solely by classroom instructional programs. Meeting these needs is essential to individual gowth, and can be accomplished through a planned educational program combining instruction and guidance.

Northside Independent School District provides a comprehensive and balanced guidance program. The *Framework* describes the elements common to the programs district-wide; however, each campus designs its own program to meet the District minimum expectations and to meet the needs of the community it serves. As each school designs its guidance program, the rationale for the local design rests on an assessment of local student and community needs.

Some specific student needs identified in 1991–92 are those for

> a sense of connection
> someone to listen
> support systems
> advocacy
> personal management skills
> career skills, life skills
> self-esteem
> valuing education as an investment in the future
> learning to give of oneself
> problem-solving skills.

Programme components The nature and structure of the delivery system for counselling and guidance (the programme components) were determined on the basis of answers to the following questions:

- Are there knowledge, skills, and attitudes needed by all students that should be the instructional responsibility of counselling and guidance programmes?

- Do students have the right to have someone in the school system sensitive to their unique life career development needs, including needs for placement and follow-through?

- Should guidance staff be available and responsive to special or unexpected needs of students, staff, parents, and the community?

- Does the school programme and staff require support that can be best supplied by guidance personnel?

The structure suggested by an affirmative answer to these four questions and by a review of the literature is a programme model of guidance techniques, methods and resources containing four interactive components: *guidance curriculum, individual planning, responsive services* and *system support* (Gysbers and Moore, 1981).

One of the assumptions upon which this conception of counselling and guidance is based is that there is guidance content that all students should learn in a systematic, sequential way. This means counsellor and teacher involvement and collaboration in the curriculum; it means a *guidance curriculum*. This is not a new idea in the United States; the notion of a guidance curriculum has deep historical roots. What is new, however, is the array of guidance and counselling techniques, methods and resources currently available that work best as a part of a curriculum. What is new, too, is the concept that counselling and guidance has an organized and sequential curriculum similar to other programmes in the school district.

The purpose of the *individual planning* component of the programme is to provide all students with guidance activities to assist them to plan for and then monitor and manage their personal–social, educational and occupational development. The focus of the activities in this component is on students' developing plans consistent with their personal–social, educational and occupational goals. Through the activities of this component, school counsellors and others with guidance responsibilities, including teachers, serve students and parents as facilitators of students' personal–social, educational and occupational development. The plans that students develop and use are both processes and instruments. As processes, students' plans evolve throughout the school years, responding to successions of guidance activities provided through the guidance curriculum and individual planning components of the programme. As instruments, plans provide structured ways for students to gather, analyse, synthesize and organize self, educational and occupational information. As processes, plans are vehicles through which this information is incorporated into short-range and long-range goal setting, decision-making and planning activities. As instruments, plans are not tracks to be plotted and followed routinely; they are, instead, blueprints for life quests.

Problems relating to academic learning, personal identity issues, drugs and peer and family relationships continue to be a part of the educational scene. As a result there is a continuing need for crisis counselling, diagnostic and remediation activities, and consultation and referral to be an ongoing part of a comprehensive, developmental counselling and guidance programme. In addition, there is a continuing need for the programme to respond to the immediate information-seeking needs of students, parents and teachers.

The *responsive services* component organizes counselling and guidance techniques and methods to respond to these concerns and needs as they occur. In addition, the responsive services component is supportive of the guidance curriculum and individual planning components. Responsive services consist of activities to meet the immediate needs and concerns of students whether these needs or concerns require counselling, consultation, referral or information. Although counsellors have special training and possess skills to respond to immediate needs and concerns, the collaboration and co-operation of teachers, administrators and parents are necessary for the component's successful implementation.

The administration and management of a comprehensive guidance programme require an ongoing support system. That is why *system support* is a major programme component. The system support component consists of management activities that establish, maintain and enhance the total programme. Also included in the system support component are those activities in the school that support programmes other than guidance. These activities could include being involved in the school testing programme (helping interpret test results for use by teachers, parents and administrators), serving on departmental curriculum committees (helping interpret student needs data for curriculum revision), and working with school administrators (helping interpret student needs and behaviours). Fair-share responsibilities, the routine 'running of the school' tasks that all members of the building take equal turns doing, are also part of the system support component. Care must be taken however, to watch the time given to system support duties because the prime focus for counsellors' time is the direct service components of the comprehensive developmental counselling and guidance programme. It is important to realize that if the programme is well run, it provides substantial support for the other programmes and personnel in the school and community.

School counsellor time allocation School counsellors' professional time is a crucial variable in developing and implementing a comprehensive developmental counselling and guidance programme. How should professional certified school counsellors allocate their time? What criteria should be used to guide the time allocations process?

The four programme components provide the structure for making judgements about appropriate allocations of counsellors' time. One criterion used in making such judgements is the concept of programme balance. The guidance curriculum, individual planning and responsive services components bring together the direct services counsellors and other guidance personnel provided to students, parents, teachers and the community, while the system support component organizes the indirect services of the programme. The assumption is that counsellors' time should be spread across all of the programme components, but particularly the first three, in an 80 : 20 or a 75 : 25 ratio.

Another criterion is that different grade levels require different allocations of counsellor time across the programme components. For example, at the elementary level more counsellor time may be spent working in the curriculum with less time spent in individual planning. In the high school, those time allocations probably would be reversed.

How personnel in a school district or school building allocate their time depends on the needs of their students and their community. Also, once chosen, the time allocations are not fixed forever. The purpose for making them is to provide direction to the programme, to the administration and to the counsellors involved.

Since the programme is a '100 per cent programme', 100 per cent of counsellors' time must be spread across the four programme components. Time allocations can be changed on the basis of newly arising needs, but nothing new can be added unless something is removed. The

Table 5.1

	Per cent		
	ES	M/JH	HS
Guidance curriculum	35–45	25–53	15–25
Individual planning	05–10	15–25	25–53
Responsive services	30–40	30–40	25–35
System support	10–15	10–15	15–20

assumption is that professional counsellors should spend 100 per cent of their time on task, implementing the guidance programme. Remember this 100 per cent includes the fair share responsibilities found in the system support component.

What are some suggested percentages? As an example, the state of Missouri (Starr and Gysbers, 1992) has adopted suggested percentages of counsellor time to be spent on each programme component (Table 5.1). These suggested percentages of time were recommended by Missouri counsellors and administrators who had participated in the field testing of the Missouri Comprehensive Guidance Programme Model from 1984 to 1988.

Programme resources

Human resources The human resources of a comprehensive, developmental counselling and guidance programme – counsellors, teachers, administrators, parents, students, community members and business and labour personnel – all have roles to play in the guidance programme. While counsellors are the main providers of guidance and counselling services and are the co-ordinators of the progamme, the involvement, co-operation, and support of teachers and administrators are necessary for the programme to be successful. The involvement, co-operation and support of parents, community members and business and labour personnel also are critical.

Financial resources Appropriate and adequate financial resources are crucial to the success of a comprehensive, developmental counselling and guidance programme. The financial resource categories required for a programme include budget, materials, equipment and facilities. A budget for the programme is needed to fund and then allocate those funds across the buildings and grade levels of the district. Materials and equipment are needed so that guidance activities across the four programme components can be fully implemented. And finally, well-designed guidance facilities in each building, organized to meet the needs of the guidance programme, are required.

Political resources The political resources of a comprehensive development, counselling and guidance programme include district policy statements, pertinent state and federal laws, state board of education rules and regulations, and professional association statements and standards. Clear and concise board of education policies are mandatory for the successful operation of guidance programmes in school districts. Since they represent courses of action, or guiding principles designed to influence and determine decisions in school districts, those that pertain to guidance programmes must take into account pertinent laws, rules and regulations and standards as they are being written, adopted and implemented.

Concluding thoughts

A comprehensive, developmental counselling and guidance programme by definition leads to guidance and counselling activities for all students. It removes administrative and clerical tasks not related to the operation of the guidance programme (remembering that fair share responsibilities that all staff members have are part of the system support component), one-to-one counselling only, and limited accountability. It is proactive rather than reactive. Counsellors are busy and unavailable for unrelated administrative and clerical duties because they have a programme to implement. Counsellors are expected to do personal and crisis counselling as well as provide structured activities for all students in collaborative relationships with teachers.

Finally, the full implementation of comprehensive, developmental counselling and guidance programmes in the schools requires that counsellors, teachers and administrators must:

- Understand that a comprehensive, developmental counselling guidance programme is *student development orientated*, not school management or administration orientated;
- Operate a comprehensive, developmental counselling and guidance programme as a *one hundred per cent programme*; the four programme components constitute the total programme, there are no add-ons;
- Start the comprehensive guidance programme the *first day of school and end it the last day of school*, not begin in the middle of October and end in April, so that administrative, non-guidance tasks can be completed;
- Understand that a comprehensive guidance programme is *programme-focused, not position-focused*; and
- Understand that a comprehensive guidance programme is *education-based, not agency or clinic-based*.

References

Ashcroft, K.B. (1966) *A Report of the Invitational Conference in Implementing Career Development Theory*. Washington, DC: National Vocational Guidance Association.

Aubrey, R.F. (1969) Misapplication of therapy models to school counselling. *Personnel and Guidance Journal*, 48, 273–8.

Borow, H. (1966) Research in vocational development: implications for the vocational aspects of counselor education. In McDaniels, C. (ed.), *Vocational Aspects of Counselor Education*. Washington, DC: George Washington University.

Davis, H.V. (1969) *Frank Parsons: Prophet, Innovator, Counselor.* Carbondale: Southern Illinois University Press.

Gysbers, N.C. and Moore, E.J. (1981) *Improving Guidance Programs.* Englewood Cliffs, NJ: Prentice-Hall.

Gysbers, N.C. and Henderson, P. (1988) *Developing and Managing Your School Guidance Program*. Alexandria, VA: American Association for Counseling and Development.

Gysbers, N.C. (1990) *Comprehensive Guidance Programs That Work*, Ann Arbor, MI: ERIC/CAPS.

Hoyt, K.B. (1974) Professional preparation for vocational guidance. In Herr, E.L. (ed.), *Vocational Guidance and Human Development.* Boston: Houghton Mifflin.

Johnson, A.H. (1972) Changing conceptions of vocational guidance and concomitant value-orientations 1920–1930. *Dissertation Abstracts International*, 33, 3292A (University Microfilms No. 72-31, 933).

Mathewson, R.H. (1962) *Guidance Policy and Practice* (3rd edn). New York: Harper & Row.

Parsons, F. (1909) *Choosing a Vocation*. Boston: Houghton Mifflin.

Starr, M. and Gysbers, N.C. (1992) *Missouri Comprehensive Guidance: A Model for Program Development, Implementation, and Evaluation*. Jefferson City: Missouri Department of Elementary and Secondary Education.

Stephens, W.R. (1970) *Social Reform and the Origins of Vocational Guidance*. Washington, DC: National Vocational Guidance Association.

Tennyson, W.W., Soldahl, T.A. and Mueller, C. (1965) *The Teacher's Role in Career Development*. Washington, DC: National Vocational Guidance Association.

Wellman, F.E. and Twiford, D.D. (1961) *Guidance, Counseling, and Testing: Program Evaluation*. Washington, DC: US Department of Health, Education, and Welfare.

Wellman, F.E. (1968) *Contractor's Report, Phase 1, National Study of Guidance*. Contract OEG 3-6-001147-1147. Washington, DC: US Department of Health, Education, and Welfare.

Zaccaria, J.S. (1966) Developmental guidance: a concept in transition. *School Counselor*, 13, 226–9.

CHAPTER 6

A whole-school approach to pastoral care

A New Zealand perspective

ROSIE ARNOTT

Introduction

Many parallels may be drawn between the British system of pastoral care and the development of the New Zealand secondary schools' guidance networks. The early New Zealand secondary schools were private institutions, based on the model of the British public school with 'house' systems, where 'house parents' offered advice and guidance to their young charges. As in Britain, the expanding state education sector adopted this model, which developed into a variety of pastoral care systems, grouping young people into form or tutor groups, 'houses' or year bands and providing a hierarchy of staff responsible for the guidance, well-being and discipline of the students. Systems in both countries expanded and developed throughout the relatively affluent and liberal 1960s and 1970s, though the New Zealand system broadened its perspective, incorporating ideas and influences from the USA (Webb, 1981) along with those of the increasingly influential Maori community. Guidance counsellors were introduced to complement the system of tutorial care, and guidance networks developed from there. More recently, a programme of 'transition' education has been incorporated into the curriculum to help young people to adjust to the challenges and demands of leaving school. State education in both countries has undergone major reconstruction over the past few years, and the rapid pace of change appears to be continuing. This reconstruction has been characterized by economic deficiencies and a political climate that favours competition and a 'market forces' approach. However, whereas the New Zealand core curriculum makes the inclusion of pastoral care a statutory requirement, the 'guidelines' for personal and social development in the recently introduced National Curriculum in Britain have no such teeth.

This chapter will outline the New Zealand system of educational guidance, comparing and contrasting it with that found in England and Wales. In particular, it will examine the relationship between pastoral systems and school counsellors – services which co-exist in most New Zealand secondary schools, unlike their counterparts in the UK. In the final section, the New Zealand situation will be illustrated through a case study of developments in a particular high school.

A brief comparison

Secondary schools in New Zealand, as in the UK, generally describe themselves as 'caring' institutions, concerned with the development of the whole child (Harris-Springett, 1985; Buckley, 1980). They substantiate such claims with descriptions of administrative structures and particular courses designed to promote the affective aims of education and the social, emotional and spiritual development of their students. In New Zealand, this 'affective' aspect of education is known as 'educational guidance' and in the UK as 'pastoral care'. Despite considerable rhetoric supporting these systems, both have suffered from a lack of conceptual clarity and the wide range of interpretation characteristic of terms which have not been clearly defined. There has been an assumption in both countries that because the administrative structures were in place, pastoral care or educational guidance was happening (Best, 1989). As a New Zealand guidance counsellor has remarked, 'The concern for children's all-round development has been implicit rather than explicit [in New Zealand education]' (Harris-Springett, 1985, p. 25).

In New Zealand the term 'guidance' is used to encompass a wide range of services, including 'pastoral care' (as it is understood in Britain), classroom programmes of personal and social education, educational and vocational guidance and specialist individual counselling. The 1973 Working Party Report, *Guidance in Secondary Schools* (Department of Education, 1973, p. 4), stated: 'When we speak of guidance we shall have in mind all the influences in a school that bear on choices and decisions that pupils make in respect of their own personal, educational and vocational concerns.'

Prior to the 1940s, guidance was implicit in the structural organization and pastoral care relationships found in the small schools of the time. Career or vocational guidance was evident as far back as 1913, with the voluntary involvement of the YMCA and the YWCA. As it developed further, by 1946 'guidance' was mostly associated with the aim of fitting students to appropriate courses and careers (Webb, 1981). Careers advisers were appointed to schools in 1948, and the Psychological Service was set up at this time. In 1959 the first two guidance counsellor positions were established in secondary schools, as an experiment to be compared with two visiting teacher positions. Visiting teachers were already an integral part of the primary sector, with one visiting teacher serving several primary or intermediate schools. They fulfil a similar role to that of the educational welfare officers found in England. However, the visiting teacher scheme for secondary schools was dropped in favour of the guidance counsellor scheme, as secondary schools preferred the idea of one person attached to each school who could be more involved with its running. 'The balance swung in favour of the Counsellor–Psychologist, rather than the Counsellor–Social Worker' (Webb, 1981, p. 18).

In the 1960s, guidance was seen as having a remedial function and the Currie Commission of 1962 discussed it under the heading of 'Delinquency in our Schools'. It was recommended for use in the large new comprehensive schools, in technical colleges and in those schools with a high proportion of Maori students. During this period of time, the Department of Education gradually increased the number of guidance counsellors in secondary schools, and by 1967, 25 full-time counselling positions had been established.

In 1973, the New Zealand government published *Guidance in Secondary Schools*. By this time, over one-third of New Zealand secondary schools had guidance counsellors and the working party set out to look for trends in guidance that were worthy of encouragement. The report recommended that guidance should be a shared responsibility between all members of staff, forming a 'network of services and personal influences aimed at helping students assess themselves, plan and make decisions on a wide range of issues that are important to them' (Department of Education, 1973; p. 57). One of the implications of this recommendation was a move towards guidance-centred rather than subject-centred schools. Other major recommendations included changes in the careers advisory service in schools. There had been concern from the business sector in New Zealand that the emphasis on comprehensive guidance in schools would be to the detriment of careers advice, and the working party was asked to look into the validity of those concerns. In fact it recommended that the part-time careers adviser positions in schools be disestablished, and that two full-time counsellors be appointed to cover the whole range of guidance issues. Although this did not become official policy, there was certainly a move in that direction with many schools adopting the recommendations in their staffing policies. Appropriate training for guidance counsellors was also an issue for the working party and it suggested that a 12-week inservice course be introduced. However, in 1972, Canterbury University in Christchurch introduced the first one-year full-time course, since when all new appointees are required to attend one of the three university courses offered.

Since the 1973 report, the Department of Education has continued to promote the role of guidance in secondary schools. It has stressed the importance of networks, not only within the schools, but with supporting agencies such as the Psychological Service. Time and finance have been made available for guidance, according to the size of the school, and a member of the inspectorate made responsible for guidance in each inspectorial area. The 1973 Johnson Report states that 'the aim of guidance is to promote the educational, vocational and personal growth of students. Every student has the right to guidance and every teacher needs to be involved in it. It should permeate every aspect of school activity and should consider the best interests of the total community, as well as of the individuals in it' (Department of Education, 1973, 2.2.2). By the mid-1980s, guidance networks in New Zealand secondary schools were well established and generally considered successful and acceptable. The guidance network in a typical form 3–7 (ages 13–18) New Zealand high school of about 800 students might be: deputy principal (guidance); one or two guidance counsellors; five year or house deans; 25 form tutors.

The Henderson High School guidance network

One New Zealand high school that has attempted to incorporate the 'guidance-centred' philosophy into every facet of its structure and practice is Henderson High School, which is situated approximately 20 kilometres north-west of Auckland city. The importance of the personal and social development of the students is emphasized from the first contacts made with them and their parents via the contributing intermediate schools and is incorporated into every aspect of school life. Strong links are maintained with the community and with local colleges of further education, and a variety of support services are welcomed into the school. A very dynamic transition programme offers specific careers advice, health and safety courses and life skills for school leavers. Henderson High School is a co-educational, multi-cultural, multi-course state school, which caters for students from form 3 to form 7 (ages 13–18) and supports a comprehensive adult student programme. The students come from a wide variety of ethnic and cultural backgrounds: indigenous Maori, Samoan, British, Dutch, Yugoslavian, Tongan, Fijian, Niuean, Cook Island, Indian, Vietnamese and Cambodian. The school is divided into five learning units, each with its own teaching and learning style, which aims to address the differing needs of individual students. Like all New Zealand state schools, Henderson is self-governing, with an elected board of trustees representing the local community, the teaching staff and the students. The school is managed by a corporate management group consisting of the principal, two deputy principals, two curriculum co-ordinators and two student directors. The guidance network consists of the deputy principal (guidance) the deans of the learning units, the form tutors and the guidance counsellor, and all teaching staff are seen as having a responsibility in this aspect of school life. The ethos of the school is embodied in the school philosophy as stated in the 1991 prospectus (Henderson High School, 1990):

Henderson High School aims to develop in all its students:

- self-respect/sense of self worth
- respect for others
- a desire to learn/urge to enquire
- an ability to make more decisions for themselves

In an environment which values:

- the uniqueness of every person
- the multi-cultural nature of the community
- equality and equity for all
- the special place of Taha Maori in New Zealand

The school is committed to:

- enabling students to become self-empowering with

the knowledge, creativity and personal skills to take a full and informed part as happy and successful citizens in the community

- acknowledging that each student has unique strengths and talents and that it is the school's task to identify these and help the student attain excellence in them

This philosophy articulates easily with Buckley's (1980) definition of a 'caring community' and may be examined in the light of Best's (1989) model. The needs of the child are placed alongside and integrated with those of the pupil or learner as with the needs of the citizen. The key to the successful implementation of this philosophy is the management structure which leads by example and is representative of all members of the school community.

The learning units

As previously explained, most New Zealand high schools have an internal organizational structure similar to that found in most British secondary schools. Students are grouped into forms or tutor groups with a further grouping into year or house bands, the most common variable being whether or not students are streamed by ability. Henderson High School is unique, in this writer's experience, in its 'schools within schools' method of organization, where students are grouped according to their preferred learning style. Buckley (1980) endorses this model as a means of fully integrating the school's care and concern for the individual within the learning–teaching situation. He emphasizes the importance of the relationship between the learner and the teacher if there is to be effective learning and that the purpose of developing positive relationships in schools is in order to enhance the learning process. The importance of effective communication, or a common understanding between the learner and teacher, is also emphasized, as is the need for the teacher and learner to spend adequate amounts of 'time' together, working at a particular 'task'. These conditions, he affirms, constitute a relationship which embodies 'pedagogic care' rather than a 'soft-centred concern'. In order for this pedagogic care to become institutionalized, he argues, the school organization needs to be designed to allow for the following (Buckley, 1980):

- a group of teachers to be responsible for the 'whole' development of a group of learners;
- dialogue between those teachers who teach the same learners;
- decision-making about those learners and their learning to take place as close as possible to those learners in the total school structure; and
- dialogue between the teachers and learners about the effectiveness of the teaching and learning.

In order to provide optimum learning conditions for this very diverse group of students, Henderson High School is divided into five learning units. This development occurred over a period of several years as the staff and principal recognized the benefits to be gained from such a move. The system was created to provide students with a choice of five different styles or emphases of learning–teaching. Each unit is headed by a dean/ co-ordinator, is made up of mixed-ability groupings (apart from the special education unit) and is served by a team of teachers. Students take the 'core' subjects of English, mathematics, social studies and science within their unit groups and mix with students and teachers from other units for a variety of 'options'. The school runs a (cross-unit) 'enrichment' programme for students identified as being very able and also offers individual programmes for students with language or reading needs.

The special needs unit   At Henderson High School, there has long been a special needs unit, previously known as a work experience unit. This forms part of the nationwide network of such provision for secondary-age students with moderate learning difficulties and serves a large area of West Auckland. The students are referred to this unit by the Education Department Psychological Service – a process which may be equated with the UK system of 'statementing'. The small numbers of pupils allows for individual educational programmes, though in recent years there has been a recognition that many of the students have particular strengths and abilities that are better served in mainstream classes. The unit therefore concentrates on a programme of personal and social education, aimed at assisting the students towards an awareness of their own strengths, raising self-esteem and promoting behaviours which will allow the students to access more readily the wider community and to live independent and fulfilled lives. The unit is now more fully integrated into the school, with all of the students participating in mainstream options. Unit staff act as an advisory resource for other members of staff. Reverse integration happens as the enrichment programme and the sixth-form life-skills programme take place within this unit. Anecdotal evidence would suggest that 'labelling' of students is no longer a problem associated with this unit.

The flexitime learning unit   The flexitime learning unit began in 1987 as a response to the particular interests of a group of teachers and students in the school. It aims to provide a peaceful, holistic learning environment in which students can develop fully – academically and socially. As the name suggests, in this unit students have some flexibility in the way they use their learning time. Specifically, the unit aims are:

- to encourage students to take responsibility for their own learning and actions;
- to encourage students to set realistic goals and evaluate their achievements;
- to encourage academic excellence and a desire to learn how to learn;
- to encourage a willingness to learn by experience and to become involved in a wide variety of learning activities;

- to encourage students to negotiate willingly and assert themselves so that their needs are met;
- to encourage tolerance of others and an appreciation of the uniqueness of all individuals.

Reo Maori Tuturu learning unit   This unit was established in recognition of the unique place of the Maori people in New Zealand society. It is for all students who wish to become fluent in Reo Maori (the Maori language). It offers varying degrees of commitment/language immersion from a full bilingual unit (Te Rito o te Reo) to an enriched/augmented Maori language programme. The aims of the unit (Henderson High School, 1990) are:

Personal:

To give dignity and self-worth by experiencing the strength and support of a whanau-based society.

To develop the ability for self-examination and accept, with whanau (extended family) support, the consequences of personal actions.

To cultivate a sense of community development and responsibility through participating in the completion of the wharenui (meeting house) with carving, tukutuku (woven panels) kowhaiwhai and weaving so that 'the house becomes imbued with the wairua [spirit] of each student who in turn becomes certain of turangawaewae [belonging] and gains respect for the wider community and property'.

Cognitive:

To provide a model based on traditional whakawa method as an alternative to the persuasive counter-culture to which many are attracted in the wider community.

To promote bilingual, bicultural students through a targeting of Maori language and culture.

Though not totally unproblematic, the success of these smaller learning units with their element of choice and specific objectives was self-evident. During the course of 1988 it was decided to experiment by dividing the remaining students in the school into two smaller units, each with a specific emphasis. Many of the teaching staff had expressed a preference for an integrated studies approach to learning–teaching, though it was recognized that this method did not suit many others who preferred a more traditional, subject-based approach. This division of opinion was also evident in the wider community, so the natural course of events was to offer students, parents and teachers a choice. Existing students were canvassed and given the chance to opt for the unit of their choice. Those who showed no particular preference were allocated to units by the members of the guidance network. Newly enrolling students and their parents were given information at public meetings and in written form, in a variety of languages, in order to assist them in making the choice. The Department of Education adviser on guidance and the liaison inspector were also involved and informed of these developments and showed a great deal of interest and support.

The team learning unit Within the context of Henderson High School's basic philosophy, the team learning unit emphasizes the wholeness of the curriculum, not fragmented by divisions of school organization, time-tabling or subject barriers. It utilizes co-operative planning and implementation of the curriculum by all of the teachers, in conjunction with the students. It aims to enable students to take increasing responsibility for their own learning and be involved with teachers in setting their own goals, organizing their own studies and activities and evaluating their own learning and achievements. The team learning unit aims to: 'provide education of the highest quality in a way that is accessible, balanced, responsive, and inclusive for the total student group, giving them opportunity for success and enjoyment as well as a life long love of education' (Henderson High School, 1990).

The focus learning unit The focus learning unit offers a wider variety of teacher contact, on an individual subject basis. This specialization appeals not only to many of the students and teachers, but also to many parents. There is a greater emphasis on catering to the individual needs of the students, within a very secure and supportive environment. Tutor groups are arranged vertically, with the older students being encouraged to share in the management of each group. The main objective of the unit again reflects the philosophy of the whole school, with positive reinforcement for academic improvement and socially acceptable behaviour. The main aims of the unit, as stated in the 1991 prospectus, are: the development of a personal values system; encouraging positive attitudes towards others; the development of learning skills; academic achievement; the development of cultural interests.

Each unit's aims and objectives are reviewed annually, both in a specific unit-based sense and in relation to the whole school. The unit Dean/co-ordinators have a timetabled meeting once a week with the deputy principal (guidance) and the school guidance counsellor.

The Henderson High School model takes the New Zealand Department of Education recommendations for a guidance-centred school quite literally. There are structures within the school that are specifically designed to meet the social and emotional needs of individual students, a thoroughly institutionalized guidance network and links with the outside support agencies and with the wider community. It appears that the Henderson High School model satisfies all criteria of Buckley's (1980) definition of a 'caring environment'. The needs of the child are met by the provision of small units of learning, offering security, warmth and guidance, and, one would suppose, love, patience and support. The needs of the pupil are similarly met as the school recognizes that students and teachers have differing preferences in learning/teaching styles (Borich, 1988). Each unit acknowledges the importance of enhancing self-esteem and increasing independence as part of the learning process (Holt, 1970)

and lists among its aims the opportunities for students to acquire concepts, learn facts, practise skills, develop attitudes, etc. The needs of
the citizen are met by the sense of participation and belonging inherent
in the unit structure, and also by the umbrella of the overall school
philosophy which is reflected in that of each of the units. The school
has a set of general school rules, clearly stated and impartially applied,
which are designed to: 'protect [you] and help [you] stay safe and keep
out of hassles' (Henderson High School, 1990). The staff and students
are also required to acknowledge and abide by a set of 'rights and responsibilities'. Specific courses, such as transition education (involving
careers information and work experience plus living skills and political
and social education), assist the students in their appreciation of the
their place in the wider community. The ethos of the school is enhanced
by the importance placed on 'peace education'. The school community
is 'a violence-free zone' where students are helped to handle conflict
in a non-confrontational, non-violent way. Students are taught anger
management techniques and assured that physical and verbal violence
are unacceptable forms of behaviour – in the school and in society as a
whole. Students are encouraged to participate in the decision-making
processes of the school, through the unit systems, and also through
representation on the school council, the corporate management team
and the board of trustees. The management of the school leads by
example. Achievements by both staff and students are recognized by the
principal, who makes a special effort to be aware of everything that is
happening in the school yet is well able to step back and delegate responsibility to others. There are open channels of communication between
management and teaching staff, and the principal has a sequence of
personal interviews, ensuring that all staff have the opportunity to
express their ideas or concerns directly to him. There are regular, timetabled inservice courses as well as structured 'teacher-only days' for
more in-depth training sessions.

Summary

Although the New Zealand system of educational guidance has many
similarities to the systems of pastoral care found in British secondary
schools, and indeed faces some of the same problems associated with
the current economic climate and prevalent ideologies, this paper has
demonstrated that there are also vast differences between the two
systems. These differences are not only historical, as New Zealand
culture has diverged from its British antecedents, but also reflects the
geographical location of a country which is closer to the influences of
the West Coast of the USA than to the 'mother country'. The increasing
influence of the tribal or family-based Polynesian cultures is also a
contributory factor. The major difference between the two systems is
that New Zealand schools utilize the role of school counsellor as well
as employing the more traditional pastoral organization of form tutor,
year or house head model seen in most British secondary schools. This
duality has developed further into a system of guidance networks, which
give weight to the importance of the affective aspects of education in

the development of whole-school policy. The care–control dilemma faced by many pastoral heads is bridged with the addition of this extra dimension. Transition from primary to secondary school, and from secondary school to further education or to the world of work or unemployment are recognized as crucial and stressful times for most young people and given appropriate attention in the curriculum.

Henderson High School is an extreme example of the philosophy prevalent in New Zealand secondary schools. Guidance is an integral aspect of the life of the school, with guidance counsellors enhancing the pastoral system and forming a network of services designed to provide optimum learning conditions for the students. The structural organization of the school reflects a contemporary theory that effective learning is enhanced when the individual learning style and associated learning behaviour of the student is taken into consideration (Kolb, 1984; Honey and Mumford, 1986). Despite the differing emphases of each of the learning units, the prevailing ethos of the whole school is one that recognizes the unique qualities and talents of each individual and professes the importance of the personal and social development of all of its students.

References

Best, R. (1989) Pastoral care: some reflections and re-statement. *Pastoral Care in Education*, 7(4), 7–13.

Borich, G. (1988) *Effective Teaching Methods*. Columbus, OH: Merrill.

Buckley, J. (1980) The care of learning: some implications for school organization. In Best, R., Jarvis, C. and Ribbins, P. (eds) *Perspectives on Pastoral Care*. London: Heinemann.

Department of Education (1962) *Report of the Commission on Education in New Zealand* (the Currie Commission). Wellington: Department of Education.

Department of Education (1973) *Guidance in Secondary Schools: Report of a Working Party*. Wellington: Department of Education.

Department of Education (1973) *Growing, Sharing and Learning: The Johnson Report*. Wellington: Department of Education.

Harris-Springett, D. (1985) Developmental group work in secondary schools: a pastoral programme for form teachers. In Codd, F. (ed.) *delta 35*. Palmerston North: Massey University.

Henderson High School (1990) *Prospectus*. Auckland: Henderson High School.

Holt, J. (1970) *How Children Learn*. Harmondsworth: Penguin.

Honey, P. and Mumford, A. (1986) *The Manual of Learning Styles*. Maidenhead: Honey.

Kolb, D.A. (1984) *Experiential Learning*. Englewood Cliffs, NJ: Prentice Hall.

Webb, S. (1981) The development of guidance and counselling in New Zealand secondary schools. Unpublished BPhil thesis, Exeter University.

CHAPTER 7

The development of pastoral care and career guidance in Singapore schools

JAMALIAH SALIM AND ESTHER CHUA

Historical perspective

The first school in Singapore was established in 1823. The pace of educational development in the country was gradual until World War II. Substantial progress was made subsequently in the provision of primary and secondary education. By the early 1980s, the targets of building a sufficient number of schools to ensure the provision of a place for every child and of establishing a national system of education in Singapore had been achieved. The focus was then shifted to improving the quality of education through excellence in schools.

Although care and concern for the welfare of pupils has always been given varying degrees of recognition in our schools, the preoccupation with providing a good academic education and securing excellent results in national examinations has tended to eclipse the guidance and caring aspect of education. In 1973, however, this aspect was eventually recognized by the government when a Social Work Unit was set up in the Ministry of Education. At about the same time, growing concern over the dearth of proper career guidance programmes for our school-leavers led to the establishment of a Career Guidance Unit in the same ministry.

The Social Work Unit, though small in size, provided a service to the schools by helping pupils to cope with socio-emotional problems. It also organized programmes to enable teachers to become conscious that their role goes beyond that of a subject instructor to that of a 'mentor' and 'human developer', responsible for the welfare and all-round development of the pupils. Teachers were encouraged to care actively for their pupils, and the role of the form teacher as being central to those caring activities was emphasized.

The Career Guidance Unit set about gathering, updating and collating information on careers, which was then made available to the pupils through their newly appointed careers teachers and the schools' careers clubs.

In 1979 the structural reorganization of the Ministry of Education had a major impact on the two units: the Social Work Unit was reconstituted as the Guidance and Social Work Unit and the Career Guidance Unit was disbanded, as it was felt that, given the prevalent teacher shortage, it was not productive to train teachers as specialists in career guidance. It was then envisaged that the dissemination of careers information could be better managed by the Ministry of Labour and the Ministry of Trade and Industry. However, manpower constraints also restricted the career guidance efforts of those other ministries and the schools were left to fend for themselves.

The Guidance and Social Work Unit conducted school-based workshops to develop teachers' knowledge and skills in pupil welfare. Most schools, however, gave pupil welfare low priority or retained a very narrow perception of it.

A reactive approach to welfare continued until 1987, when a group of 12 secondary school principals visited successful schools in the UK and USA, and made several recommendations in their report *Towards Excellence in School* (1987), including one for the introduction of a proactive approach, through pastoral care and career guidance (PCCG), to enhance the quality of education in Singapore. The report pointed out that 'pastoral care and career guidance [were] major weak areas' in our schools, and recommended that 'a well-planned comprehensive pastoral care and career guidance programme be introduced in each school', with teachers as pupil counsellors. It further recommended that the schools be provided with the 'necessary manpower and expertise to develop proper programmes for pastoral care and career guidance so that the pupils would be better prepared for the world of work and be able to choose careers and occupations in keeping with their respective abilities'. The Guidance and Social Work Unit was then reorganized, upgraded and renamed the Pastoral Care and Career Guidance Section.

Pastoral Care and Career Guidance pilot scheme

In January 1988, 17 schools – a representative cross-section of secondary schools – were selected as pilot schools for the Ministry of Education's Pastoral Care and Career Guidance pilot scheme. In January 1989, 12 more secondary schools were included, followed by another 19 schools in January 1990. Six more secondary schools have been chosen for inclusion from January 1991.

Meanwhile, in late 1987 the Ministry of Education invited Peter Lang, Senior Lecturer in the Department of Education at Warwick University, England, to be the consultant for pastoral care. At the same time, Anthony Watts, Director of the National Institute for Careers Education and Counselling, Cambridge, England, was appointed to be the consultant for career guidance.

Aims and structure

By January 1990 the number of schools on the PCCG pilot project totalled 48. During the first two years of the project, the pilot schools evolved the following aims:

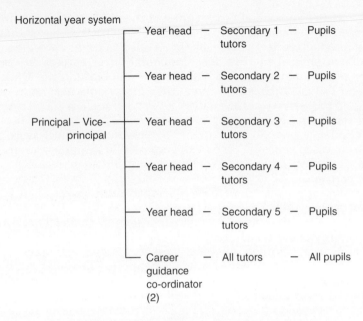

Figure 7.1 Horizontal year system. (HOD = head of department)

- to foster a caring and orderly environment in which pupils are able to exercise initiative, responsibility and self-discipline;
- to develop the child socially, mentally, morally and spiritually to realize his fullest potential to become a well-balanced person, who will derive maximum benefits from a changing society and make a maximum contribution;
- to establish and develop a close rapport and effective working relationship between the school and the community.

To meet these aims, most of the 48 schools adopted and adapted the horizontal year system, used in the United Kingdom. Figure 7.1 typifies the structure.

One school has adapted further by pairing each year head with a head of department (HOD) of an academic area (Figure 7.2).

In the project schools the principals are much involved with PCCG although they have delegated day-to-day administration of it to one of the following: the vice-principal, senior assistant, chief co-ordinator of year heads, or a head of department for PCCG. This overall PCCG co-ordinator also looks into areas related to pastoral care, such as moral education, religious knowledge, ethics and civics.

Although our project schools have not adopted the vertical house system found in some UK schools, some schools have combined it with the horizontal system. In the combined structure, pupils are allocated to houses under the charge of house masters. This allows for social interaction among pupils of different age groups. At the same time, every level (Secondary 1 to 4) is under the charge of a year head. Table 7.1 illustrates the combined structure.

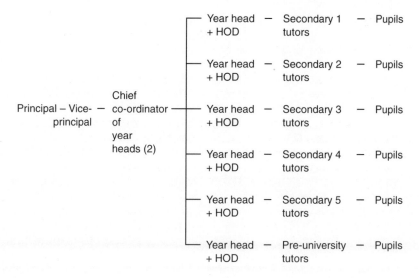

Figure 7.2

Programmes

When the project was launched, the Ministry of Education did not want to prescribe a common PCCG programme for the pilot schools, but decided to leave the schools to develop their own, based on the identified needs of their pupils. Each school decided the direction of its programme and the pace of its development. Thus, there are variations in the pilot programmes. It is hoped that a few distinctive pilot programmes might be highlighted for use as models by schools to be phased into the PCCG project. Aspects of programmes developed by some pilot schools are discussed below.

Personal and social education (PSE)   The introduction of PSE lessons by all the pilot schools immediately caught the interest of both teachers and pupils. Most schools have one or two periods (35–70 minutes) a week for PSE.

The key PCCG personnel in the pilot schools were enthusiastic about planning and preparing the PSE lessons. Some even sacrificed their

Table 7.1

House group and House Master	Red	Blue	Yellow	Green
Year groups and year heads	Mr Ali	Ms Goh	Mr Raj	Mrs Koh
Secondary 1, Ms Uma	1A	1B	1C	1D
Secondary 2, Mr Wee	2D	2C	2B	2A
Secondary 3, Ms Tan	3A	3B	3C	3D
Secondary 4, Mrs Teo	4D	4C	4B	4A

school holidays. Many made use of resource materials (mainly from the United Kingdom and Australia). What is encouraging to note is that schools have taken pains to select materials that could be modified to meet their pupils' needs. For example, one school in which the pupils are academically able and a high percentage of them come from middle-class homes focuses its PSE lessons on the inculcation of positive values such as humility and caring for others, in particular for those who are less fortunate. In another school, where the academic ability of the pupils is average, the focus is on building the pupils' self-esteem, developing a sense of belonging to the school and inculcating respect for school property.

Regular reviews of their PSE programmes have been conducted by the schools and, over the past two years, the key PCCG personnel have refined the PSE materials. The PSE programmes have generally been well received by the pupils, even though lessons in some schools are conducted outside curriculum time. The teachers and pupils particularly like the group processing skills approach that is used during the PSE lessons. This new way of teaching and learning has promoted teacher–pupil rapport and understanding.

Career guidance (CG)   From 1979 to 1987, schools were left to decide how to provide career guidance; but in 1988 it was recommended (in *Towards Excellence in Schools*) that career guidance should be given greater emphasis.

In March 1989, the Ministry of Education jointly sponsored a successful, comprehensive careers convention, comprising a careers exhibition and a series of seminars, which attracted an estimated 242,000 visitors. During this period every secondary school was instructed to nominate two CG co-ordinators. The CG co-ordinators went through a two-day workshop on the management of career information to help prepare them for their role, which is primarily to co-ordinate career guidance activities in the school.

Some of the pilot schools have also initiated work experience and work shadowing schemes. The response from both the pupils and their parents has been very encouraging. Two of the pilot schools shared their experiences with the CG co-ordinators during the workshop in April/May 1989 and one school has published a handbook on work experience for schools interested in such a scheme.

The pilot schools are now introducing career guidance during PSE lessons. There have also been attempts by some schools to integrate career guidance into the academic curriculum. These have proved successful.

Peer support programme   Two of the pilot schools have initiated the peer support programme, which trains older pupils (15-year-olds) to adopt and guide younger pupils (12-year-olds) to help orientate them into secondary school life. The programme originated in Australia and in May 1990 two trainers from Australia (jointly sponsored by the rotary clubs of Changi,

Singapore and of Fukaya, Japan) conducted workshops for teachers in the remaining pilot schools.

In addition, many of our schools hold annual camps focusing on themes such as self-awareness, study skills and leadership skills as well as on personal grooming courses for the pupils.

Training In order to implement the schools' PCCG programmes, initial training is given to all teachers in the pilot schools, by the Institute of Education (IE) or by the PCCG Section of the Ministry of Education.

The training provided by the PCCG Section is categorized into four types and the courses are school-based (i.e. take place in the schools as and when schools request for them). The courses range in duration from 3 to 12 hours and include the following:

Introduction to pastoral care
Personal and social education
Group processing skills
Career guidance
Discipline

When PCCG was introduced in Singapore, the guidance officers in the PCCG Section first underwent training by our consultants, Peter Lang and Anthony Watts, in pastoral care and career guidance respectively, and later Trish Nova, an Australian specialist, gave group skills training.

In June 1988 18 educationists, comprising guidance officers, IE lecturers, principals and vice-principals, visited the UK to study models of PCCG in 16 schools. Their report has since been published. In June 1990 some guidance officers were sent on attachment to Germany and Switzerland to study how career guidance is provided for secondary-level pupils. In January 1990 Norm Hyde of Australia was invited by the PCCG Section to conduct training for the guidance officers in monitoring and evaluation. Our aim was to have a comprehensive evaluation of the PCCG programme in April 1991 based on a study of the effectiveness in the 29 pilot schools following close monitoring in 1990.

Outcomes

Since the project was launched in 1988, each school has monitored its PCCG programme through an annual self-review. Some common ways of obtaining feedback have been through regular scheduled meetings or sharing sessions with tutors. Pupils' responses, and often also the responses of teachers, were usually collected through questionnaires. Annual reviews have resulted in revised and improved PSE materials being produced by the schools.

In August 1988, the PCCG Section wanted a formal review of the PC programmes in the pilot schools. The first 17 schools in the project conducted reviews and submitted individual reports to Peter Lang. Subsequently he visited 10 of the 17 schools, where he held separate discussions with senior staff, PC co-ordinators, tutors and other class teachers and pupils, and studied the overall school organization and observed some examples of pastoral activities. On the basis of the individual school reviews, his school visits and discussions with the guidance officers, Peter Lang prepared a report on the development of PCCG in Singapore, which was submitted to the ministerial committee in February 1989. He noted in the report that teachers felt that PC enhanced the effectiveness of the teaching–learning process as teacher–pupil relationships were more relaxed and pupils were more forthcoming. Feedback from pupils indicated that PC had a significant and positive effect on both their relationships with and their feelings about the teachers. However, their expectations of these teachers had also become greater; they were generally enthusiastic about the PC programme and expressed positive feelings towards it. They expressed interest in having more PSE lessons. Also, the pupils were able to know their teachers better and have a better dialogue with them. Their criticisms were often directed at the ways in which PSE was delivered rather than at the content of the course.

In May 1989 another formal review was conducted by the PCCG Section. The guidance officers interviewed 245 key teachers and 232 pupils in the 17 schools. Based on these interviews, an assessment of the PCCG project was made and a report submitted in June 1989. The assessment confirmed the pupils' point of view obtained from the previous feedback in September 1988. Pupils felt that they had a better understanding of their teachers, enjoyed their PCCG sessions and appeared to be more confident in expressing themselves. Several schools reported a general improvement in pupil discipline. One school included class committees in the referral system itself. These committees decided whether or not students should be referred to tutors for discipline.

There seemed to be a trend in a number of schools to have referral systems where the form tutors, instead of the discipline master, were at the forefront of discipline. The project had focused more attention on preventive measures such as fostering a sense of belonging to the school. A disciplinary structure, however, still existed for dealing with recalcitrant pupils.

The report highlighted the attitude of the teacher, the supportive role played by the principal and the co-operative efforts of the year head as being crucial to the success of the PCCG programmes.

Another significant finding was that communication with parents was better and more frequent, and parental involvement in schools activities had increased.

In the area of career guidance, schools have made an effort to set up career guidance corners in their libraries and some have gone beyond this to provide sophisticated career guidance centres.

Although the pilot schools are developing their programmes to serve as models for other schools intending to provide pastoral care for their pupils, some non-pilot schools are so enthusiastic about implementing pastoral care that they have started on their own.

Future directions

The pastoral care programme in Singapore is in its third year of implementation and a number of the pilot schools are already moving in the direction of making pastoral care a whole-school responsibility. For example, some of them have attempted to integrate pastoral care with academic subjects, particularly subjects such as English Language and the humanities. Others have involved every teacher, whether form tutor or not, in pastoral care by having two tutors for each pastoral group.

Training has always been provided for all teachers, including non-form tutors.

The provision of both moral education and PCCG in the pilot schools has led some of the PCCG teams in the pilot schools to introduce PSE activities into the moral education curriculum.

Our long-term aim is to implement PCCG in all secondary schools in phases, followed by the primary schools and finally the junior colleges. We would like to see PCCG permeating every aspect of school life and involving every member of the school community to the benefit of all pupils.

PART II

Applications

CHAPTER 8

The pastoral care and career guidance programme in an independent school in Singapore

T.C. ONG AND L.H.L. CHIA

Introduction

One of the traditions of British education, exported to a number of other countries, is that the school is concerned with the pupils' all-round development. This chapter is concerned with developments in one school in one such country.

A team of educationists commissioned by the Minister of Education, Dr Tony Tan, visited some 13 UK and 12 US schools in 1986; it was noted that all schools visited had a comprehensive programme to provide for the personal growth and development of every child. Pastoral care formed an integral part of each school's programme and was built into the organizational structure. There was provision for guidance in the choice of subjects and careers, and in social and moral development; and there was a stress on discipline to cultivate the total person. It was noted that a comprehensive system of pastoral care and career guidance (PCCG) was essential to provide guidance on subject combinations, advice on careers and higher studies. A milieu for emotional and social growth of pupils was also seen as being vital for the success of schools.

The above observations were confirmed when another team of educationists visited 16 UK schools in 1988, and the concepts developed in the Singapore context, with the advice of two Ministry of Education consultants, Peter Lang for pastoral care and Anthony Watts for career guidance. As a result of these experiences, it was decided that pastoral care and career guidance should be part of Singapore schools' programme.

The task of implementing the PCCG in our schools started in 1987. With the unfailing support of the Ministry of Education and the expertise, encouragement, training and advice of the above-mentioned consultants from the UK, some 17 pilot schools were selected to evolve and implement the programmes.

Anglo-Chinese School (ACS), one of the leading and oldest schools in Singapore, was given the mandate to become an independent school (i.e. run and managed by the principal under a board of management instead of under the sole control of the Ministry of Education). It was selected as one of the 17 schools to implement a PCCG system for the pupils in early 1988. Within the space of some 20 months, a comprehensive structure and programme emerged.

The school and its philosophy

Founded in 1886 by Bishop William FitzJames Oldham, ACS is built over an area of 4.3 hectares of prime land of the Republic of Singapore and currently has about 1800 pupils. There are three main blocks of buildings, housing some 56 classrooms. The upper school comprises pupils aged 14 to 16 in Secondary 3 (14 classes) and 4 (O-level students, 14 classes) and functions from 7.30 am to 1.00 pm from Monday to Friday. The lower school has 28 classes, Secondary 1 (14 classes) and 2 (14 classes) which function from 1.00 pm to 6.25 pm with pupils in the age range of 12 to 14 years old. The facilities include laboratories, an auditorium, AVA room, music room, art room, an Olympic-size swimming pool, playing fields, tennis courts, gymnasium, project adventure course, counselling room and a PCCG resource centre. Hostel living is provided for a limited number of students in the adjourning premises of the school.

The medium of instruction is English, the main working language in our multi-racial and multi-lingual society. The school offers a wide range of subjects including English (compulsory), Chinese as First Language, Second Language (Chinese, Malay or Tamil), Additional Mathematics, Elementary Mathematics, Physics, Chemistry, Biology, Physics with Chemistry, Literature, History, Geography, Religious Knowledge, Music and Art. In addition, a number of our students also offer foreign languages such as French, German or Japanese in their GCE O level exams. There is also a Gifted Education Programme for specially selected and very bright pupils. The Extra-Curriculum Activities (ECA) in the school include a wide range of activities: sports and games (swimming, water-polo, rugby, soccer, table-tennis, basketball, volleyball, tennis, badminton and athletics), numerous clubs and societies, choir and uniformed youth organizations (Boys' Brigade [the largest in Singapore], St John's Ambulance Brigade, National Cadet Corps, National Police Cadet Corps and Scouts Troops) and the military band.

The school was founded with the vision of providing pupils with the opportunity to learn the Christian principles and values. At the same time, it caters to the needs of the pupils from all walks of life in the multi-racial, multi-religious and multi-lingual society of Singapore. The school has through the years been providing education of the highest standard and to date has an illustrious list of local, Commonwealth and Rhodes Scholars associated with it. The emphasis on the intellectual, moral and spiritual has been the hallmark of the school, which is well known for providing a good balance between academic and sporting activities.

The school's pastoral care and career guidance

The school views the tripartite relationship among the academic, disciplinary and pastoral care systems as inseparable (Best and Ribbins, 1983). Mutual support and a complementary relationship and harmony between these systems are of paramount importance to ensure success in achieving our aims and objectives. In ACS, the term 'pastoral care' includes both pastoral care and career guidance (PCCG). The overall school philosophy is to foster a caring, sharing, educated, united and orderly community consisting of individuals well-grounded in moral and spiritual values which will help them attain a wholesome, balanced adult life.

PCCG aims and objectives

Broad aims   The ACS pastoral care system aims to foster a caring and orderly environment where each pupil can exercise his initiative and responsibility to:

- attain excellence in every aspect of his education;
- develop his potential to the fullest irrespective of his background and abilities;
- grow physically, intellectually, socially, emotionally and spiritually (morally) as a responsible, sensitive and well-adjusted individual, better prepared for adult life after school.

Other objectives   The pastoral care system also seeks to

- provide a point of personal contact with every student;
- provide a point of personal contact with parents;
- offer support and guidance to students on any issue which affects their development and achievement;
- promote the development of curriculum, organization and pedagogy which meet the cognitive, affective and vocational needs of all students;
- monitor the progress and achievements across the whole curriculum of all students as individuals;
- provide staff with relevant knowledge of students so that their teaching efforts can be adapted for greater success;
- mobilize the resources of the wider educational and welfare network to meet the needs of all students;
- promote a partnership between students, teachers and parents and the wider community within which all students are enabled to make the most of their opportunities;
- evaluate the operation of the structure and processes which will be set up to ensure the effective achievement of the goals listed above.

These aims and objectives are contained in our teacher and student handbooks and displayed on the notice boards.

PCCG structure

Basically, the PCCG structure is a horizontal system as shown in Figure 8.1. A whole-school approach is adopted in implementing the PCCG programme activities. Each of the four levels of the school (Secondary 1 to 4) has a head of level (HOL) or head of year and an assistant head of level (Asst HOL) and under them are the form (i.e. class) teachers and assistant form teachers and subject teachers. A majority of the 59 classes in the school has two teachers (form teacher and assistant) who act as facilitators during formal PCCG contact time. Secondary 1, 2 and 3 have 30 pupils in each class; Sec 4 has about 40 pupils in each class. Two periods each of 40 minutes' duration are provided each week in Secondary 1 to 4 for formal contact time in which PCCG activities are conducted by form teachers or assistant form teachers.

Teachers' roles in PCCG A recent survey showed that teachers perceived their PCCG roles to be a mixture of the following: tutor, mentor, moral educator, friend, role model, adult-figure, confidant, guide, facilitator, encourager, supporter, and helper. Staff members generally wish to get to know students as individuals to help them develop their potential and to encourage the development of self-esteem and self-awareness. The need to guide pupils in the academic, social, emotional and spiritual aspects of their lives is seen as being essential. For example, many teachers felt the need to be able to identify students facing problems with their schoolwork, and to promote in their class a sense of security and belonging.

Of equal importance was the consensus that was arrived at in wanting to inculcate civic consciousness and to establish a 'care and share' attitude among pupils so that they will learn to contribute to society, care for the less privileged and be involved in community services, and to serve the nation with loyalty and enthusiasm. A good number of staff members also see the necessity to create awareness of issues pertaining to growing up and to assist pupils in learning to prepare for further studies, for work and for the future.

The staff are of the view that the channels of communication between school administration and the staff, and between staff and students, are varied, adequate and effective. Many make themselves readily available to students and often spend off-duty hours interacting with pupils. Of course, the formal contact time provided in the PCCG programmes, which forms part of curriculum time, has enabled teachers to get to know pupils well through the existing PCCG activities, group work and discussion.

Head of PE/extra-curricular activities (ECA) and ECA teachers Since the extra-curricular activities (ECA), which includes the different uniformed youth organizations, sports and games and clubs and societies, form an important part of the school life, the head of ECA, assisted by an assistant co-ordinator and teachers in charge of various ECA, form part

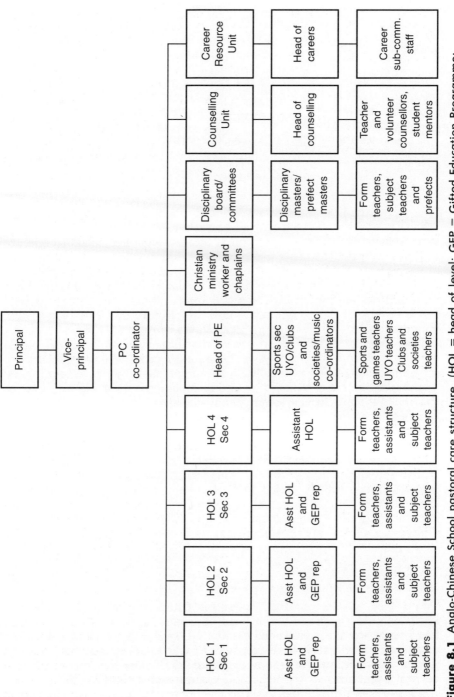

Figure 8.1 Anglo-Chinese School pastoral care structure. (HOL = head of level; GEP = Gifted Education Programme; UYO = Uniformed Youth Organization)

of the PCCG structure as well. We believe that ECA provides a rich avenue for teacher-pupil interaction and point of personal contact between teachers and pupils. The ECA also includes a house system, which, however, exists mainly for the administration of track and field activities.

Christian ministry Since ACS is a mission school, with daily devotions, weekly chapel services (one for the upper and one for the lower school), Christian fellowship groups, religious emphasis weeks and the teaching of Bible knowledge, it is natural to include the Christian ministry staff and the chaplains as part of the PCCG structure as well. The Christian ministry worker and the chaplains also assist in the counselling of pupils and parents.

Disciplinary board The inter-relationship between academic, pastoral care and discipline areas of schooling is of vital importance. Each has activities specific to itself as well as activities that are seen to be common to two or all three (Best and Ribbins, 1983) and needs to operate in harmony with the other areas for the total development and nurture of each pupil. From the onset of implementing the PCCG programme, it was recognized that discipline of pupils is crucial to bring about an orderly environment in which the aims and objectives of the school can be realized. A disciplinary board (see Figure 8.2) was formed and included as part of the overall PCCG structure.

The principal oversees the school disciplinary structure; the actual administration and execution of disciplinary procedures and measures, including referral for counselling, are undertaken by the vice-principal (pastoral care). He is assisted by two disciplinary masters (DMs), one for the upper and one for the lower school who are senior teachers appointed to assist the vice-principal in investigation of disciplinary offences.

The DMs could work independently, but more often than not, they work closely with the disciplinary committees, each headed by a senior assistant who discusses disciplinary cases with the heads of level of the Upper School and Lower School. The school also has a board of student leaders or councillors called prefects. The prefects are placed under the charge of two teachers called prefect masters. The prefect masters and the head of Physical Education and ECA as well as the Christian ministry staff are also members of these two disciplinary committees (see Figure 8.2).

The PCCG programme

The programme for our PCCG resulted from suggestions made by our staff members, especially the head of levels, as well as ideas gleaned from seminars and workshops conducted by the Ministry of Education consultants, Ministry of Education PCCG training and Institute of Education training workshops and courses. The school has conducted several school-based inservice courses on understanding the concept, framework and implementation of a PCCG programme and the role of

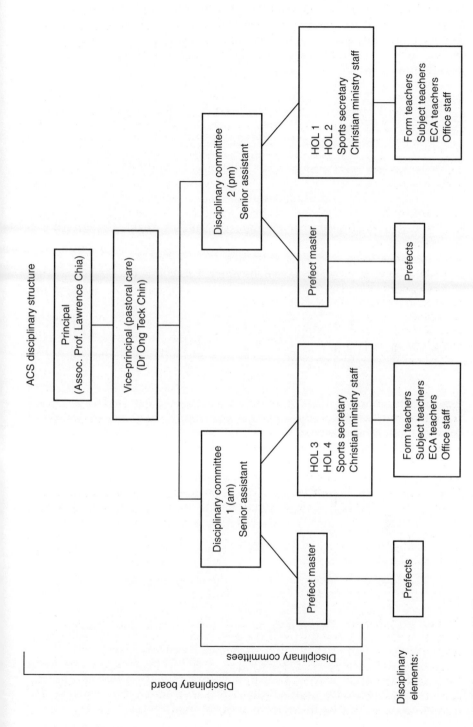

Figure 8.2 Anglo-Chinese School disciplinary structure.

tutors. The programme includes the use of group work and active tutorial work, spanning five key areas:

- **Self-awareness:** self-knowledge, building self-esteem, personal values, personal strengths and weakness, personal interests and aptitude, role in the class, school, family and community and learning to cope with crisis.

- **Personal skills:** time management, coping with homework, study skills, examination techniques, problem-solving, decision-making, social skills, stress management, parenting skills, use of leisure, communication skills, goal setting and conflict management.

- **Interpersonal relationships and social responsibility:** loneliness, friendship, peer groups, support groups, team-building, sexuality and adolescence, love, courtship, and marriage, relationships with parents and family, caring and sharing concepts, caring for the underprivileged, caring for the community, welfare work, community services and cultural awareness.

- **Health and hygiene:** physical fitness, learning a game or sport, forms and values of exercise (aerobic, non-aerobic), energy requirements, sleep and relaxation, how to referee a match, nutrition and diet, sex education, grooming and etiquette.

- **Careers and vocational guidance:** interests inventory, occupational surveys, choice of subject combination, role of the mass media, understanding and finding a place in the world of work, jobs and sex stereotyping, job application skills, interviewing for jobs, work experience, shadowing and observation, and learning to use career resources.

The staff members worked in teams and produced detailed lesson plans for each level of students to cover the whole school year. Constant review, usually annually, is carried out to modify the topics for formal contact time and teachers are encouraged to solicit feedback from students on new topics or improvements of the set topics.

Co-curricular activities Apart from the formal contact time/PCCG lessons, the programme includes activities for both students and staff members that are known as co-curricular activities.

- **Christian Education activities:** weekly chapel services, daily devotions, Christian fellowship meetings and Bible knowledge lessons.

- **Talks, films and videos:** on careers education and pastoral care topics or personal and social education topics.

- **Camps:** Secondary 1 Discovery Camp, Secondary 3 Adventure Camp and Secondary 4 Study Camp, run annually for the students.

- **Meet-the-parents sessions:** special meetings held at school two or three times a year where parents meet the teachers on an individual basis to discuss the progress and development of their children.

- **Visits and tours:** for pupils to local places of interest, companies and institutions as well as overseas educational tours.

- **Welfare visits:** each level of pupils adopts one welfare home or institution for the handicapped or underprivileged, and regular fortnightly visits are made by groups of pupils to these institutions to help the people there as part of our school's community service.
- **Seminars and workshops:** for pupils and teachers on PCCG matters and topics.

These activities have proved to be popular among students, staff and parents, especially the camps and the meet-the-parents sessions. The latter, organized two to three times per academic year, have contributed to fostering strong and intimate home–school links, which are important in giving both parents and teachers a better understanding of the children.

- **Project adventure:** Project adventure has been introduced recently as a co-curricular activity. It consists of a series of adventure-based activities, which could be used to foster team-building, provide practice in problem-solving, build better self-awareness and self-esteem and help develop confidence and leadership skills.

Counselling A Counselling Unit comprising staff members and volunteer counsellors was set up in June 1988 to look into the needs of pupils with behavioural and emotional problems, or who have difficulty fitting into the school and coping with the work. Study skills and time management are included as part of the counselling program. The school has several overseas-trained counsellors as well as volunteer counsellors drawn from the teachers and the community at large. The aims and objectives of the Counselling Unit are:

- to build pupils' self-esteem and self-worth;
- to help pupils to manage time and develop sound study skills;
- to provide mentors to boys who need friendship and assistance in their academic work; and
- to counsel pupils with maladjustment, behavioural and emotional problems.

The following schemes are provided by the Counselling Unit:

- Individual counselling
- Group counselling
- Buddy system (this is a simplified support system where older students with good leadership qualities are hand-picked to help younger pupils who are experiencing difficulties)

Integration of pastoral care and career guidance

Watts (1983) stated that increasingly there is a need for careers education to be linked to the curriculum of the school so that a comprehensive PCCG programme can be developed to cater to the wide-ranging needs of pupils and career planning can begin at an early stage of a pupils' schooling. Steps have been taken in ACS to make careers education an integral part of our broad programme of personal and social education. This integration is reflected in the formulation of the PCCG structure and development of PCCG syllabuses for all pupils.

Career guidance has been integrated into the PC syllabus at all levels; for example, in the area of developing self-awareness and discovering personal strengths and weaknesses, in drawing up interests inventories, encouraging opportunities awareness and knowledge of the world of work. This would include job interviews, job application, decision-making, occupational preference system and work experience. The emphasis is on creating experiences for the pupils which help towards future career decision-making. A comprehensive range of literature and information on careers, job opportunities and further education has been acquired. These are made available in a Career Resource Unit which is open to all staff and students in the school.

The aims and objectives of our career education and guidance are:

- to develop self-awareness;
- to develop educational awareness;
- to supply information with regard to options upon leaving school;
- to provide practice in decision-making; and
- to provide opportunities for pupils to be involved in work experience.

A successful scheme has been initiated (1989), which gives Secondary 3 students two weeks of work experience at the end of the academic year. The aims and objectives of the work experience scheme are:

- to give pupils an insight into the world of work;
- to inculcate work and social skills;
- to give pupils a broader view of possible job and career opportunities.

Our resources

Michael Marland (1986) has stressed the need for a school to build up supporting services and resources to help the PCCG programme. At ACS, steps have been taken to ensure adequate physical resources for a proper PCCG programme, such as adequate classroom and activity space, a counselling room and a career resource room. Resources for our PCCG programme include the expertise on offer from old boys of the school, parents, supporters, friends, experts from the tertiary institutions, government and public sectors, church members and members of our boards of governors and management.

We have also acquired resource and reference materials (worksheets, books, guides, film scripts, videos, AVA materials, cassettes) and have developed our own handouts and lesson plans.

Staff development

The teacher is an irreplaceable agent of the educational process at all levels of the educational system, and the quality of education depends to a decisive extent on the quality of the teacher's personality. Teachers are able to fulfil their educational duties only when they are both well prepared for the profession and able to improve their skills through education. Thus we have embarked on a programme of inservice training conducted locally or overseas.

The purpose of the inservice training is to enable us to meet the following challenges:

- the changing requirements imposed by society;
- the changing requirements imposed upon education system and teachers;
- the requirements imposed upon the teacher's qualifications by the educational sciences and improvements in the level of performance of the teaching profession, and
- the need to prepare teachers to be tutors and to assume leadership in our PCCG.

Such training, we believe, will improve the quality of the education system by making teachers better tutors for PCCG and encouraging them to assume proper attitudes, and thus improve the standard of teaching as the education system changes and innovations are introduced.

Many teachers have been encouraged to enrol for courses both in PCCG and in academic areas. This will in the long run contribute to the upgrading of our teachers in their profession. Having a good inservice training programme not only will help boost staff morale but also will motivate them towards giving their best in order to enable our pupils to achieve excellence in education.

Strengths and weaknesses of our PCCG

Feedback obtained through two surveys conducted among all the staff members and pupils in the school in 1988 and 1989 indicated the following:

Strengths

Training of teachers provided through workshops.

Importance given to it in terms of curriculum time.

Most teachers see the need of programme.

Heads of level friendly and approachable.

Closer rapport between students and teachers that have developed.

Recognition that pastoral care is responsible for it.

Adequate and useful training programme. Training occasionally on Saturdays.

Strong direction from the top. Effective pastoral care structure or framework.

Programmes and activities outside the classrooms.

Pastoral care included in curriculum time.

Helpful staff – co-operative teachers.

Contact time with pupils as class teacher.

Structured syllabus – know what to do in each pastoral care period.

Good relationships between students, staff and students and staff and parents.

Meaningful activities.

Enthusiasm of pastoral care team and class teachers.

Pastoral care programme has created (aroused) awareness among teachers: more sensitive to students' needs.

Staff involvement: many teachers are interested in the personal welfare of the students.

Willingness to experiment.

Flexibility in using the set syllabus.

An elaborate and flexible programme that can be modified to be relevant to the needs of the students.

There is sincerity on the part of the people involved who want to make it work and improve on it.

Meet-the-parents sessions – foster good rapport with parents; supportive parents.

Weaknesses

The following weaknesses were identified:

Insufficient time to prepare good lessons.

Teachers have really too much to do apart from pastoral care to be able to carry out pastoral care effectively.

More co-ordination on the topics to be covered.

Pastoral care is a new subject and teachers are not expert at conducting it. Little time for counselling.

Pastoral care takes up more time than recognized for preparation, etc. Most teachers are not able to cope effectively with heavy overall programme of school. Is the school expecting too much from its teachers?

Pastoral care periods are an added burden to teachers' workload.

General indifference and disrespect of boys for pastoral care. Some students are negative.

Too many pupils to handle, class size too big so students find it hard to open up.

Difficulty of making the lessons interesting.

Lack of background reading materials which are short, concise and interesting.

Personal inadequacies.

Difficult topics like 'My Body and I'.

Insufficient resources materials for outdoor activities.

Unable to keep close supervision of groups of boys during pastoral care lessons.

Emotionally demanding on the teacher.

This information has been useful to us in reviewing our PCCG programmes. Adjustments and modifications based on the above feedback have been made to the existing structure and programmes and syllabus in our PCCG system.

Conclusion

Button (1983) emphasized the need for those planning the pastoral programmes to bring to the surface and to make explicit the unseen influences of the activities of such programmes that have an impact on experience and attitudes of all concerned.

Paul Nash is quoted by McGuiness (1982) as stating, 'If educators confine their attention to the intellectual developments of their pupils, they will find that their failure to regard the whole personality vitiates even their attempts of intellectual learning.' Success of the planned pastoral care scheme has been demonstrated in a number of UK schools. It remains the case that unless schools demonstrate a capacity for care and understanding and unless they are places where children can discover objectives beyond the self-seeking attitudes that are so prevalent, then there seems to be little to replace the work ethic of earlier decades. Hughes (1983) argues that pastoral care may prove to be essential for the future of our society in providing children with self-esteem and value, apart from material considerations.

We believe in the importance of a good pastoral care and career guidance programme that will help meet the varied needs of individual pupils and staff of our school. Obviously it will also contribute positively to the tone and climate of the school. It is important to realize that PCCG objectives may not be fulfilled unless all teachers or members of staff involved believe in the usefulness of the programme and wholeheartedly give their attention and support to applying the principles of care in their work. A whole-school approach is vital for success.

While the PCCG programme may not provide an instant change in the school climate, pupil behaviour and staff morale, a balanced and relevant programme of pastoral work applied consistently over at least several years could result in changes for the better in the school. It would allow teachers to express concern and stimulate coping in ways which foster self-respect in pupils while simultaneously supporting teachers in their arduous task. Hamblin (1984) enumerated the rewards for pupils from the PCCG as a continuity of concern, the growth of a sense of mastery and escape from stagnation. Teachers' rewards stem from the satisfaction brought by a more professional level of communication and interaction with pupils plus the recognition that the programme wrestles with the forces which alienate pupils and create stress for the teacher. We concur with Himmelweit and Swift (1969) and Rutter *et al.* (1979) in believing that the school and its PCCG programme can have a positive impact on each pupil.

Pastoral care in its present form is relatively new to us. We are thankful that the government and the Ministry of Education have recognized the need for all schools to emphasize this neglected area within the school curriculum. With the keen support given by the Ministry of Education, our school's board of management, our Old Boys' Association and our principal, we are able to develop a comprehensive programme to help meet the needs of our students. The journey towards our goals has just begun but we are confident that, given the supportive resources from both within and outside the school, we will be able to achieve much in providing realistic pastoral care to each pupil.

The review of 1989 opened our eyes to some areas within our pastoral care system that needed our attention. It has helped us to focus on the identified difficulties in the hope that we will be able to fine-tune the many processes that make up the total pastoral care programme in ACS. Some of these processes are in their infancy in terms of implementation. One such process is setting up of a resource library for staff and students specializing in pastoral care and career guidance. Others include the formalizing of our pastoral care programme and the evolution of our pastoral care structure which needed regular review and adjustment for improvement.

The road before us may be long and difficult, but we are certain that, with God's help, the support of many and with 'the best is yet to be' as our motto, we will surmount any obstacle and achieve our aims and objectives.

We acknowledge the unfailing support and guidance of the Ministry of Education, ACS board of governors and ACS board of management for our PCCG. Special thanks also go to Mrs Tan Lee Yong and Miss Ong Pheng Yen from the Ministry of Education, Pastoral Care and Career Guidance Section and staff of Anglo-Chinese School, especially Mrs Fanny Tan, our pastoral care co-ordinator, and the heads of levels, Ms Bok Hai Choo, Mrs Yoon Lay Beng, Mrs Tessie Cheng and Mrs Jeann Woo, Head of Counselling, Mr Peter Lim and Head of Career Guidance, Mrs Florence Lim, who have all contributed to the success of our PCCG.

References

Best, R. and Ribbins, P. (1983) Rethinking the pastoral–academic split. *Pastoral Care in Education*, 1(1), 11–18.

Button, L. (1983) The pastoral curriculum. *Pastoral Care in Education*, 1(2), 74–82.

Hamblin, D. (1984) *Pastoral Care: A Training Manual.* Oxford: Blackwell.

Himmelweit, H. and Swift, B. (1969) A model for the understanding of the school as a socializing agency. In Mussen, P., Langer, J. and Covington, M. (eds), *Trends and Issues in Developmental Psychology*. New York: Holt, Rinehart & Winston.
Hughes, R.A. (1983) The case of Upbury Manor: a plan for pastoral care. *Pastoral Care in Education*, 1(2), 107–13.
Marland, M. (1986) *Pastoral Care: Organizing the Care and Guidance of the Individual Pupil in a Comprehensive School*. London: Heinemann.
McGuiness, J.B. (1982) *Planned Pastoral Care*. Maidenhead: McGraw-Hill.
Ministry of Education (1987) *Towards Excellence in Schools: A Report to the Minister of Education*. Singapore: Ministry of Education.
Ministry of Education (1988) *A Report on Pastoral Care and Guidance in Sixteen Schools in the United Kingdom*. Singapore: Ministry of Education.
Rutter, M., Maughan, B., Mortimore, P., Ouston, J. and Smith, A. (1979) *Fifteen Thousand Hours*. London: Open Books.
Watts, A.G. (1983) Changing structures and conceptions of career guidance in British schools. *Research in Counselling*, (8), 14–26.

CHAPTER 9

A pastoral care programme in a government primary school

ELEANOR WATSON

Introduction

This chapter describes the setting up and piloting of a structured and formalized pastoral care programme in a government primary school in Western Australia. The school, because designated a Priority School, attracted extra Commonwealth funding by way of a special programme called Participation and Equity, which is aimed at increasing participation in education (particularly by the most educationally disadvantaged groups) and at introducing greater equity in educational provision.

The school's students came from a cross-section of the community, reflecting a range of value positions, socio-economic situations, lifestyles, ethnic backgrounds and educational aspirations. The Priority Schools Programme Submission (1987) included the following family profiles:

- 45 per cent of students come either from a broken home or had single parent background;
- 16 per cent of families had both parents unemployed;
- 27 per cent of students had both parents working.

Some students came from the semi-structured caravan parks. Their stay at the school was on a short-term basis. The majority of teachers felt that some students raised in such disadvantaged circumstances were incapable of benefiting from the general academic programme offered.

In 1987, as a result of a school needs assessment among the teachers, concern expressed by parents wishing to become involved in the educational experience, and stated teachers' concerns in relation to discipline, low academic achievement and related stress, a whole-school approach to the needs was adopted. This was embodied in the notion of actively identifying the school as a 'caring' school, as identified by Beazley (1984, p. 149):

> the provision of an environment in which it is possible for each person associated with the school (staff, pupil, parent) to fulfil their basic

personal needs and expectations as defined in experiences of self-worth, adequacy, security and warmth of relationships.

The teachers decided to concentrate on what they could modify: school organization and environment. Beazley had defined his 'caring' school concept in terms of the importance attached to the school environment. He argued that this should include such components as pastoral care, codes of behaviour, pupil–teacher relationships, and the values system underpinning the school organization. The implication of his argument was that these aspects of school life were *not* being addressed generally within the school system.

In view of the decision to become a 'caring' school in Beazley's terms, a pastoral care programme was developed, based on the assumptions that:

- 'Positive self-concept [i.e. the beliefs, hypotheses and assumptions that students hold about themselves] and healthy levels of self-esteem are fundamental for the optimal development of students' (Beazley, 1984);
- self-concept is influenced by the way people see students and what is expected of students;
- over time students will internalize the feedback received from others and will behave as the models; and
- 'The feedback students get from "models" relates to their effectiveness in dealing with the physical world and this, in turn, affects their self-perception' (Hattie, 1988).

The specific intent of the programme was to:

- instil in students a sense of being accepted and belonging in relation to both individuals and groups;
- develop their sense of competency and of their ability to exercise influence on what happens in their lives;
- reinforce the belief that they are worthwhile and special because of being their unique selves;
- expose students to models to whom they can relate.

The pastoral care programme was intended to operate as a separate entity under the umbrella of the 'caring' school concept.

During 1987 the school was also involved in policy and curriculum change in response to the Ministry of Education's document, *Better Schools in Western Australia* (1987). This document was intended to initiate change, but had no stated outcomes. It did, however, focus on a number of key issues, including the idea of the 'self-determining school', the maintenance of educational standards, community participation, equity responsiveness and the teacher's professional role.

These focuses were intended to provide the structure on which to develop the 'caring' school. The Better Schools Programme and its devolution of autonomy to schools imposed heavy pressures to incorporate ongoing evaluative structures. Mainstreaming of the physically and intellectually handicapped into schools meant that programmes had to be further individualized, and not necessarily with the provision of extra funds.

The elimination of school catchment boundaries meant that the schools were free to present themselves in such a way as to attract students from other areas. This was of interest to the school under discussion as it had already been down-classified owing to declining enrolments. In keeping with the general trend in Australian education, the area was seeing an accelerated movement of students from the state to the private system. As there were a number of private and non-state schools in the area, the school was in danger of becoming a dumping ground for the poor and socially rejected.

The concept of the self-determining school had implications for the pastoral care programme. The School Grant and the Priority School funding ensured that programmes had to operate within well-defined economic parameters. However, the entrepreneurial spirit embodied in the Better Schools Programme was, by and large, lost on this community, which had few avenues for revenue raising. For this community, the Better Schools Programme was merely a method by which the school had to deploy existing resources, and was made more accountable for them into the bargain.

Needs identification

Some specifics identified in the needs survey undertaken at the school included the following:

Poor school tone and a lack of school ethos. An attitude list (Self-Esteem Inventory List, compiled by the Curriculum Branch of the then Education Department of Western Australia), when applied across the school, showed several students exhibiting low self-esteem and poor attitudes to school in general. Further investigations, such as the comparison of test marks, and general teacher interchange of ideas, showed a high correlation between low esteem/poor attitude and low academic results in the literacy and numeracy areas.

Lack of stated policy. Teachers stated that they were frustrated and stressed by the absence of a formulated discipline policy to deal with students who severely and blatantly transgressed school and societal rules.

Lack of induction procedures for new students. There was agreement among teachers that the transient students exhibited especially poor attitudes to school and society in general. The length of their stay varied, but the stream of students was constant and the disruption to the school community as a whole was real. There was a support service in place, consisting of a guidance officer and a school nurse who visited the school each week for a couple of hours. These services were perceived by the staff as not meeting the needs of the students. In fact there was antipathy towards the delivery of the service, because

- only a few students who were already in a crisis situation received any support;
- these students were the most poorly behaved or from the most traumatic home environments;
- teachers were powerless to change these external factors to accommodate these students in any meaningful way;
- teachers were suspicious of the constant testing that went on. The lists of test scores created an air of mystique in which teachers were made to feel ignorant and de-skilled;
- reports prepared by the guidance officer were often of little benefit to the teachers (when programmes were suggested they often required supervision and extra resources which were not available);
- some teachers had been criticized by the guidance officer for the way they handled problem students.

The underlying problem here was that the roles of the student support service personnel were ill-defined. Significant numbers of students were alienated from the school process. The presence of the student support service merely created the impression that something was being done for the welfare of the students.

The new reforms under the Better Schools Programme gave the impetus to set up a school-level programme that reflected the aspirations of the school community and provided positive policies aimed at establishing a 'caring' school.

Developing the pastoral care programme

To provide for the development and ongoing evaluation of the programme, Hodgkinson's P3M3 (1981) model was adopted as it was considered to be flexible in providing a skeleton upon which the direction, purpose and strategies of the programme could be built. It also allowed for the needs and priorities set by the Ministry of Education and the school to be met, and some consideration of budget. Also it carried the expectation that monitoring and evaluation would be ongoing.

This model has six administrative phases (philosophy, planning, politics, mobilizing, managing, monitoring), which are not necessarily sequential; fluctuations back and forth between the phases are allowed.

In the philosophical stage the 'idea generators' and the 'synthesizers' generated abstracted thought. This philosophical rhetoric was essential as the programme had to line up with the School Development Plan, which declared the school a 'caring' school.

The principal at the school had been greatly influenced by the writing of Lapate et al. (1969), which focused on the concept of destiny control and urged parent involvement in education. Lapate argued that if parents are involved in the life, work and programmes associated with the school and by their actions show they can change the status quo, children will themselves believe it. The principal believed that parent involvement was perhaps the single most important prerequisite to the development of an effective pastoral care programme.

In addressing the priorities in the document *Better Schools in Western Australia* and in particular those that related to Maintaining Education Standards, Community Participation in School Management, and Equity, the following general aims for the programme were set:

- students were to have the opportunity to be presented with a set of alternative behaviours and attitudes through the medium of a pastoral care curriculum;

- students experiencing academic problems were to have the opportunity to have help in further acquisition of cognitive skills through a structured support programme;

- students were to be given the opportunity to develop self-discipline in a progressive manner as an outcome of an effective discipline policy.

At the planning stage specific allocations of time were made for specific tasks with stated objectives. The components of the pastoral care programme were specified as:

- the rationale of the programme;

- the structure of the programme, including the role of the pastoral care co-ordinator;

- various procedures associated with the programme:

  (a) staff referral network

  (b) support service procedures

  (c) students referral procedures for the academic support programme

  (d) induction of new students

  (e) crisis care, including suspected cases of child abuse

  (f) parent involvement

  (g) parameters of legal liability of teachers

- inservice training for the co-ordinator and other teachers;

- details of the pastoral curriculum programme;

- criteria for the referral of students to the academic support programme;

- training of parents as para-professionals;

- budget;

- method of delivery of the formal and informal pastoral curriculum programme;

- evaluation;

- discipline policy;

- the processes to be used in the cases of suspension, including the rights of the parties involved, viz. parents, students, teachers and the principal.

At the politics stage, the co-ordinator and the principal had the task of 'selling' the programme to the teachers, parents and the district superintendent, who had to be convinced of the need for extra staff allocation.

The mobilization and management phases came next. The para-professionals were trained, the support teachers implemented the academic programme and the pastoral care curriculum sessions started. These required management of the timetable, parent interviews and school support services case conferences.

Finally, the programme was monitored using Scriven's widely accepted model of evaluation (1967) with its emphasis on the roles and goals of the programme.

The pastoral care programme

Discussion among the staff led to the conclusion that a school could contribute to change in the status quo of the community. There was an avowed concern for the individual students and this found expression in the establishment of a formal pastoral care programme. The school institutionalized this concern by declaring that the school was a 'caring school', in line with the recommendations of the Beazley Report (1984). All submissions made to the Grants Committee were developed under this title of a 'caring' environment.

The School Development Plan identified the following objectives:

- developing a school commitment to all students and not only those in a crisis situation;
- speaking in an encouraging manner in such a way as to reflect respect for the students and for each staff member;
- having open communication channels among the staff;
- monitoring parental attitudes and opinions in order to act appropriately and with empathy;
- to show justice and consistency towards rewards and punishment;
- to encourage self-discipline;
- to provide the students with basic skills for effective living in society.

To these ends the administration was to:

- provide open leadership;
- communicate its visions and expectations to others;
- recognize the unique abilities of individual students and also those with specific learning difficulties and ensure the opportunities for these students to learn.

Students were to be expected to:

- value the worth of others;
- relate with their peer group;
- take responsibility for learning;

- be accountable for their actions;
- appreciate their own ethnic and cultural background (based on *Pastoral Care Support Document No. 1* (1986)).

The pastoral curriculum

The pastoral curriculum at the school was largely based on the Ministry of Education's *Health Syllabus K-10*, published by the Curriculum Branch. This, based on sound theory and on experience, possessed much potential to contribute to the pastoral needs of the school. The strands extracted were 'Mental and emotional health', which recognized the importance of a positive self-concept. This was reflected in the development of satisfying relationships, and in the responsibility needed for personal decisions and behaviour; second, 'Societal health issues', which assisted the individual to recognize that behaviour in general is influenced by a variety of societal factors.

Much of this material was somewhat controversial. Many parents and teachers held the view that such imparting of knowledge should remain the responsibility of the family. As a consequence, in many schools this section of the *Health Syllabus* was often deleted or very superficially addressed.

The aims of the pastoral curriculum were to encourage:

- a positive self-concept;
- a sensitivity to, acceptance of, the feelings and needs of others;
- a willingness to become involved in group and community decision-making;
- a responsibility for personal actions, and an acceptance of the consequences.

The pastoral curriculum covered the following areas:

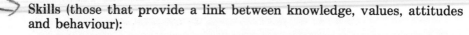

Skills (those that provide a link between knowledge, values, attitudes and behaviour):

- to be able to interact effectively with others;
- to be able to analyse and justify personal values.

Understandings

- a positive self-concept is fundamental to whole-body development;
- social networks can help satisfy many needs;
- an ability to cope with changing life situations is essential.

Content

- self-concept and self-esteem;
- self-management;
- assertiveness;
- family life;

- human relationships;
- the peer group;
- coping with loss, grief and change;
- value awareness and analysis;
- decision-making;
- stress management.

The pastoral care programme in operation

The general intent of the programme was to create and maintain a 'caring' climate that provided a stable, constant and non-threatening environment for the entire school community. Pastoral curriculum sessions represented the core of the programme in that they were structured as proactive activities to provide students with alternative behaviours. These used library sessions led by the pastoral care co-ordinator as an avenue of contact with every student for 80 minutes per week.

The pastoral curriculum was scheduled for eight successive weeks in term 1 and term 4. The programme presented covered the following themes:

- conflict resolution;
- development of assertion skills;
- problem resolution;
- value clarification;
- cultural stereotyping.

The same topic was presented to each class several times, broadening the coverage at each level. This allowed for themes to be followed up in the general life of the school and in particular in the classroom. On occasions when a particular problem was obvious (for example, an outbreak of bullying), an incidental theme was presented for that week.

The pastoral care co-ordinator was given administrative time which was used as follows:

- students were counselled if a problem had arisen with which the class teacher wanted intervention or extra help;
- parents were interviewed;
- the support services were co-ordinated at case conference-type sessions;
- a 'Growing Up' course for Year 7 was organized;
- para-professionals were trained for their role;
- in conjunction with the support teachers, remedial type programmes were organized.

Several innovations were made to the programme over a period as the need became apparent. These were as follows:

(a) A comfort zone was instituted. The symptoms of social upheaval frequently manifested themselves at school. Many children came to school distressed, depressed, hungry or just unhappy. A partitioned-off section of the library formed a special room and students were able to see the pastoral care co-ordinator at any time. There were several fold-up beds available. Through the pastoral curriculum sessions they were invited to share their problems with either their teacher or the pastoral care co-ordinator. The promise of confidentiality was given. This arrangement was formalized to the extent that the pastoral care co-ordinator made herself available each morning prior to school starting.

(b) A sick bay was established. At times students came to school ill, sometimes even chronically ill. Parents were working or out of the house and could not be contacted. Staff members tended to share the responsibility for the 'caring' aspect of this section of the programme; they included the secretary, the library assistant and the teachers' aide. Teachers also tended to use the area for students who were not physically ill but obviously in need of comfort and care.

(c) An after-school care centre was set up. Many of the students came to school very early and were in the school grounds late in the afternoon without supervision. With a grant from OOSCA (a government organization), a formal centre was established and staff hired to supervise the students until parents collected them. Students were given afternoon tea, homework sessions were organized, play was supervised and television was available.

(d) A discipline role was established for the pastoral care co-ordinator as a sympathetic listener rather than as someone directly involved. The assumption underlying this policy was that if a student was referred it was because the teacher believed there to be some underlying personal problem of which poor behaviour was but a manifestation. Perhaps the teacher felt the situation required more in-depth counselling, or was serious enough to warrant the attention of the principal and of parents.

There was an assumption that the staff would provide support for each other in this area, with the principal accepting ultimate responsibility for punitive actions.

The role of the para-professionals in the pastoral care programme

At the beginning of the 1987 academic year the principal of the school sent a letter home to invite parents interested in helping on the programme to become active participants. A basic screening of potential candidates took place. The guidelines for acceptance of volunteers as para-professionals were that the candidates should

• possess a warm attitude towards all students;

- be literate;
- be able to appreciate the need for confidentiality;
- have a positive attitude towards the school and in particular be supportive of the teachers;
- be in a position to attend the school on a regular basis.

All candidates attended formal training sessions run by the pastoral care co-ordinator. They were briefed on the aims and objectives of the programme. Materials to be used (e.g. reading and spelling programmes that had already been prepared by the pastoral care co-ordinator) were explained.

The candidates were then given experience of working in a one-to-one relationship with a student. They were shown how to monitor and record results and were shown where material was placed. The support teacher demonstrated a teaching lesson with the candidates seated with their charges. The para-professionals were part of the lesson and they were then given the responsibility of taking the student on their own and reinforcing the main elements of the demonstrated lesson.

From this stage on a support teacher took responsibility for the running of the academic support, monitoring the para-professionals, checking their day-to-day reports and supplying materials and programmes.

During the year the para-professionals were involved in a full-scale two-day seminar run by staff from the West Australian College of Advanced Education. They were introduced to a basic philosophy of literacy and numeracy, and taught specific skills, and they took part in a practical workshop on making resource material, financed through the school. The seminar was requested by the para-professionals themselves as they wanted a deeper understanding of the curriculum taught at school, mainly for their own satisfaction. It was assumed that all students would gain from para-professionals' having a broader experience and knowledge in the area in which they are assisting the support teacher.

The role of support teacher

The enrolment policy of the school at this stage was that any student could be enrolled, provided that there were the facilities and the places available. Students from other boundary areas were enrolled, including a significant majority of 'problem' students.

On the basis of a formal report submitted to the Ministry of Education during the early stages, a part-time support teacher was allocated to the programme. The report supplied evidence of a significant number of students who:

- were tested and perceived to require extra support because of learning difficulties;
- had been moved from other schools because of behavioural problems;
- were under the care of welfare agencies and had identified associated needs such as extra academic and emotional support;

- were on drugs for such conditions as epilepsy;
- were physically handicapped and needed to be integrated into the mainstream of the school community.

The support teacher was responsible for taking small groups of students and providing a programme in literacy and, to a lesser extent, numeracy. This was made possible by the help of the para-professionals. These teaching sessions were highly structured and constantly evaluated. There was a constant transient group passing through the programme and the challenge was to 'teach' a set of skills. The support teacher kept records of student progress and conferred with the pastoral care co-ordinator, class teachers and parents.

Discussion

A number of factors were identified as having important effects on the implementation of the programme at the school. These included:

- the role of the principal, whose commitment to the programme, management style, willingness to sell the concept and ability to transmit the vision were essential to its success;
- maturity of the staff in terms of flexibility, expertise, personalities and a commitment to the general welfare of all students;
- the qualifications of the co-ordinator, who had experience in the special needs of students and formal training in assessment, lending credibility to her role;
- the existence of a stated policy on pastoral care that outlined the development of the programme in explicit terms;
- the building of an evaluative procedure;
- the design of a pastoral curriculum to address the needs of all students in a formalized structured way;
- the delivery of student services which were complementary to the pastoral care programme with the school determining the support needed so that de-skilling of the teachers did not take place;
- a time allocation was essential so that the pastoral curriculum was accepted as part of the whole curriculum;
- staffing levels had to be sufficient to allow the academic support programme to function;
- the careful selection and formal training of para-professionals ensured the quality of their contribution;
- the provision of a room as a base for the pastoral care programme;
- the involvement of all teachers in the selection of new students, who were attending from outside the boundary areas specifically to take advantage of the programme.

The programme itself was a planned response to a needs assessment. Change strategies were implemented and a continued evaluation programme was followed. During the planning stage every effort was made to ensure that all crucial elements were included in the evaluation, with Hodgkinson's P3M3 providing the conceptual framework. There was a clearly defined rationale, a strong underlying philosophy and a clear idea of the aims of the programme. Although staff interpretation varied, the staff settled to a generally shared view of the programme in terms of students' needs and teachers and pastoral care staff seeing their role in relation to these needs.

Over a period of some 12 months, greater responsibility was placed on students to perform in both the affective and the cognitive areas. Given the growing confidence of the staff in meeting student needs, and in the light of the positive first evaluation, all students in the school became part of the programme via the pastoral curriculum. Staff gave status to the programme by accepting the time allocated of 80 minutes per week per class. However, this very success brought with it certain costs. As the programme gained acceptance within the wider community, excessive demands were placed on teachers as students from outside the school boundaries enrolled at the school. Some of these students were very talented but the majority had severe behavioural and academic problems. Teachers had little say in their admission and this created tensions between administration and staff.

The para-professionals quickly settled into a structured pattern and with the allocation of their own base room the tensions caused for teachers by their presence in the staff room or close to classrooms disappeared. They had become a close group with their own identity and they too appreciated being able to 'breathe'.

Training and using parents in this way brought a heightened awareness of community in the broad sense. This building up of the community did not just happen; using the school facilities in a planned way encouraged a sense of obligation to develop in the para-professionals and other community members were drawn into this ethos.

The extra staff person was crucial to the programme because of the high number of problem students. The personality factor was important here as this teacher had to be able to express warmth and empathy. However, she was perceived as needing more training, so she enrolled in a pastoral care unit at a tertiary institution.

The structure for the pastoral care programme was created and the work was defined, but the commitment of the school as a whole was essential to make it work. At times this was difficult and differences of opinion occurred, in particular over discipline. However, in the final analysis the staff pulled together and shared a common attitude. It was a compassionate approach in many ways, as teachers felt justice was important, and the planned policy of support meant that no student was left to struggle through his or her problems alone.

References

Beazley, K. (chairman) (1984) *Education in Western Australia. Report to the Ministerial Committee into Education.* Perth: Education Department of Western Australia.

Hattie, J. (1988) *The Enhancement of Self-Concept in Schools Involved in the Priority Schools Programme.* West Australian Centre for Education and Training (unpublished).

Hodgkinson, C. (1981) A new taxonomy of administrative process. *Journal of Educational Administration,* XIX(2), 141–52.

Lapate, C., Flaxman, E., Bynum, E. and Gordon, E. (1969) *Some Effects of Parent and Community Participation on Public Education.* New York: Eric Information Retrieval Center on the Disadvantaged, Teachers College.

Ministry of Education (1987) *Better Schools in Western Australia.* Perth: Western Australian Ministry of Education.

Scriven, M. (1967) Methodology of evaluation. In Tyler, R., Gagere, R. and Scriven, M. (eds) *Perspectives of Curriculum Evaluation.* Chicago: Rand McNally.

The Catholic Education Commission of Victoria (n.d.) *Pastoral Care in Catholic Schools.*

CHAPTER 10

Sharing the task

Your problem or *our* responsibility?

ELSPETH O'CONNOR AND NANCY PATERSON

Introduction

While schools strive to provide an effective education for students, rapid social changes mean that greater social responsibilities are involved. Increasingly teachers are being asked to undertake many of the functions that families traditionally performed. Families are sometimes unable to provide the stability, assistance, discipline and emotional support and structure which are essential to a child's physical, social, emotional and spiritual development. Often it is left to the school to meet these needs.

The title of this chapter was chosen because for these authors it captured the essence of the differing models of social work. Previously, students with problems were referred to social workers to 'fix them', with the referring person then thinking it was no longer their problem. However the way we now work in Catholic schools reflects the idea of pastoral care as an attitude in which all students are a shared responsibility. The social worker liaises with others in the school community to find an effective solution to whatever problem arises.

When clarifying our concept of pastoral care, we chose to use Kevin Treston's definition (Treston, 1983):

> Pastoral care is the school's expression of concern for the development of the child. It is the response of the school to the various needs of the child ... an holistic education centered on the human person of the child made in the image of God.

Pastoral care was given emphasis in the 1980s as a response to criticism of schools as having an outdated or irrelevant curriculum, of being alienated from the community, of being unable to deal with student disruption, and of being unresponsive to teacher stress (Morgan, 1985).

The social work programme in Catholic schools in Western Australia

In 1983 the Catholic Education Office appointed Mary Dynan as a part-time consultant for developing student welfare services. Her research, *Do Schools Care?* (Dynan, 1980), led her to conclude that there was a need for specific action to be taken to extend the caring atmosphere of schools. From her experience she thought social workers had skills and attributes useful to facilitate the necessary changes.

In 1984 the appointment become a full-time one and school-based social workers were established. Participating in the programme were 21 schools which employed social workers either part- or full-time. There was one other Catholic school in Perth, catering for disturbed adolescent girls, which had access to a social worker from the early 1970s but this school was not originally part of the social work programme. Currently there are ten social workers, working in 17 Catholic schools in the metropolitan area.

With the emphasis on pastoral care in the early 1980s schools were being asked to strengthen school–family–community links. It was thought that a more structured, integrated and professional approach was required to deal with the social and emotional development of students. Social workers would collaborate with the school principal, teachers and other professionals to extend the caring role of the school.

Initially there were two barriers to the programme; one was lack of funds and the other the outdated view of social work, identifing it with the 'charity–welfare' model, in which the social worker was perceived as one who 'fixes' problem children.

Dynan's (1986) research suggested that there were two dimensions of pastoral care improvement that social workers needed to tackle:

- Casework with students and families.
- Co-operation of the social worker with teachers, students and the parent community to improve the pastoral climate in schools. This would include both preventive programmes and improved consultation with administrators and teachers, contributing towards more effective classroom management and the development of improved organizational procedures.

For these tasks, social workers needed a wide range of interpersonal and organizational competencies. A set of impact and service objectives were formulated and the social work service became operative. Its philosophy was to be inclusive, holistic, integrative and normative. Eight key values underpin the philosophy developed:

1. Uniqueness of the individual

According to Mendelsohn (1982, p. 184), social work's purpose is to 'promote or restore a mutually beneficial interaction between individuals and society in order to improve the quality of life for everyone'. This definition takes into account the individual and the wider society and the interaction between the two. Institutional structures often militate against the individual's needs, and this is as true of schools as of any other institution.

Both church and social work practice recognize and understand that each client has unique qualities, and that an individual must be free to become the person that he or she was created to be – not anyone else, no matter how alluring that ideal might be. The purpose of instruction at school is education; that is, 'the development of man from within, freeing him from that conditioning which could prevent him from becoming a fully integrated human being', according to *The Catholic School*, Sect. 29 (Society of St Paul, 1977). Thus 'individualization is based on the right of human beings to be individuals and to be treated not just as *a* human being but as *this* human being with his personal differences' (Biestek, 1957, p. 25).

In Catholic schools the social worker also recognizes and upholds the spiritual dimension of the individual as he or she strives to integrate faith and life and culture. This has implications for the way we work. As St Paul says (Romans 14 and 1 Corinthians 12), 'we were all given different gifts and we use these in accordance with God's grace, each serving a different purpose'. So if we value the uniqueness of the individual, one of our tasks as social workers is to develop and affirm that uniqueness, recognizing that individually we cannot do much but together we can accomplish great things.

Therefore, in the school setting we recognize that teachers, parents, special education consultants, physical education teachers, guidance consultants and all other personnel in the school community have their special role to play and a different gift or talent. We endeavour to work together wherever possible and, if we have fully utilized our resources within the school community, then we refer to outside agencies to obtain their help and assistance.

Upholding this value – the dignity of the human person – entails accepting the other values listed below.

2. Confidentiality

Confidentiality underlies everything social workers do, as it is on this value that we build trusting relationships with our clients. Most of a social worker's time is spent in making contact. If clients are comfortable in the relationship and feel they can trust the worker they are more likely to share information and thus the work may be more effective.

> Confidentiality is the preservation of secret information concerning the client which is disclosed in the professional relationship. Confidentiality is based upon a basic right of the client; it is an ethical obligation of the social worker and is necessary for effective casework service. The client's right however, is not absolute. Moreover the client's secret is often shared with other professional persons within the agency and in other agencies, the obligation then binds all equally. (Biestek, 1957, p. 121)

Social workers in schools must be very conscious of this value as dilemmas arise in deciding exactly what information can be shared and with whom. This is always done with the client's permission except when confidentiality needs to be broken, when a child is 'at risk', and even then the principle of client consultation is usually employed.

3. The non-judgemental attitude

This value is both a church and social work value. In the Bible we are admonished not to judge others so that God will not judge us (Matthew 7:1), while in social work theory, we are advised that

> The non-judgemental attitude is a quality of the social work relationship; it is based on the conviction that the casework function excludes assigning guilt or innocence, or degree of client responsibility for causation of the problems or needs, but does include making evaluative judgements about the attitudes, standards or actions of the client; the attitude, which involves both thought and feeling elements, is transmitted to the client. (Biestek, 1957, p. 90)

Within institutions, this is a particularly difficult attitude to maintain as it is so easy to fall into the trap of stereotyping individuals. I am sure we are all familiar with *the* 'problem kid', *the* 'Aboriginal family', *the* 'aggressive parent', and *the* 'new teacher'. We judge others as either worthy or unworthy of our help and assistance, often denying assistance to persons we judge as 'those who do not wish to help themselves'. Withholding services to groups and individuals who do not qualify as 'needy' flies in the face of justice and equity. Social work recognizes and accepts the Christian concept that it is possible to love the sinner without loving the sin.

4. Client self-determination

> The principle of client self-determination is the practical recognition of the right and need of clients to freedom in making their own choices and decisions. Social workers have a corresponding duty to respect that right, recognize that need, stimulate and help to activate that potential for self-direction by helping the client to see and use the available and appropriate resources of the community and of his own personality. The client's right to self-determination, however is limited by the client's capacity for positive and constructive decision-making, by the framework of civil and moral law and by the function of the agency. (Biestek, 1957, p. 103)

We do not see ourselves as telling others what to do or giving advice; we try to empower others, to assist them to make their own choices by offering options. Sometimes it is very hard to accept the choices individuals make but choosing is tied to the exercise of responsibility, which, when accepted, is one of the ways in which a person can grow and mature. Thus one of our tasks as social workers is to affirm and support others when they make their choices and take what might be difficult steps for them, in changing their behaviour patterns.

Parents and teachers often seem to be protective of their children, trying to prevent them from making mistakes. They sometimes do things *for* them to perhaps 'help' them achieve success. But the underlying message sent is that the individuals are not capable of doing it for themselves and this does not foster growth in the individual. It does not encourage empowerment, the active use of resources to meet one's own needs and the growth of independence and competence necessary for an individual to function well in contemporary society.

5. Acceptance: starting where the client is

The client may be the student, parent, teacher, school or system. Acceptance means taking the client as he or she is without any 'shoulds' or 'oughts'. The social worker's task is to assess:

- where the client is, recognizing both strengths and weaknesses;
- where the client is ready to begin working;
- where the goal is that the client wants to attain.

To facilitate the process, the social worker needs empathy, i.e. working *with* the other person. We do this by putting ourselves in the other's shoes, to understand things from that person's perspective, maintaining at all times the other's dignity and personal worth. From a church perspective that means having compassion for one's fellow man.

6. Social justice and equity

These values are highly esteemed by both church and the social work profession. Thus for us to promote these values there must be an integration of theory and practice at all levels in our work – we call this 'praxis'. It calls for reflection and integration of both head and heart. In upholding the values of social justice and equity, social workers need to maintain a keen awareness to look for those structures, policies and practices at both micro and macro levels that might militate against these values. They do this not only by looking outward but also by looking at their own practice and the prejudices that might influence the way they work. They look to their peers for supervision and support to enhance their work and develop themselves professionally, and try continually to evaluate their own performance to see whether they are being fair to their clients, selves and agency.

7. Parents, the primary educators of their children

In both church teaching and Catholic school policy, parents are recognized as the primary educators of their children. Therefore, they have the ultimate responsibility for decisions made about their children, especially in primary school. Yet as Don Edgar, Director of the Institute of Family Studies, points out (1988, p. 1):

parents have little authority over those with whom they share the task of raising their children and are today in some ways like executives in a large firm – responsible for the smooth co-ordination of the many people and processes that work together to produce the final product. This assumes that all parents have the necessary know-how and resources to choose and co-ordinate, which manifestly some have not.

Therefore, one of the tasks of the social worker in Catholic schools is to provide, wherever possible, the necessary resources for families to be in a better position to make informed choices.

8. Building community

In contemporary urban society much of the population lives in large cities, and our school communities have become very diverse in terms of social class, ethnic background and geographical boundaries. This poses a challenge for principals and parish priests who endeavour to build 'community'. In community work processes in the past, family and community were seen as embodying a common relationship. However, because of the social differentiation that has occurred in cities, recent community work techniques have separated these two into primary and secondary relationships. The greater the amount of differentiation, the greater the need for intervention both within and between levels. Reintegration is seen as one of the central issues in our society today (Cox *et al.*, 1977) and it is certainly one of the key problems for us working in the school setting.

Social workers focus on communication between home and school to raise consciousness of differing needs. Unless there is a sense of shared goals or common values between both it is very difficult to build a sense of community in the school. The family in modern society, while it may have lost some of the functions it has traditionally performed, still plays a crucial role in consolidating, co-ordinating and integrating information to provide children with important life chances.

From values to practices

We approach our task in schools from a collaborative, integrative and holistic perspective which not only focuses on crisis intervention but also on prevention and development. The fence at the top of the hill might be better and more effective than the ambulance at the bottom. American research shows (Edgar, 1989, pp. 43, 44) that early intervention and support is better than costly cures that come too late.

Each member of the school community contributes to the development of the school climate and the quality of the relationships within it. The social work service, working co-operatively and collaboratively, aims to strengthen and enhance those relationships.

Our concept of the school community may be illustrated as in Figure 10.1. Our work is in the six inter-related areas.

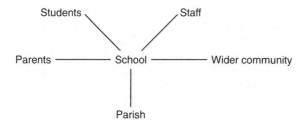

Figure 10.1

Students

Individuals The social work service is available to each student. Students are made aware of the social worker's role and the means of making contact for individual counselling in a casework relationship. A most important value at work in this setting is the need for self-fulfilment of the child without violating the rights of others. This work recognizes the goal of the agency (the school), in promoting the growth of self-understanding and problem-solving skills in the child.

For example, a child's disruptive behaviour in the classroom may reflect family circumstances over which he or she feels powerless. In casework, the social worker recognizes the child's uniqueness, giving him the opportunity to describe and explore his own perceptions of his behaviour and situation. His frustrations and needs can be more clearly understood, and with the adults about him – parents, teachers and social worker – he can work at improving his life.

In order for the child to trust the social worker, confidentiality is assured; he must understand that his private thoughts and fears will not be widely discussed. He also needs to know the limits of confidentiality: that some specified information must be passed on to others to resolve the problem he describes.

Acceptance of the child and a non-judgemental attitude are essential values when working with children. It is important that the social worker conveys these attitudes to establish a relationship where change can be possible, even where it is obvious that the child's behaviour may have harmed or disadvantaged others.

Group work Sometimes the value of acceptance means that we work with groups of children, rather than with the individual. For instance, a child may avoid a one-to-one counselling relationship to deal with his problems with bullying, or with getting on with peers in general. A group work intervention, in a setting managed by the social worker, may better deal with the student where he is experiencing the consequences of the behaviour. Such groups have been used to enhance self-esteem and peer support among students, and to deal with issues such as racism.

Working within groups managed in this way can enable students to attain goals in their future lives. Social workers value self-determination, and through seminars on, for example, transition from primary to secondary school are offering the means and resources for students to learn coping skills for application to many areas of their lives.

Every adult in the school models certain behaviour and values which children can readily observe. The social worker recognizes this, and her behaviour towards individual students, staff and others demonstrates those values of the dignity and uniqueness of the individual in any situation – the playground, the classroom, assembly time or on outings. At the same time the social worker supports the efforts of other school staff in her encouragement of the child's learning of self-discipline.

Staff

Staff as individuals The social worker–staff relationship is obviously critical to the working of this service in schools, and is one reflection of the school's commitment to pastoral care. It is desirable that the relationship is mutually supportive, with co-operation and exchange of skills and information (within the bounds of confidentiality) working in the child's best interests.

Where teachers and the social worker work together to assist a student, the confidentiality of the child's information is maintained. As mentioned, however, the child is made aware of that information which must be passed on to the teacher so that they can work together effectively towards coping with the problem. This process of co-operation and consultation demonstrates the value of the uniqueness and dignity of both individuals, for the teacher's personal qualities and requirements are taken into consideration, as well as the needs of the student.

The teacher–social worker relationship does not develop overnight, but can be most effective for students when there is sound trust and co-operation. The social worker recognizes the demands on the teacher's time and the limitations that exist in the busy timetable of the school, where so many individuals, subjects, duties and tasks compete for a teacher's time and energy. This demonstrates the value of acceptance, of acknowledging the reality of the other's position.

In any profession where there is a commitment to sound and caring relationships, the extra component of stress must be recognized. Teaching is no exception, and the social worker's role is to share and relieve some of this stress.

Confidentiality is paramount also in helping individual teachers deal with stress. For instance, the teacher may wish to express feelings of anger, frustration or uncertainty in her work with a student, parent or colleague. It may be unacceptable to give expression to these feelings to the individual concerned, but the social worker – operating from non-judgemental values and concern for this individual's self-determination – can assist the teacher to clarify, explore and resolve the problem.

The teacher's relationship with parents is an area where conflict and misunderstanding can arise. In using a non-judgemental approach, recognizing each party's needs and employing sound communication skills, the social worker can promote a better understanding between these two most important adults in a child's life. For example, in preparing for a parent–teacher interview the teacher and social worker can rehearse and use those skills and behaviours which achieve co-operation and mutual respect.

In thus empowering others to manage such situations, preventive work is taking place, and contributing to a more positive atmosphere for dealing with conflict. At best, this can have the effect of strengthening the generativity of a teacher's love and concern for a child, and is important in re-affirming self-worth.

Staff as a group Stress has been mentioned already. Some social workers have arranged stress management courses for staff; others have recognized secretarial and support staff needs which may have been overlooked by the behaviour and demands of others, and advocated change in this.

In assisting to resolve these issues, the social worker operates from the values of social justice and building community, and contributes to an atmosphere where relationships with one another are more likely to be nurtured and developed.

Social workers in schools recognize the cumulative effect of demands and expectations of others in society on our teachers. In some such areas the social worker can outline reasonable expectations and courses of action. For example, all adults have a responsibility to protect children from abuse; a teacher, in his day-to-day contact with a child, is sometimes seen as having a responsibility next in importance to that of the parent. The responsibility in such a case can be shared with the social worker, who provides staff inservice training on identifying children at risk of abuse, appropriate responses to this, and liaison with the relevant authority. Social justice and equity are the values demonstrated in this example.

Administrative staff The social worker's accountability rests not only with her professional code of ethics, but with her employers in the form of administrators. Most social workers liaise closely with the principal and other executive staff on a teamwork basis; at a minimum, regular meetings with the principal keep her informed of social work activities. In turn, the social worker accepts direction by the principal to those areas of work which best suit the needs of the school.

In this aspect of social work in our schools, building community and confidentiality, and promoting parents as primary educators, are values always to the fore.

Parents and families

The social worker contributes specific expertise in the understanding of family functioning to the school's response to a child's needs.

One important task for the social worker is to challenge notions of a 'normal' family; judgements of the child's family arrangements can have serious implications in the way he views himself and is viewed by others. By providing research data and other expert opinion to staff, the social worker can enhance the school's acceptance of cultural differences which influence a child's behaviour and performance.

Family therapy and family counselling are skills which social workers add to the school's ability to offer help to families in need. While the school itself is not seen as a treatment centre, school-related needs can best be met by these methods. When this is not indicated, it is important that appropriate and effective referrals be made.

Family referral may be needed in a variety of circumstances. These include occasions when children suffer the death of a family member, when schoolwork is disrupted by a child's feelings of loss and confusion at parental separation, when a child experiences difficulty in accepting standards of discipline which are at odds with those at home, when a child shows symptoms of stress in excess of usual expectation because of his own perceived failure, or when, in general, the school's best efforts to help the child overcome a particular difficulty are showing no effect. Referrals of this kind are made in a spirit of collaboration with parents, i.e. 'Let us work together to overcome this problem', rather than 'Please come and take responsibility for something which is beyond our control'.

In recognizing the stresses in family life, preventive programmes are offered in the form of parenting skills groups, or information evenings on subjects requested by parents. Resources such as literature, tapes and films are made available to parents.

The social worker can give the skills and time to family members to explore and resolve important issues. In so doing, the social worker affirms the parents' primary role in the child's education – not simply in academic areas, but in life – and acknowledges the uniqueness of the individual and his family and culture.

Parish

The parish priest is a vital part of the school community, and the social worker recognizes his work for all connected with the school. Referrals are made to the parish priest, and his consultation and guidance are valued by the social worker. Others within the parish, such as specific service groups, are also referred to where appropriate, thus making some families aware of the network of care to which they belong.

The wider community

In pastoral care children become aware of the communal nature of being a person in our world through interactions with the wider community. While teachers chiefly address this need for their students, the social worker interacts with other professional or interest groups on behalf of the school, e.g. local committees on services for children in the area; a committee dealing with prevention strategies for child abuse.

It is the social worker's responsibility to be familiar with the various services and resources available in the wider community, and to use these effectively for members of the school community. The social worker values social justice and, for example, lobbies relevant authorities and acts to support other agencies when services (e.g. marriage guidance) for local families in need are threatened with closure.

The school

The pastoral care climate in a school is affirmed by its organizational structures. These

- allow for those inter-related groups within the school to share in decision-making affecting its members;
- are based on social justice and concern for the dignity of the human person; and
- develop an awareness of, and sensitivity to, cultural and other differences.

The social worker, with all staff, has a responsibility to participate in formulating and evaluating the effectiveness of these structures. In some schools, this has meant distinguishing the aims of these structures from the methods they use, and ensuring that school personnel understand their individual responsibilities in carrying these out.

As an example, a school's discipline policy is an area where social workers have a part to play. In addition to giving attention to the value of the dignity of the individual in extant discipline procedures, the social worker can extend the values of the school's policy in providing parenting programmes which are consistent with this policy. Similarly, with this profession's commitment to the care network, the social worker can assist in the formulation of effective measures, such as referral procedures and resource dissemination in the school, to cater for the self-determination and empowerment of others with particular needs.

Conclusion

It is our belief that social work values fit comfortably in pastoral care in education. Moreover, their influence on all areas of school life can demonstrate how sometimes rhetorical policies can be translated into effective action.

It must be noted that not all of the activities described are undertaken by all social workers in Catholic schools. Rather, this outline includes the variety of interpretations individual social workers give to their role in pastoral care. It is, however, true to say that the values described are held by all social workers in Catholic schools. All recognize and work with the six inter-related groups who make up the school community, and all work to balance the short-term and long-term objectives of its members in providing for students' needs.

It is not our view that the social worker's role in pastoral care is more prominent than any other's. Instead, the social worker seeks to strengthen and develop those skills and relationships within the school network, so that every member of the school can develop as an individual, and experience a sense of belonging to a caring community.

References

Biestek, Felix P. (1957) *The Casework Relationship*. London: Unwin.

Catholic Education Commission of Victoria (1983) *Pastoral Care in Catholic Schools*, draft statement. Melbourne: CEC.

Cox, F.M., Erlich, J.L., Rothman, J. and Tropman, J.E. (1977) *Tactics and Techniques of Community Practice*. Itasca, IL: Peacock Publishers.

Dwyer, B. (1989) *Parents, Teachers, Partners*. Rozelle, NSW: Primary Teachers Association.

Dynan, M. (1980) *Do Schools Care?* Co-operative Research Series Report No. 6. Perth: Education Department of Western Australia.

Dynan, M. (1986) *Enhancing Pastoral Care*. Perth: Catholic Education Office, Western Australia.

Edgar, D. (1988) Children need pride of place in family policy debate. *Family Matters: Australian Institute Family Studies Newsletter*, April, Issue No. 20, 1-6.

Edgar, D. (1989) Family problems: the cost benefit of prevention. *Family Matters: Australian Institute Family Studies Newsletter*, December, 25.

Mendelsohn, R. (1982) *Fair Go: Welfare Issues in Australia*. Ringwood, Victoria: Penguin Books, Australia.

Morgan, J. (1985) *School Social Work: Towards Developing a Model*. Perth: Catholic Education Office, Western Australia.

Society of St Paul (1977) *The Catholic School*. Homebush, NSW: Society of St Paul.

Treston, K. (1983) *Renewing the Vision*. Sydney Parish Ministry.

CHAPTER 11

Towards pastoral care

A Catholic school perspective

A.C. CURTIS AND SR A. WILLMOTT

Introduction

This chapter outlines how one school has developed its policy of pastoral care, and has endeavoured to identify and carry out its pastoral care objectives. It will focus on the outcomes of seven years of developing a pastoral care policy. Although the whole process involved was demanding and very important for the school, only a few of the steps in the process will be highlighted. It is a reasonable assumption to say that the approach to pastoral care represented in this paper is fairly typical of Catholic schools generally.

Early history of pastoral care at Corpus Christi College

Corpus Christi College is a new Catholic, co-educational, secondary school located in the Perth suburb of Bateman. It is in its eighth year of operation, with a student population of just over 800. From its first year of operation, in 1983, the original teaching staff of six planned for the implementation of a strong pastoral care programme. This was seen to be critical if the newly established school was to have a truly Catholic identity – especially so, since it was the first new, co-educational, secondary school founded by the archdiocese and not owned by a religious order. Fr Robert McCormack, O. Carm., the foundation principal, was a man thoroughly committed to pastoral care. This concern found expression in the ongoing, everyday, face-to-face dealings with students on campus, and in a more structured course for students in Year 8–10 focusing on those areas of curriculum devoted to life skills and the personal development needs of the students. This course was called Personal and Vocational Education, commonly referred to as PAVE.

About this time, the Catholic Education Office began the development of a set of PAVE guidelines for each year level. Two staff members from the college, Mrs Robyn Quinn and Sr Anita Willmott, participated in the process, which helped to refine the college's own

PAVE programme. At the same time, a formal support network was initiated with the appointment of year co-ordinators, student counsellor/careers adviser, and the establishment of a work experience programme.

Problems with the PAVE concept

PAVE topics were taught by home-room teachers for two periods per week. This seemed to work well until 1986 and 1987 when the school expanded to Year 11, then to Year 12, with a five-stream intake.

Unfortunately, in these two years, the initial strong commitment to pastoral care seemed to wane. Key contributing factors seemed to be:

- the explosive growth of staff numbers from six to sixty;
- the time needed to plan and set in place the curricula for the inaugural Year 11 and 12 courses;
- planning for the introduction of Unit Curriculum for Years 8–10;
- many new teachers were confronted with the task of teaching a formal PAVE programme without understanding its rationale, or being committed to its delivery; and
- not all teachers taught PAVE.

There was a feeling that 'pastoral care' equated with what was happening in the formal PAVE programme only and didn't happen anywhere else. Also significant was the fact that some teachers who felt unskilled in this area tended to trivialize the class sessions, so that many topics were treated in a perfunctory manner.

In 1987 it became evident that there was a need to clarify our understanding of pastoral care and to articulate this understanding in the form of a pastoral care statement that could be owned by all staff members.

Process of reviewing pastoral care

Perhaps the most important step taken during 1987, in reviewing our understanding of pastoral care, was the involvement of all staff members in a whole-day discernment process facilitated by Brendan McKeague and Peter Hann, who initiated and developed the PAVE guidelines at the Catholic Education Office. This process broadened the notion of pastoral care from a narrow focus on PAVE classes to a more holistic, whole-school concept, and identified student and staff needs, basic principles, and possible strategies.

Because the PAVE classes were judged not to be working satisfactorily, they were discontinued in 1988. This, however, led to concern that material vital to the students was not being covered at all.

During 1989, therefore, further staff meetings identified specific pastoral care needs of students in each year level. By the end of the year, staff had worked out a 'programme of ownership' by which these needs could be met. These 'pastoral objectives' are proving important guidelines for year co-ordinators and home-room teachers.

The term 'pastoral curriculum' has recently been adopted to include these elements, and was expanded to embrace other informal, school-based activities that were already an integral part of the College's school life.

In the mean time, from 1987, various draft statements regarding pastoral care were developed and subjected to critical staff analysis. The final draft was endorsed as reflecting a common understanding of the principles articulated, with a general commitment to the structures, initiatives and practices contained in it.

The outcomes of this long process have been articulated in the following pastoral care policy statement.

PASTORAL CARE POLICY

'I have come that you may have life, and have it to the full'. (John, 10:10)

Pastoral care in a Catholic school

In a Catholic school, pastoral care is based upon the Christian belief in the fundamental dignity and worth of each person.

In this context, pastoral care is Christian formation in a community setting, enlivened by the Gospel spirit of freedom and love. It encompasses the total climate of care which reflects the broad Christian ethos of individuals caring for and respecting one another.

It includes a pastoral curriculum which provides opportunities for students to achieve an understanding of themselves, and a realization of their potential.

Principles underlying pastoral care

In order to build an effective climate for pastoral care,

- all groups within the school community need to work together;
- all staff members need to be committed to this common vision;
- each child needs to be a member of a small group which has a close personal relationship with a significant adult; and
- all staff members need to be supported in the carrying out of their pastoral role.

Pastoral care at Corpus Christi College

In Corpus Christi College, pastoral care includes a structure in which

- all staff members are responsible for the social, emotional, spiritual, intellectual, and physical development of each student;
- strong relationships are established between the staff, students and their families, in a Christian community setting;

- clear, consistent, firm and just discipline is practised in an environment which facilitates the development and experience of responsible self-discipline; and
- students and staff are able to appreciate the care that they experience.

This person-centred philosophy is an expression of faith that begins in the classroom, and is reflected in all facets of the school experience, including contact with non-teaching staff and the school's enrolment policy and practice.

The goals of pastoral care at Corpus Christi College

At Corpus Christi, pastoral care refers to the total care of each member, expressed through

- the establishment of an effective care network,
- the provision of satisfying learning experiences, and
- the development of quality relationships.

Initiatives in the establishment of an effective care network

- Subject teachers are responsible for the pastoral care of students belonging to their classes.
- Home-room teachers are responsible for the pastoral care of a specific group of students.
- Year co-ordinators are appointed to co-ordinate the pastoral care of each year group.
- The assistant deputy has a special responsibility to co-ordinate pastoral care initiatives within the school.
- The student counsellor is employed to provide personal, educational and vocational counselling.
- Year teams facilitate the liaison between home-room teachers with year co-ordinators.
- A pastoral council meets to co-ordinate planning between year co-ordinators and principal, deputies, religious education co-ordinator, and student counsellor.
- Clear definition of the pastoral aspects of the roles of all staff is provided for in this statement.
- Regular parent contact avenues are important: especially courier, telephone, formal/informal parent/teacher meetings, student reports, homework diary, pro-forma letters to parents.
- Clear internal referral network re discipline, crisis situations, external assessment is co-ordinated by the assistant deputy.
- Effective liaison with community referral agencies has been established by the student counsellor.
- Regular, formalized year student reviews are initiated by principal and/or year co-ordinators.

- Informal and formal student interviews – 'getting-to-know-you', or discussion of academic progress can be organized by all staff members.

Initiatives in the provision of satisfying learning experiences

- Regular review of school curricula to ensure the provision of relevant learning occurs, at the levels of staff meetings, academic council, and executive meetings.
- Each classroom teacher is responsible for the teaching of the appropriate curriculum content within their subject area.
- The deputy has a special responsibility to co-ordinate curriculum matters within the school.
- An academic council meets to co-ordinate planning between departmental/subject co-ordinators with principal, deputies, librarian and careers adviser.
- Religious Education classes provide co-ordinated experiences to assist faith development.
- Personal development, community health and vocational education issues are key areas dealt with at each year level.
- Library services provide essential resources and scope for individual learning.
- A careers guidance service is available to all students.
- Educational support classes, e.g. teacher-assisted learning (TAL), small focus classes for basic skills development, ESL tutorials for Aboriginal students have been established to assist students in need of additional help.
- A Special Education Centre with integrated classes has been established to provide for handicapped students, especially those with mild to moderate intellectual disabilities.
- Evaluation reviews of pastoral care initiatives occur from time to time.

Initiatives in the development of quality relationships

- Home-room groups – where each student belongs to a regular group with a focus person – provide an important occasion for pastoral care activities.
- Home-room teachers, who teach students for a variety of subjects, can extend their pastoral care.
- A house (faction) system used for intra-school sporting events has been established.
- Clear discipline policy and procedures provide orderly teaching and learning environments.
- Regular formal/informal assemblies – whole-school, year, class, special ceremonies – assist in developing identity and corporate spirit.

- Occasional masses, liturgies – celebrating together as a school/year/ class are essential faith development experiences for students and staff.
- Involvement of parents – formal/informal, sports coaching/managing, camps, fêtes, adult education evenings, school board, P & F, canteen, clothing stores, library assistance, school-based social activities – is a feature of school organization.
- Student involvement in student-organized activities is encouraged.
- The student council – facilitating involvement of students in real decision-making is an important exercise in leadership training.
- Camps, retreats, excursions, sports carnivals, mission days are essential and integral to the life of the school.
- Social education – school balls, dinner dances, dancing classes, year socials are important planned activities for students.
- Regular social gatherings, staff meetings and planning days assist in fostering the development of the staff as a team.

Pastoral care roles

The overall pastoral care and development of the students is the responsibility of all staff in the school. This is expressed through each staff member's commitment to the students, through acceptance, respect, understanding and service, whether in the classroom, library, front office or College grounds.

The **subject teacher** is the first person in the network of pastoral care. The relationship between the subject teacher and each individual student in the class is at the heart of the pastoral care programme. No other pastoral strategies can compensate for a failure in the caring approach of the teacher to each student in the class.

The subject teacher is responsible for programmes of work within the subject area under the direction of the subject co-ordinator, and is a member of that department. The subject teacher liaises with the students' home-room teacher in matters relating to the students' progress and welfare.

The **home-room teacher** is a special focus person who is responsible for the pastoral care of a specific group of students, and is the significant adult to whom the members of that group relate, fostering a sense of belonging within that group. The home-room teacher is also responsible for reporting on the general progress of students to parents.

The home-room teacher works in close consultation with the appropriate year co-ordinator and the student's subject teachers. Each home-room teacher is a member of a year team assisting the year co-ordinator.

The **subject co-ordinator** is responsible for the planning, implementation, and review of all courses of study within the department, monitoring the progress of all students in their work within those courses, counselling them in their choices where appropriate, and providing adequate advice and support to their subject teachers.

The subject co-ordinator works in close liaison with the principal and deputies, and is a member of the academic council.

The **year co-ordinator** has the overall responsibility for the pastoral care needs of the students in a particular year group, integrates the work of that team of home-room teachers, and supports them in their care for individual students.

The year co-ordinator works directly with the students in the year group, in close consultation with the home-room teachers, as well as other appropriate pastoral care personnel. The year co-ordinator works in close liaison with the principal and deputies, and is a member of the pastoral council.

The **student counsellor** is responsible to the principal for the planning and conduct of those aspects of pastoral care which will meet the personal needs of individual students.

The student counsellor works in close consultation with the principal and deputies, the year co-ordinators, and the student's family where appropriate, and is a member of the pastoral council.

The **careers adviser** is responsible to the principal for the planning and conduct of those aspects of pastoral care which will meet the vocational needs and aspirations of the students.

The careers adviser works in close liaison with the principal, deputies, and the year co-ordinators where appropriate, and is a member of the academic council.

The **assistant deputy** takes a particular responsibility for matters pertaining to student welfare, integrates the work of the year co-ordinators and student counsellor, supports them in their care for individual students, and liaises closely with students' families. The assistant deputy chairs the meetings of the pastoral council.

The **deputy principal**, in consultation with the principal, is responsible for the day-to-day planning and implementation of the school's curriculum, the overall discipline, and the efficient running of the school within a pastoral care context, recognizing and appreciating the differing needs of individual staff members and students.

The deputy principal works in close liaison with the subject co-ordinators, and chairs the meetings of the academic council.

The **principal** has the direct responsibility to ensure that the policy and practice of pastoral care permeates all areas of school life, responding, appropriately to the individual needs of students, parents, and teachers in accordance with the common good.

The principal works in close liaison with the deputy principal and the assistant deputy, forming the administration executive team, as well as with the year and subject co-ordinators, the student counsellor, and the careers adviser.

Pastoral curriculum at Corpus Christi College

The College's pastoral curriculum comprises those learnings and experiences which will enable students to develop an understanding of themselves, and assist in their personal growth.

Our pastoral curriculum focuses on

self-knowledge, and covers a range of general areas such as self-concept, human physiology, psychology, sexuality, gender, family, relationships, society, and ethnicity;

self-management and self-appraisal within a social context (the school community and society), and includes the treatment of moral development, study skills, information-handling skills, communication skills, time management, drug education, and social etiquette;

the concept of a satisfying Christian life style, including the student's self-awareness (personality, interests, aptitudes, abilities), vocational development, career education as an interpretation of the needs and demands of occupations and fields of work, and the practice of decision-making skills;

affective development, where students are able to express their feelings, and respond in a personal, sensitive manner, be it through music, dance, the visual arts, or spoken language.

leadership development, through the student representative council, mission days, fund-raising activities, and other opportunities for service.

This pastoral curriculum is delivered *formally* in class sessions of a developmental nature, for example, in religious education, health education, and career education classes, and in organized home-room activities.

It is also pursued *informally*, by means of extra-curricular activities. This informal pastoral curriculum allows students to express their gifts and strengths, in their own area of competence, and to turn these talents to service. Examples of such activities are sports days, athletics and swimming carnivals, cross country runs, sports and games, music festivals, school bands and orchestras, fete and mission days, excursions, camps, retreats, assemblies, and the student council and other leadership activities.

Pastoral curriculum objectives of each year group

The following pastoral curriculum objectives have been identified by year group teams as important for particular year groups:

Year 8

The pastoral curriculum will enable students to:

(a) make a successful transition from primary to secondary school;
(b) learn the social skills needed to relate to their peers;
(c) develop a sense of belonging by fostering a significant relationship with at least one staff member;
(d) become aware of the rights and responsibilities of individuals and groups;
(e) learn appropriate decision-making, study and organizational skills.

Year 9

The pastoral curriculum will enable students to:

(a) develop respect for themselves, others, property, and the environment;
(b) understand and develop the skills needed to deal successfully with their own sexuality;
(c) communicate maturely with others, dealing appropriately with conflict, peer pressure, and study demands;
(d) understand and appreciate that rights and responsibilities include the need for structure and authority;
(e) begin to focus on their future in relation to career choice and further study.

Year 10

The pastoral curriculum will enable students to:

(a) develop further their self-esteem, their skills in communication, assertiveness, and appropriate social etiquette;
(b) make decisions about their sexuality, and how they express themselves as males and females in relationships;
(c) make informed, realistic decisions regarding their future career paths and life styles;
(d) develop the qualities needed for acceptable peer leadership;
(e) be aware of the effects of drugs in our community.

Year 11

The pastoral curriculum will enable students to:

(a) be confident, competent, and considerate in their relationships with others, demonstrating self-motivation and independence;
(b) commit themselves to an organized programme which achieves a balance between studies and social activities;

(c)   identify their academic strengths and apply them realistically to their career goals;

(d)   participate in and contribute to the life of the school and the wider community;

(e)   accept leadership challenges and respond to them effectively.

Year 12

The pastoral curriculum will enable students to:

(a)   accept themselves as worthwhile persons with the potential to shape their own lives;

(b)   be comfortable in authentic relationships, and appreciate the values of openness, acceptance of others, and the rejection of prejudices and stereotypes;

(c)   be flexible, realistic, and adaptable when considering career choices and inevitable life changes;

(d)   demonstrate effective and responsible leadership, presenting themselves as quality role models to the rest of the school community;

(e)   deal resolutely and successfully with the pressures of external examinations, school and societal expectations.

Pastoral curriculum programmes

At the end of 1989, the members of the pastoral and academic councils worked together to co-ordinate the delivery of new and existing programmes. A detailed scheme indicating how and when specific elements of the pastoral curriculum objectives could be dealt with was drawn up.

Year 8

The **Year 8 co-ordinator, home-room team** and **religious education team** are responsible for the organization and delivery of the following programmes:

(a)   The induction into secondary schooling (Term 1)

(b)   Study skills (Term 2)

(c)   Community living skills (Term 1 – Year 8 camp)

(d)   Rights, responsibilities, rules (Term 3)

(e)   Life skills, decision-making, bicycle education (Term 4)

The **Year 8 religious education team** is also responsible for the

(f)   Human sexuality programme (Term 4).

Year 9

The **Year 9 co-ordinator** and **home-room team** are responsible for the organization and delivery of the following programmes:

(a) Relationships, community skills (Term 1 – Year 9 camp)

(b) Study skills (Term 2)

(c) Social conscience – poverty, drugs, social behaviour (Term 3)

(d) Career education (Term 4)

The **Year 9 religious education team** is responsible for the

(e) Human sexuality programme (Terms 1 and 2)

The **Year 9 physical education team** is responsible for

(f) Alcohol and smoking education

(g) Life-style diseases education

(h) Fitness programme.

Year 10

The **Year 10 physical education team** is responsible for the organization and delivery of the following programmes:

(a) Drug education (Term 1)

(b) Career education (Term 2)

(c) First aid (Term 3)

(d) Life-style diseases (Term 4)

The **Year 10 religious education team** is responsible for the treatment of

(e) Human sexuality (Term 4)

(f) Relationships (Term 4)

The **Year 10 co-ordinator** and **home-room team** are responsible for the organization of and assistance with the processes involved in

(g) Dance and social etiquette programme (Term 2)

(h) Subject selection (Terms 2 and 3)

and assist the work experience co-ordinator with the

(i) Work experience programme (Terms 1–4).

Year 11

The **Year 11 co-ordinator** and **home-room team** are responsible for the organization and delivery of the following programmes:

(a) Study skills (Terms 1–3)

(b) Time-management and organizational skills (Terms 1–3)

(c) Leadership training (Terms 1 and 3)

and, assisted by the student counsellor/careers adviser, help the students in their

(d)   Course and career decision-making (Terms 1–4)

The **Year 11 religious education team** is responsible for the treatment of

(e)   Issues of justice and peace (Term 1)

(f)   Christian view of love (Terms 1–4)

(g)   Goal-setting and stress management (Terms 1–4).

Year 12

The **Year 12 co-ordinator** and **home-room team** are responsible for providing experiences in

(a)   Independent learning and living (Terms 1–4)

(b)   Dance

and, with the assistance of the student counsellor/careers adviser, help the students in their

(c)   Course and career decisions (Terms 1–4)

(d)   Guest speaker programme (Terms 1–4)

The **Year 12 physical education team** assists the year team with

(e)   Leadership training (Terms 1–3)

The **Year 12 religious education team** assists the year team with

(f)   Human relations and commitment programme (Term 1–3).

Pastoral care and discipline

The school's discipline policy has been developed as a separate statement. However, both the policy and the practice of discipline are based on this pastoral care statement.

The discipline policy should be read in conjunction with this pastoral care statement.

The policy in practice

Understanding of pastoral care: enabling

The basic attitude towards pastoral care at the College is expressed in the term 'enabling', as exemplified in the New Testament text: 'I have come that you may have life, and have it to the full' (John 10 : 10). This Christian stance underpins the school's whole approach to education and pastoral care.

Principles underlying pastoral care

The process of teasing out this basic Christian stance led to certain fundamental principles that needed to be articulated. These were:

- All groups within the school community need to work together.
- All staff members need to be committed to this common vision.

- Each child needs to be a member of a small group which has a close personal relationship with a significant adult.
- All staff members need to be supported in the carrying out of their pastoral role.

Organizational structure at Corpus Christi College

To ensure that these principles operated, a particular tone or climate had to be maintained, and this climate had to be underpinned by a supportive organizational structure where all staff members are responsible for the personal growth of each student in a relational setting, where just discipline facilitates the development of self-discipline, and where both students and staff are able to appreciate the care that they experience.

Three elements emerged as being essential for the implementation of these pastoral care initiatives. These were:

- the establishment of an effective care network;
- the provision of satisfying learning experiences: and
- the development of quality relationships.

These initiatives have been noted very explicitly in the policy statement.

Pastoral care roles

The overall pastoral care and development of the students is the responsibility of all staff in the school. This is meant to be expressed through each staff member's commitment to the students, through acceptance, respect, understanding and service, whether in the classroom, library, front office or College grounds.

However, some staff members have been identified as having more specific pastoral care roles, and these have also been articulated in the policy statement.

Pastoral curriculum

Over the past two years, a considerable amount of effort by the staff has been devoted to the area of pastoral curriculum, including the development of pastoral care objectives and pastoral curriculum programmes.

A significant achievement has been the identification of pastoral curriculum objectives for each year group. These objectives highlight areas of development considered to be important learnings for students as they progress through the school.

Pastoral curriculum programmes

Who does what, and when? are important questions if the pastoral curriculum objectives are to move beyond being mere statements of intent.

At the end of 1989, the members of the pastoral and academic councils worked together to co-ordinate the delivery of new and existing programmes. A detailed schema indicating how and when specific elements of the pastoral curriculum objectives could be dealt with was then drawn up.

This approach to planning pastoral curriculum objectives is unusual, and indicates the extent to which staff members are committed to pastoral care.

Conclusions

Three areas are worthy of comment as a conclusion to this chapter.

The first is that Catholic schools generally would share the fundamental approaches taken by Corpus Christi. For all, pastoral care is an integral part of being a Catholic school. However, their methods of implementing pastoral care strategies could be somewhat varied.

The second is to continue to evaluate and ask ourselves: Where to from here? As a school, we need to work further on:

• considering and firming up the time allocation given to covering life skills and personal development programmes for students;

• developing and owning a common understanding of pastoral care, particularly as new staff members move into the school community;

• seeing whether or how parents should be involved in the process; and

• sustaining our basic commitment to the concept of pastoral care.

The third is a brief attempt at estimating the extent to which rhetoric is translated into action at the College. We suspect strongly that the rhetoric is a major concern of ours – whilst most other staff members *do* pastoral care. The most recent example of this is the move to provide leadership experiences for students, and to support these experiences with practical assistance and encouragement. Overall, the climate of care at the College is strong and all-encompassing; that is, it really does pervade the operation of the school. It is self-evident that any perception of the effectiveness of the school's pastoral care policy depends essentially on 'how we operate' rather than on 'what we say'.

CHAPTER 12

The organization of pastoral care in independent secondary schools in Australia

DAVID C. MARTIN

Introduction

In 1984, I conducted a survey of the organization of formalized pastoral care in 77 independent secondary schools in Australia (see pp. 152–6). The schools varied in size from under 400 to over 1200 students and included 26 boys' schools, 16 girls' schools and 35 co-educational schools. In March 1989, I sent a further questionnaire (pp. 156–8) to each of the 77 schools seeking information on any changes that might have been implemented over the previous five years. Replies were received from 59.

Considerable development has taken place in the organization of pastoral care in Australian independent secondary schools in recent years. The 1984 survey indicated that 37 of the schools had instituted or significantly altered their pastoral care systems in the preceding ten years. Significant modifications to the system during the five years prior to this survey were indicated by 52 of the schools.

Experience in both Britain and USA has influenced the approach taken in Australia. The historical pattern in schools in USA has involved the use of specialist personnel while that in Britain has tended to place more emphasis upon the use of the resources of the teachers themselves. While specialist services have tended to serve those students with special and obvious needs, pastoral care, which utilizes a larger proportion of the personnel of the school, attempts to reach all pupils.

In the USA, increasing concern about the effectiveness of counselling services has seen, in some schools, a shift towards teacher–adviser programmes. In 1975, the Report of the California Commission for Reform of Intermediate and Secondary Education (see Carey, 1977, p. 7) recommended that 'a sufficient number of adult advisers should be provided from the instructional and support staffs so that each learner can identify with and relate to at least one adult on a one-to-one basis'.

In nineteenth-century Britain, the public schools saw dramatic changes with the humanizing efforts of Thomas Arnold and other reformers. The emphasis on manliness which grew in the latter part of the century saw the increasing importance of organized games in these schools. House structures in the schools were often convenient means for dividing students into teams.

House systems have been a part of the life of independent schools in Australia, particularly boys' schools, for some time. Apart from in the boarding situation, their main purpose has not always been the administering of pastoral care. Even where the principal purpose has become pastoral care, houses can be involved in keen competition. Some would argue that this reinforces the identity of the unit, while others agree with Miles that the idea of each house striving to be the 'best' house does not add to real educational and social development (Miles, 1968, p. 30).

Very few schools in Australia have the large boarding populations which characterize the English public schools. A school with a large boarding component lends itself far more naturally to a house system than a school which has a predominance of day pupils. Compensatory factors must be included in the latter case for the system to be effective. One major advantage of the boarding schools, and particularly those run by religious orders, is the large number of staff members who are strongly committed to the full life of the school.

Division into groups

Of the 77 schools surveyed, 22 (29%) indicated that pastoral care was based solely on some vertical house structure, while 20 (26%) based theirs solely on some type of horizontal division. The remaining 35 (45%) employed a combination of horizontal and vertical groupings. Within this latter group, four schools indicated that one section of the school was divided into houses while in another section or other sections of the school – for example, first year of entry into secondary school or the last two years of secondary school – year or class groupings were used. The other schools ranged from those which based most of their individual pastoral care on a house system, using the horizontal structure for specific group purposes such as subject selection, to those which made little use of houses for pastoral care programmes.

Pastoral care organization based solely on a house system was strongest in boys' schools with 42 per cent indicating such use compared with only 13 per cent of girls' schools and 26 per cent of co-educational schools. All 13 Catholic schools indicated use exclusively of a horizontal system apart from in boarding sections.

In the follow-up questionnaire, 49 schools indicated no significant change in their structure since 1984, although some had introduced modifications to strengthen their existing systems. Seven schools have either moved from a horizontally organized system to a house system or some other vertical structure, or changed the emphasis from horizontal to vertical. One school experimented for a year with a vertical structure but many teachers found it difficult to operate in a less structured context and the school returned to a grade-based system. Another school, which uses a vertical (house) system has supplemented this with a horizontal, form structure.

In a system based on horizontal (year) groupings, the base unit is usually a class, although sometimes this may be divided into smaller units. Thus its membership is dictated by factors other than purely pastoral concerns. It would be possible to argue that this is not a bad thing. The group, as a teaching unit, has already established a certain identity of its own and this may be an advantage. No additional activities need to be contrived to establish an identity. On the other hand, it may be that teachers consider pastoral care to have a low priority and thus devote increased time to the teaching function.

It is possible, however, that in a horizontally based system, base units could be constituted so that they cut across teaching units. Thus there is the possibility of mixed-ability groups and some, although limited, scope for choice. If the major division is based on vertical groupings such as houses, the choice still remains for base groups to be either horizontal or vertical in their structure.

Staff involvement

Use of all or most teaching staff enables base groups to be kept as small as possible. The inclusion of other staff within a school can further reduce the size of the group. There are compelling reasons for wishing for the formal involvement of all staff but it is clear that not all staff in every school will be either willing or capable participants in such a programme. Class size tends to determine base unit size in schools organizing their pastoral care horizontally. Base units within houses, especially if arranged vertically, tend to be limited by staff availability. Nash (1979, p. 6) suggests that base groups of 15 or less are preferable.

The survey sought to determine the proportion of staff whose role in the pastoral care organization could be seen as formal. Out of 74 schools which responded to this question, 35 (47%) indicated that all teaching staff, with the possible exception of some senior administrative staff, were involved in the pastoral care programme. A further 32 (43%) indicated that a majority of the teaching staff were involved. Only 7 (9%) indicated that less than half of the staff members were involved in the programme.

Those schools which chose to organize their pastoral care along class lines only were less likely to involve all teaching staff in their programme. Only 5 of the 35 schools that indicated use of virtually all staff organized their pastoral care along horizontal lines, while 12 of them based their organization solely on house lines. Eight schools indicated that staff involvement in the programme was voluntary, although one admitted to 'pushing'.

Group size

The size of groupings based on school classes is often determined by factors which are not related to the pastoral care functions of the group. Various factors, chief among which are timetabling and subject selection, may determine class sizes. Generally schools using this type of structure base the groupings on actual academic classes.

Houses varied widely in size between schools. They ranged from 30 members to 400, but of 47 responses, 25 schools (53%) indicated houses of 60–100 members. The responsibility of an individual housemaster thus differs quite markedly between schools.

The survey indicated that the most common number of houses (15 schools: 32%) in any one school was four; other arrangements ranged from three to sixteen houses. Obviously, even numbers are preferred where there is any programme of inter-house competition. Only seven schools indicated an odd number of houses.

Houses were in most cases divided formally into smaller base groups: 40 schools indicated that houses were subdivided and 8 schools reported either that the houses were left undivided or that any division was at the discretion of the housemaster. Although the information was not specifically sought, it appeared that the majority of schools using house-based systems divided their base groups along grade lines.

It was clear that divisions of houses in the schools surveyed led to smaller-sized base groups than in those schools basing their organization on grades: the most common size in the former fell between 16 and 20, in the latter between 26 and 30.

Seven schools indicated that, since 1984, they have considerably reduced the size of their base groups, in many cases from c. 30 to about half that number. In some of these schools, this has been as a result of a complete restructuring of the system; in others it has been achieved by the splitting of existing groups.

Allocation of time

Schools were asked to indicate how formal pastoral care activities were timetabled in the school week. Four schools gave no details of any formally structured time for pastoral care. In many schools, such time is allocated at the beginning or end of the day or, particularly in the case of class-based groupings, both. The frequency of contact as well as the total time allocated for pastoral care are both important.

Schools with pastoral care based on class or year groups indicated greater frequency of daily meetings (68%) than schools using house groups (41%). On the basis of the information provided by schools which stated the actual time set aside for pastoral care activities, the average time devoted to such activities was approximately 75 minutes per week.

In the follow-up questionnaire, 26 schools indicated changes in either the time allocated to meetings or the frequency of meetings. Several schools indicated increased time to include new aspects in the programme, such as a peer support scheme or a personal development programme. Almost all of the 26 schools indicated that significant additional time had been made available for pastoral care group meetings. How much of this time is actually used for pastoral care activities and how much for other administrative purposes is not clear. There appears to be a tendency to increase the length of each contact session.

Specialist services

Linked with the pastoral care programme, or an integral part of it, are the specialist professional services relating to the health and welfare of the students. Most of the schools surveyed were affiliated to religious bodies and 51 indicated that at least one full-time chaplain was employed, while in 10 schools, the chaplaincy is a part-time position. Three schools reported that they used community services in this regard. In the recent survey, one school indicated that a full-time chaplain has since been appointed.

Strong support is evident for the incorporation of any professional guidance and counselling programmes into the pastoral care programme. Experience in the USA, where extensive counselling services were set up in school, showed the possible difficulties. Carroll (1981, p. 17) points out that guidance services have met with criticism ever since they were introduced into schools. He cites the fact that a 1971 Gallup poll seeking recommendations for economizing education recorded that removal of counselling from schools was given fourth place out of a total of sixteen recommendations.

Sprinthall (1980, p. 485) comments on the rather episodic nature of contact between counsellors and students and the client-centred approach of counsellors as contributing factors to the problems: the tendency has been 'to separate the psychology of the pupil from the psychology of the school. The pupil's mind remained in the classroom and the soul in the counselling office.' Many of the advisement programmes set up in the USA have attempted to incorporate professional counsellors as part of an integrated programme where the contribution of the specialist can be much more effective. In this way, counsellors have the potential to work with staff and support them in their pastoral role. A division between counselling staff and teachers increases resentment, counsellors often being seen in the 'good guy' role. Thus communication between the groups becomes restricted. Such a situation reaffirms the teacher's perception of his role as being strictly instructional.

One of the areas of weakness in pastoral care systems cited by Best *et al.* (1980, p. 273) is the inadequate or inappropriate use of the 'expert'. Dyer (1979, p. 8) points to a need for all schools to couple the work of the housemaster, tutor or form master with that of properly trained counsellors. It would be false to assume that any pastoral care programme eliminates the need for properly trained counsellors.

In 1984, responses indicated that 40 of the schools had the services of a full-time counsellor, vocational guidance officer or psychologist; 31 indicated that such a position was part-time; 3 used external services. In the follow-up questionnaire, 7 schools indicated that they had appointed a full-time counsellor; 6 others indicated increased use of a counsellor, in some cases using external resources on a contract basis.

As well as counsellors, there are many other specialists available either within the school or in the community. These include school nurses, doctors, dentists and therapists of various kinds. All these

personnel ought to be seen as participants in the pastoral care programme. A few schools listed special education teachers and librarians
as providers of services related to pastoral care.

Training

For effective pastoral care programmes it is essential that the staff
participants are prepared for their role. Many writers on the subject
indicate a feeling of inadequacy on the part of many teachers when
placed in the pastoral care situation.

Rogers (1983, p. 26) points to a survey of 633 Inner London teachers
which found that only 6 per cent of teachers, 3 per cent of senior teachers
and headteachers and 8 per cent of deputy heads had attended pastoral
care inservice courses. Problems reported in the USA also indicated
little or no pre-service training for teacher–advisers. The expectations
placed upon teachers are sometimes under-estimated. It is unrealistic
to expect every teacher to form an effective relationship with each of a
group of students in her care without first having adequate preparation.

In 1984, 27 schools indicated that there had been little or no inservice
training of staff in relation to pastoral care in the preceding two years.
In 19 schools some staff had attended externally-run seminars on
pastoral care-related topics. For 20 schools pastoral care had been a
component of internally run seminars during that period. In 14 schools
staff members were cited as running the seminars. Nine schools
indicated some form of on-the-job training for teachers by the principal,
chaplain or counsellor. In 25 schools there had been, over the past five
years, a significant increase in inservice training for staff in pastoral
care-related issues. In several cases this training had been specifically
related to newly introduced features, such as peer support programmes.
Many schools have brought in specialist personnel to run seminars.
There certainly appears to be increasing recognition of the importance
of training in this area.

Other aspects

An important feature of effective pastoral care is the development of
trust between staff member and student. This is more likely to develop
where some choice is available on the part of either or both of these
participants. Class-based systems tend to be less flexible than house-
based systems in this regard unless they are not specifically based on
teaching groups. Where a student joins a house on entry to a school,
very few criteria are usually available on which to base a choice. Often
family tradition plays a part in the decision. It is rare for students to
change houses. If the house is divided along year lines, the choice is
restricted. If the house is divided on a vertical basis, then a choice may
be possible.

Five schools specifically indicated that students were able to express
a preference for membership of a particular pastoral care group. The
majority (53%) of schools reported that the division into groups was

random, apart from the placing of siblings in the same houses or basing choice upon family traditions.

The concept of an individual member of staff having responsibility for a particular student throughout his or her schooling is difficult to achieve within a horizontally based organization. Certainly it is unlikely that a class teacher would be equipped to move with a group throughout the secondary school, although, in the more recent survey, one school indicates that it tries very hard to achieve this. Eighteen schools indicated that the responsibility of a staff member for a particular student lasted only for one school year. A housemaster would generally have responsibility for a student throughout his secondary schooling, but a tutor associated with the house might not.

In all but five schools, physical facilities of some description were allocated for pastoral care group use. Such facilities could be seen as reinforcing the identity of a group. In the case of class groups, home-rooms with associated notice boards and locker areas were available. House groups in most schools also had access to classroom areas. Where schools indicated a high proportion of boarding students, house areas were available for use. House ties, house badges, honour boards for house captains, daily bulletins, a courtyard, seating area in the assembly hall and change rooms were each listed once by different schools.

Physical facilities identified in the follow-up questionnaire included senior common rooms, locker rooms, notice boards, and creation of a tutor group 'home area' and lunch areas. One school mentioned plans to build day house centres. Nine schools in all indicated increased facilities during the past five years.

The majority of schools use their pastoral care groups for various administrative purposes such as absentee checking and dissemination of information. While such activities can increase the importance and cohesion of the group, schools must be careful that they do not eclipse its pastoral function. Several schools have indicated that, although groups are used for such activities, the time set aside for them has been separated from the time set aside for pastoral care.

All schools indicated that pastoral care groups were involved in activities beyond timetabled meetings (e.g. sport, music, drama, debating, lunches, assemblies, chapel services and social activities). Some of these activities relate closely to pastoral care, but all could be considered to strengthen the identity of the group and, in some cases, provide opportunities for pastoral care to take place on a less formal and, possibly, more individual basis.

Other activities listed by some schools included community service, camps and excursions. One school reported that each group has responsibility for a particular area of the grounds of the school. Schools adopting exclusively a class-based pastoral care structure indicated less involvement in these activities. Some schools indicated that, although their pastoral care was organized by classes, a house system was employed for competitive activities. If such activities are seen as strengthening the identity of the group, then they are perhaps less necessary with class groupings because the class is generally already established as a teaching unit with its own identity. Of 53 schools which stated that pastoral care units were involved in some competitive activities, only 5 were schools organized solely along class lines. Such competition in these schools was restricted to year-level activities in sport or music. In other cases, competition varied from fund raising for charity to a broad range of sporting and other activities.

Special considerations

Special arrangements for students in the first year of secondary schooling were indicated by 19 schools in 1984. Often this included greater use of home-room teachers, i.e. ensuring that they teach a number of subjects to their class. Occasionally, first-year students were kept separate from the pastoral care programme employed for the remainder of the school: in such cases their programme usually included orientation activities and, sometimes, some form of outdoor education. The 1989 survey shows that more schools are following this pattern. One school divides Grade 7 into house groups for teaching purposes.

One school indicated the use of a pastoral care curriculum. Personal development programmes have been introduced as part of the pastoral care programmes of a few schools during the past five years.

Leadership training of some senior students was considered a part of the pastoral care programme by two schools, while three indicated that senior students assisted with junior tutorial groups. Sixteen schools have introduced peer support schemes involving leadership of groups of junior students by senior students. All of these have been introduced in the past five years and are considered to be an important part of the pastoral care programme. In 1984, only one school indicated that it was setting up a peer support scheme.

One school reported the setting up of a contact group chaired by the year level co-ordinator. This group consists of form teachers at that level together with those subject teachers who are most likely to be involved with that year. A second school mentioned parent evenings, held for parents of children in particular year levels on such topics as human sexuality and social issues. The school also had a weekly programme for parents dealing with parenting skills and issues.

In the follow-up questionnaire, three schools indicated the introduction of mentor systems to help junior students. An increase in the effort with the orientation of new students at various levels was also mentioned by several schools. Other areas where special attention has been given include strengthening of pastoral care programmes in boarding houses. Some schools have created separate boarding facilities for junior students and one has removed boarders from day house groups and placed them into two houses consisting only of boarders. Two schools indicated that day school parents are invited to assist with the care of boarders.

Change

The first survey revealed that the length of time pastoral care structures had been in place in the schools varied from one year to over 100 years. At that time, 11 schools reported that they were reviewing or evaluating the system currently in use.

Apart from those changes already mentioned, the 1989 survey indicated that several schools are providing more material for tutors to use in their pastoral sessions. In some cases short lessons are prepared; in one school the Director of Student Support Services co-ordinates the teaching by tutors of life skills. An increasing amount of resource material is available and being used in schools.

One school indicated that after a meeting of its pastoral care committee it was decided that questionnaires should be sent to all parents asking them to detail certain aspects of their children – their strengths, etc. as parents see them. Almost 80 per cent of these were returned, giving excellent detail. Another school described the formation of parent house committees to support the house structure, but more importantly to allow parents to mutually support one another.

Fifteen schools indicated that the overall administrative authority for the co-ordination of the pastoral care programme had changed in the past few years. In some schools it had been transferred from the school principal to his or her deputy, but in four schools the position of pastoral care co-ordinator had been created. In another two schools, a pastoral committee now co-ordinated the programme. The school counsellor and the chaplain, respectively, were listed by two further schools.

Summary

It is clear from these surveys that there is an increasing acceptance of the importance of pastoral care programmes in independent secondary schools. A wide range of practices is evident, often reflecting the unique features and traditions of the individual schools.

The special needs of sections of the school body, such as boarders and those in their first or last year of secondary schooling, appear to be catered for in the pastoral care organization of most schools. Those schools with large boarding enrolments are in a position to develop their pastoral care programme more fully because of the facilities available and the increased time spent by students, and some staff, within the school community.

Time allocated to pastoral care varies greatly both in length and frequency. There is no evidence to suggest that the success of a pastoral care programme is in any way proportional to the time allocated to it. Much of the effective pastoral care may, in fact, take place outside any formalized meeting time. On average, the time given to formal pastoral care would be approximately one-third of that normally devoted to any one of the traditional 'core' subjects during the school week. The time segments devoted to pastoral care in schools are often at the beginning or end of the day, which would tend to suggest that much of the time could be spent on administrative matters such as attendance.

Over one-third the schools indicated use of virtually all staff in the pastoral care programme. In independent schools, the principal generally has the freedom to appoint those whom he or she chooses. There is thus the opportunity to appoint those who are prepared to extend their commitment to the school to include formal pastoral care activities. Most of the schools are church-affiliated and, although the majority of them do not place religious restrictions upon their staffs, the expectation would be that staff appointed to such schools would be in sympathy with the religious aims of the school. Thus the caring aspect of such schools could be expected to be strongly supported

Independent schools tend to demand a strong commitment from teaching staff; thus staff may be prepared to accept a pastoral role on top of their primary function. Acceptance, however, does not mean that they are able to find the time fully to develop this pastoral role. Probably the most frequently mentioned problem in the literature is that of insufficient time given to staff to work in this area. In very few of the cases reported in the survey was compensation (in terms of teaching load or money) given to those in charge of base units.

The other commonly reported deficiency in the pastoral care systems in the USA and Britain is the lack of proper training for those engaged in pastoral care activities. This was also reflected in the responses to the 1984 questionnaire. Many of the respondents acknowledged this as a problem, and improvement of training was often listed as an aim for the future. It is clear from the follow-up questionnaire that many schools have begun to address this problem.

Very few schools reported that a choice was available to students or staff with regard to membership of base units. This, however, would seem to be a feature of several of the programmes reported as being successful in the USA and Britain. Absence of choice produces some mismatches and personality conflicts, although schools may be prepared to tolerate this if adoption of freedom of choice means a significant and undesirable change to other aspects of the programme. Several schools obviously made a concerted effort to maintain continuity of the care of a student by allowing tutors or class teachers to follow a group through more than one year. School reports, absentee checking and follow-up, dissemination of school information and maintenance of record cards were by far the most commonly indicated extra activity of the pastoral care group. Each of these was listed by over half the schools as being the sole prerogative of the formal care structure. All of these involve particularly time-consuming procedures and, although they can give important support and strength to a pastoral care programme, allowances need to be made for this time.

Time for actual pastoral care can also be lost through the necessity to organize competitive activities. It is clear, from the survey, that the schools see this aspect as important, but the programme has to be carefully co-ordinated to ensure that such activities remain means to an end rather than becoming the end itself.

There seems to have been a shift toward vertical structure in pastoral care organization but its acceptance is not universal and many schools remain committed to a horizontal structure. Vertically arranged base units need not be linked to form houses but very few schools have introduced systems in which base units are not joined together to form houses.

The impression was given in responses to the questionnaire that many schools would be keen to devote further time to such programmes and to provide increased time for staff members to carry out their pastoral roles. All these schools, however, are constrained by budgets; it is often difficult to justify to a governing body expenditure on an aspect of the school which is not readily evaluated. Virtually every other aspect of schooling can be evaluated, although not necessarily in a desirable way. External examinations, sporting competitions and eisteddfods are examples of measures of success of school activities. Pastoral care programmes need to be promoted strongly if they are to succeed in gaining a realistic proportion of the budget. Full support at all administrative levels is essential.

There is no evidence which would lead us to conclude that there is one best way for the organization of pastoral care. What is clear, however, is the need for any structure for the administration of pastoral care to be organized with this purpose, rather than administrative convenience, being paramount.

Careful consideration needs to be given to the size of the base group and how base groups are to be co-ordinated. Timetabling of pastoral group meetings is an important and also a potentially difficult area because of the pressures from so many other areas within the school. Teachers must be given adequate time and administrative support. Training is essential if large numbers of teachers are expected to be successful in their pastoral roles.

It is important that any programme of pastoral care should be an integrated part of the school organization rather than an appendage, otherwise the programme is likely to be vulnerable to pressures from other areas within the school.

I would like to conclude by quoting from two respondents to the follow-up questionnaire:

> I would say that 'pastoral care' is a very strong element of this school. Almost every teacher would know very personally the sixteen/seventeen students for whom he/she is responsible and would take a caring and concerned interest in her and her development in all facets of her life – spiritually, physically, academically, what other strengths she may have.... Obviously it is on-going and there is much that can still be done. However, what is achieved is quite remarkable.

> The secret of a good school is to have a successful and well-balanced pastoral care programme.

Appendix

QUESTIONNAIRE (1984)

The organization of pastoral care

Name of school: _____

The following questions relate to the *secondary* section of the school. Please feel free to give further details in response to any questions.

1. (a) Number of students in the secondary school: Girls __ Boys __
    (b) Number of boarders: Girls __ Boys __
    (c) Number of teaching staff members: Full Time __ Part Time __

2. List the administrative posts within the school and indicate how many of each there are. (e.g. principal, deputy, subject department heads, housemasters, etc.)

    _____   _____   _____
    _____   _____   _____
    _____   _____   _____
    _____   _____   _____

3. Into which of the following are the students divided to facilitate pastoral care? (Please tick one or more.)

    _____ houses

    _____ years

    _____ upper/lower/middle schools or similar horizontal grouping of sections of the school

    _____ other (please give details) _____

    _____

4. Briefly describe the number and size of each pastoral care unit (house, tutor group, year, etc.) and the general way in which it is organized. (e.g. Are houses or years divided into smaller units?)

    _____
    _____
    _____
    _____

5. Give details of any special pastoral care arrangements made in specific areas of the school. (e.g. For first-year students, for senior

students, boarding students. Are boarders in separate pastoral care units from day students?)

_____

_____

_____

_____

6. How are formal pastoral care activities timetabled within the school week?

_____

_____

_____

7. How many members of the teaching staff are formally involved in the pastoral care programme? _____

_____

8. If all staff are not involved, on what basis is selection made, e.g. voluntary or selected on such grounds as ability, seniority, etc.?

_____

_____

9. What is the normal size of the group for which an individual member of staff has direct pastoral care responsibility?

_____

_____

10. Which member of the school administration has overall responsibility for the co-ordination of the pastoral care programme?

_____

_____

11. Which members of the pastoral care team are given allowances for their pastoral care work in terms of
    (a) reduction of teaching load? _____
    (b) money? _____

12. In the past two years, what training in pastoral care has been undertaken by staff members within the school or externally? Please indicate the proportion of staff members involved.

_____

_____

_____

_____

13. How are students allocated to pastoral care units? (e.g. at random, by choice of student or staff member, are siblings placed within the same unit? etc.)

_____

_____

_____

14. Please give details of any student responsibilities within the pastoral care units (e.g. house captain, class secretary).

_____

_____

_____

15. Does the staff member with immediate responsibility for a student's pastoral care expect to take that responsibility for more than one school year?

_____

_____

16. What physical facilities, e.g. room, locker area, lunch area, notice board, etc. are seen as belonging to a pastoral care unit? Has the unit sole or shared use?

_____

_____

_____

17. Please indicate the extent to which the following can be seen as responsibilities of the pastoral care unit.

	Always	Mostly	Sometimes	Never
Attendance checking				
Absentee follow-up				
Discipline				
Dissemination of school information				
School course guidance				
Vocational guidance				
Record cards				
Medical cards				
School reports				

18. In what activities are pastoral care units, i.e. houses, tutor groups, year groups, etc., involved which might be seen as reinforcing a sense of 'belonging' to those units? (Please tick.) Please give details if appropriate.

Sporting activities _____

Music, drama, debating _____

Lunches _____

Assemblies (routine or special) _____

Chapel services _____

Social activities _____

Other _____

19. Is there any sense of competition between pastoral care units? If so, please give details _____

_____

_____

20. If parents wish to discuss the welfare of their child, with whom is first contact generally expected? (principal, deputy principal, house master/mistress, house tutor, master/mistress of lower/middle/upper school, year master/mistress, class teacher, etc.). Are there differing expectations in this regard at various levels in the school?

_____

_____

_____

21. Indicate, in the following table, what other services relating to pastoral care are available.

	Full-time	Part-time	External, community resources
Chaplain	_____	_____	_____
Nurse	_____	_____	_____
Counsellor	_____	_____	_____
Psychologist	_____	_____	_____
Vocational guidance officer	_____	_____	_____
Others (please list)	_____	_____	_____

22. What routine guidance-related testing is carried out? How often?

_____

_____

_____

_____

23. How long has the present system of pastoral care been in use at your school? _____

_____

24. Give details of any major changes in the pastoral care system in your school during the past five years. _____

_____

_____

_____

_____

25. Give details of any plans for future major changes in the organization of pastoral care in your school. _____

_____

_____

_____

_____

I would welcome copies of relevant pages from the magazine, prospectus, staff notes, etc. of your school.

THANK YOU FOR YOUR CO-OPERATION

THE ORGANIZATION OF PASTORAL CARE

Follow-up questionnaire (1989)

Please indicate whether there have been any significant changes in the organization of pastoral care in the _secondary_ section of your school during the past five years.

If you have time, an outline of any such changes would be valued.

Name of school: _____

Changes?

1. Organization by grades or houses etc. (vertical/horizontal) Yes/No

   _____
   _____
   _____

2. Subdivision of grade/house units into smaller groups, e.g. tutor groups. Size of groups. Vertical/horizontal structure. Yes/No

   _____
   _____
   _____

3. Timetabling of pastoral care activities, i.e. length and frequency of meetings. Yes/No

   _____
   _____
   _____

4. Administration responsibility for the co-ordination of the programme. Yes/No

   _____
   _____
   _____

5. Utilization of specialist support services, e.g. counsellor, psychologist, etc. Yes/No

   _____
   _____
   _____

6. Training in pastoral care undertaken by staff. Yes/No

   _____
   _____
   _____

7. Physical facilities, e.g. room, locker area, lunch area, notice board, etc., seen as belonging to a pastoral care unit. Yes/No

   _____
   _____
   _____

8. Use of pastoral care units for various aspects of school organization, e.g. attendance checking, dissemination of school information, etc.
Yes/No

_____

_____

_____

9. Special pastoral care arrangements for specific sections of the school, e.g. first-year students, senior students, boarding students.
Yes/No

_____

_____

_____

Please make any further comments on changes in the structure or emphases in the organization of pastoral care in your school which you would like to convey.

THANK YOU FOR YOUR CO-OPERATION

References

Best, R., Jarvis, C. and Ribbins, P. (eds) (1980) *Perspectives on Pastoral Care*. London: Heinemann.

Carey, R. (1977) Trends in counselling and student services. *NASPP Bulletin*, **16** (Sept.), 3–10.

Carroll, R. (1981) End the plague on the house of guidance: make counselling part of the curriculum. *NASPP Bulletin*, **65** (Oct.), 17–22.

Dyer, D. (1979) Creating a caring environment. *VATIS Journal*, **4**(2), 7–12.

Miles, M. (1988) *Comprehensive Schooling*. Harlow: Longman.

Nash, A. (1979) Care of kids. *VATIS Journal*, **4**(2), 5–6.

Rogers, R. (1983) The caring bit. *Times Educational Supplement*, 25 February, p. 26.

Sprinthall, N. (1980) Guidance and new education for schools. *Personnel and Guidance Journal*, **58**, 485–9.

CHAPTER 13

Skills for life

The internationalization of guidance

STUART WARE

This chapter critically reviews the adaptation of life-skills approaches by TACADE (UK) from a programme originally developed by Quest International (USA) to enhance the personal and social skills of school-age pupils. The programme is conducted by ordinary teachers and has proved very popular with them. It is currently in use in a large number of schools in countries on both sides of the Atlantic.

Until 1985 TACADE (The Advisory Council on Alcohol and Drug Education) produced educational materials and training courses for teachers which were based mainly on the preventive approach to alcohol, drug and other sensitive health issues. This model, which is still regarded in many circles as the traditional and orthodox approach to health education, is concerned with persuading an individual to take responsible decisions and adopt acceptable behavioural patterns.

There are several levels at which this model operates. If we take the use and misuse of drugs for example, the first level (primary) seeks to discourage a person from becoming involved in risk or harmful activities. This is followed by what is known as 'secondary', which is concerned with minimizing or reducing the risk or harm to a person who is misusing drugs. The third level of prevention (tertiary) is concerned with persuading a person from further deterioration, by abandoning the harmful lifestyle and receiving treatment.

One of the concerns over this model, especially when used to present sensitive health issues such as drug misuse, is that it tends to drift into an information/shock horror approach at the primary prevention level that is often reactionary and problem-focused. It also ignores the welfare and pastoral needs of the pupil. It is a popular method when a school curriculum timetable is too full to accommodate such sensitive health issues within the context of a whole-school health policy.

Modern primary prevention approaches to health education for children are a development from the philosophy and methods of the Christian revivalist era of the eighteenth and nineteenth centuries, which carried through the Victorian and Edwardian periods. Particularly prominent in the USA, the UK and Scandinavian countries was a concern with the prohibition of alcohol. The church-based temperance movement worked through groups such as the Band of Hope (in the UK), which employed full-time 'educators'.

During the eighteenth and nineteenth centuries various other educational philosophies were also being expounded which were to influence modern education practice and produce an approach to education on health and life skills quite different from the moralist approach. Tones *et al.* (1990) drew attention to the important influence of the progressive movement:

> The child-centred progressive philosophy of education had its roots in the eighteenth and nineteenth centuries in the writings of Rousseau, Froebel, Pestalozzi and others. It gradually made an impact on education in this century, particularly in the primary sector, and the 1960s have been described as a high point of progressivism in British schools. The concepts of progressivism – child-centredness, autonomy, and developmental approach to learning – contributed to the climate in schools in which health education slowly developed.

The important link between education, health and life skills is demonstrated in the goals for school health education proposed by Kolbe (1982):

> First, we can expect school health education to increase understanding about the philosophy and science of individual and societal health;
>
> Second, we can expect school health education to increase the competencies of individuals to make decisions about personal behaviours that will influence their health;
>
> Third, we can expect school health education to increase skills and inclinations to engage in behaviours that are conducive to health;
>
> Fourth, school health education programs, strategically with other school and community health promotion efforts, can be expected to elicit behaviours that are conducive to health; and
>
> Fifth, we can expect school health education to increase the skills of individuals to maintain and improve the health of their families, and the health of the communities in which they reside.

Skills for adolescence

The first major attempt to introduce a comprehensive skill-based programme of personal and social education in UK schools, and one which sought to deal with sensitive health issues, took place in 1985. TACADE, with the support of the Lions Clubs, adapted under licence from the Quest International (USA) the 'Skills for Adolescence' (SFA) programme.

According to TACADE, SFA is a curriculum programme for 11- to 14-year-olds which attempts to help young people learn how to deal with the challenges of our complex society by providing opportunities for personal growth and development through:

- building self-esteem,
- learning about emotions,
- improving peer relationships,
- exploring family relationships,
- developing decision-making skills,
- exploring the challenges of early adulthood.

There is a comprehensive package of materials comprising:

- a *curriculum guide* which contains structured classroom lesson plans and suggestions for community involvement;
- an *activity and assignment book* which contains photocopyable student material for classroom and home use;
- a *student textbook* raising issues about growing up;
- a *parent textbook* which helps parents to explore and understand young people's physical, personal and social growth patterns;
- a *manual of helpful guidelines* to assist schools organize parent meetings.

A major element of the SFA programme is the insistence by TACADE that the materials can only be issued to teachers through a training course, which is aimed at enabling them to develop confidence and competence to use the approach in their schools. This is because both the classroom materials and methodologies promote a participatory and active style of learning.

Not only have the curriculum materials required adaptation from the American education system, but this has also applied to the training of teachers who will use the programme. This raises issues which I know TACADE is trying to address. Content, style and methodology require modification in order to be relevant to teachers operating a different education system.

The participatory methodology and the training activities are not positively received by all groups or individuals (both teachers and pupils). This in turn affects life-skills content and there is a risk of falling back into the preventive model of information-based approaches.

SFA is appropriate to the requirements of section 1 of the UK Education Reform Act 1988, which places statutory responsibility upon schools to provide a broad and balanced curriculum which 'promotes the spiritual, moral, mental and physical development of pupils at the school and of society', and 'prepares students for the opportunities, responsibilities and experiences of adult life'. However, the reality is that the current emphasis on subject-based approaches in UK secondary schools, focusing on written examination results and attainment targets (thus putting increased pressures on time-tabling) means that life skills and participatory approaches will have an uphill battle to survive.

However, I can find no better way for a school to introduce life-skill approaches to 'sensitive' issues, such as drug use and misuse or AIDS and sex education, than through the SFA programme. Addressing a European Symposium on Drug Education Lee (1986) suggested:

> [drug education] should be involved in promoting knowledge and information (their own and new information), understanding attitudes and values (their own and others), and in developing the skills that are necessary to promote confidence and competence to make positive and healthy choices and so avoid the misuse of drugs. It changes the emphasis from drugs to people.

This approach is endorsed by research in England. Wright and Pearl (1986) offered the the following summary of the 'type' of drug education that is needed:

> In summary, based on our research and experience and on other studies, we would endorse the following points:
> a. the 'facts alone' approach is not effective;
> b. the 'shock horror' approach has no lasting effect and may be harmful;
> c. there must be careful selection of target audience;
> d. goals must be clearly defined;
> e. the source of information must be credible;
> f. 'drug education must be part of a wider programme of health and social education;
> g. such a programme must aim to enhance self-esteem and life skills and must be sensitive to locality, ability and culture.

In observing several SFA programmes since its introduction in Hertfordshire schools, I have noted that it has operated best when the above concepts have been incorporated as a whole package. SFA has failed when only selected aspects of this approach have been used, especially where the timetable or lack of skilled staff has limited its effectiveness. This calls for the need of careful planning and training of key members of staff. TACADE have been right to insist on both these crucial aspects.

A major weakness of SFA is the lack of resources to support the 'whole community' approach, which is 'to involve the school, home and community'. This requires intensive inservice training for teachers, which is ongoing and is regularly updating them with information and skills on these sensitive issues, enabling them in turn to have the confidence to develop these skills with their pupils.

One of the major concerns of this programme has been the expectation of some schools that it would have an impact on the incidence of alcohol and drug-taking behaviour. What the schools were able to provide were opportunities in which the teachers and pupils could explore their understanding and feelings surrounding the issues of drug use and misuse, including the consequences of misuse.

A further concern highlighted in the Hertfordshire evaluation (Ware, 1989) is that teachers require more than the three days' high-quality training offered by TACADE at the introductory stages of SFA. Unless there are follow-up school-based training programmes to assist in its implementation and in training other members of staff, it will not be fully taken on board. The enthusiasm generated by the initial three-day training offered to those who participated in the course is generally not transferred to others.

SFA offers a highly structured programme which places significant demands on teachers to adopt new roles and relationships. Some will not be able to make this adjustment and certainly will fail unless there is training and ongoing support within the school. Because the approach involves non-didactic methods some teachers will find themselves exposed and threatened.

However, the Hertfordshire evaluation did find that, following training, most teachers who attended the training sessions gained in confidence and skills, which enabled them to develop closer and more trusting relationships with their pupils. This in turn had spin-offs in other aspects of the curriculum, including pupil confidence in academic achievements, especially those with special needs.

A key aspect in favour of SFA is its adaptability to meet the varying needs of a school, community or country. The benefits of 'ownership' of this approach outweigh its weaknesses.

In times of recession and cutbacks, it is life skills that take a back seat. But this is short-term thinking, offering little practical help to the number of children who are struggling with adolescenthood or have special needs.

The current dominance of academic values creates an unnecessary tension between life skills and study skills, between 'pastoral care' and support for a child and 'remedial education'. Bell and Best (1986) emphasize that while there are basic divisions between the 'pastoral' and 'remedial', there are aspects of common concern and interdependence:

> While pastoral care staff remove the personal, emotional and psychological impediments to learning, the remedial department sets about clearing the undergrowth of reading difficulties and the weeds of innumeracy from the field wherein the seeds of geography, history, English, mathematics and science may be sown.

Those schools seeking to retain a caring and pastoral ethos as a matter of policy and practice recognize that it is through life skills that pastoral care can complement mainstream and academic and remedial work.

> The institutionalisation and separation of the 'pastoral', the 'academic' and 'remedial' has failed to recognise that a child's whole school experience is dependent on the presence of all three at various stages of development.

To support this further I would like to refer to a more comprehensive evaluation study carried out in the UK by Parsons *et al.* (1988) between November 1987 and April 1988. This identified the potential of SFA to bridge the gap between the social and psychological aspects of education,

Teachers reported knowing their pupils better through SFA and finding discipline easier. It was reported that improved relationships led to a less hectoring and confrontational approach in disciplining pupils. Teachers felt the tenor of relationships for whole classes and year groups had improved ...

In the best instances, lessons were focused, structured, varied and fast-moving ...

SFA has appeal for teachers interested in active learning and new styles of teaching, as reported by teachers and as seen in action ...

Whilst impact here is clearly dependent on changes in teachers and in the development of skills in pupils, this area was the single most impressive feature of SFA in use both within classrooms and its reported impact across the school. Through community building, the development of relationships and skill development the social atmosphere of whole year groups was apparently improved ...

There are reported beneficial effects in each of these [pupils' feelings about self, social attitudes, pupil skills and peer relationships] which could only be confirmed by testing and longer-term observation. In ordinary lessons apart from SFA, improvement in all of the above areas is important.

Table 13.1, taken from the same study, speculatively sets out what SFA

Table 13.1

	Judgement of *importance* of having an impact on this feature	Judgement of *likely* impact of this feature
Teacher attitude	3	3
Teacher strategies	3	3
Teacher–pupil relationships	3	3
Pupil feelings about staff	3	2
Pupil 'social' attitudes	3	2
Pupil skills	3	2
Peer relationships	3	2
Adult–adolescent relationships	3	?
Family relationships	3	?
Community action	3	?
Making reasoned and positive decision regarding health	3	?

Importance: 3 Very important, 2 Of moderate importance, 1 Of little importance
Likely impact: 3 Likely strong impact, 2 Likely moderate impact, 1 Likely little impact
Source: Parsons *et al.* (1988)

is seeking to achieve and the likelihood of having the impact hoped for on the range of relevant programme elements.

One of the current difficulties facing pastoral care and life skills in British mainstream schools results from management pressures and the effects of the National Curriculum. Conformity and maintaining a peaceful atmosphere are important; the 'problem' and non-compliant pupils are 'managed' or removed (Hamblin, 1986):

> There is a danger of growing imbalance between technology and education of the emotions. Whether we acknowledge it or not, the thrust of pastoral effort has been towards reinforcement of the status quo; attainment of an overtly tension-free state of equilibrium between staff, pupils and parents.

However, one of the strengths of the SFA programme is that it assists teachers to introduce health, social and moral issues through a variety of life-skills approaches but within a curriculum framework and time-tabling structure.

There is a need to revise SFA in order to respond to the changes taking place within education in the UK. With some modification the programme would fit in well with the aims defined in section 1 of the Education Reform Act 1988 in the UK which lays down a framework for education. The National Curriculum Council states in *Curriculum Guidance 3: The Whole Curriculum* (NCC, 1990a) that the Act places a statutory responsiblity upon schools to provide a broad and balanced curriculum work which

(a) promotes the spiritual, moral, cultural, mental and physical development of pupils at the school and of society;

(b) prepares pupils for the opportunities, responsibilities and experiences of adult life.

The Act includes the revised Statutory Orders for Science together with the non-statutory guidance which identifies cross-curricular themes to promote the aims of the Act. Health education is identified as one of these themes. The National Curriculum Council has identified that themes, such as health education, form an essential part of the curriculum. To quote from *Curriculum Guidance 5: Health Education* (NCC, 1990b):

> They are inter-related. They share many features, for example, the capacity to promote discussion of questions of value and belief, and to extend knowledge, skills and understanding.

The promotion of discussion, knowledge, skills and understanding is also an identifying feature of SFA. Further, turning specifically to health education, the *Guidance* identifies other strong characteristics which can also be found in the life-skills approaches found in SFA,

> Essential features of health education are the promotion of quality of life and the physical, social and mental well-being of the individual. It covers the provision of information about what is good and what

is harmful and involves the development of skills which will help individuals to use their knowledge effectively. (NCC, 1990b)

Skills for the primary school child

In 1990 TACADE, together with Re-Solv (the Society for the Prevention of Solvent and Volatile Substance Abuse) and with the support of Lions Clubs International, introduced 'Skills for the Primary School Child' (SPSC). This programme is aimed at a younger age group but emphasizes skills-based approaches similar to those developed through SFA. However, while not losing sight of personal, social and health education, SPSC introduces a further key aspect: promoting the protection of the child. In this respect the programme seeks to help children develop positive self-esteem to resist pressures which may lead them into difficult situations, including abuse in its many forms. As with SFA, Skills for the Primary School Child includes a key element by emphasizing the need for schools to work in close co-operation with parents and people at home. In theory, 'promoting the protection of children will be most effective when home and school support and complement each other in close partnership'. However, in practice, do all parents have the necessary confidence and skills to manage sensitive issues in the home, particularly concerning abuses within the family?

The adaptation process from one education system to another

Even though the UK and USA use the same language, the transfer of a written or education strategy, such as SFA, from American to British use is fraught with problems. This has been the experience of TACADE from the outset.

This transfer includes not only language but also concepts, systems, methodologies, models and styles of training, cultural attitudes and norms. This is further complicated by the fact that any adaptation for the British system has to accommodate the multi-cultural context of our society. (Lee, 1991)

However, there are elements which *can* be transferred from one culture and education system to another, such as encouraging the development of self-esteem, self-confidence, a respect for others and life skills.

A further problem with the American SFA programme is its abstinence approach to all drug use, including alcohol, whereas the British system is geared more towards awareness-raising as to the risks and consequences of abuse of drugs, such as alcohol. In the UK there is also greater emphasis in helping young people to have the knowledge and skills to make informed decisions.

However, there is constant pressure in the UK for SFA to follow the American pattern and become more problem-based, with a concentration on drug-related issues. The programme would lose its uniqueness if it lost sight of the pupil/teacher-centred skills approach.

There is a question of ownership and control of the programme structure and framework by the host country. The American model will present problems to British teachers if taken on board without adaptation. The same applies to training, which is a key element to the programme: the content, style and methodology will require adaptation in order to comply with the models of inservice training of the host country.

There are, then, three basic factors that need to be kept in mind when transferring SFA from one culture to another:

* the need for ownership of the programme by the host country and its education system;
* the requirement to adapt the programme and training model to meet the needs and demands of the host country;
* the importance of mutual respect for the skills of teachers and trainers of the host country who will be expected to implement the programme.

There are some positive lessons to be learned from the UK experience when transferring SFA from one country to another:

* The credibility, reputation and experience of TACADE as the implementing agency in the host country.
* The adaptation and 'ownership' of the programme which made it acceptable to UK teachers and pupils. As a result, since its implementation in 1986 over 7500 teachers have attended TACADE's SFA training courses. By March 1991 over 3500 schools and over 90 per cent of local education authorities had become involved with the programme.
* The partnership arrangement with a community service organization to assist in resourcing the programme, particularly start-up funding. In the case of the UK the valuable and ongoing contribution of the Lions Clubs of Great Britain and Ireland in support of TACADE.
* The willingness to have the programme evaluated and, as a result, to revise and update it to reflect changing patterns in the education system. In the case of the UK and the TACADE–Lions partnership, it is a matter of building on the experience gained since 1986. This involves a life-skills approach which will encompass the wider range of 11- to 16-year-olds within a National Curriculum framework.

It will be extremely difficult for many schools to continue with the life-skills approach when there are result-based pressures on the curriculum. However, if we are to continue with any semblance of the pastoral and caring aspect in education, we must continue to promote life skills. Our children will need life skills that address the needs of life in a multi-cultural, multi-lingual Europe. They will require cross-curricular skills which are transferable from one subject to another, such as communication, numeracy, problem-solving and decision-making.

The world is a smaller place than it was in the 1960s in terms of the speed and ease of travel. There are new economic problems which will affect the employment expectations of young people. Our children need help in coping with new health and social issues, such as HIV/AIDS, new 'designer' drugs, crime and homelessness.

The environment – the future of the planet and of its wild and cultivated life – is a matter of great import for our future and thus needs to be addressed by young people in schools as part of their life-skills education.

As we face the complexities of the twenty-first century, the internationalization of skills for life fulfils a universal need in the educational development of young people.

References

Bell, P. and Best, R. (1986) *Supportive Education*. Oxford: Blackwell.

Hamblin, D. (1986) *A Pastoral Programme*. Oxford: Blackwell.

Kolbe, L.J. (1982) What can we expect from school health education? *Journal of School Health*, 52.

Lee, J. (1986) Skills for adolescence: an approach to drug education for 11- to 14-year-olds. Conference paper for European Symposium, Scotland.

Lee, J. (1991) *Adapting the Lions/Quest Skills for Adolescence Programme for the UK Environment*. Salford: TACADE.

NCC (1990a) *Curriculum Guidance 3: The Whole Curriculum*. York: National Curriculum Council.

NCC (1990b) *Curriculum Guidance 5: Health Education*. York: National Curriculum Council.

Parsons, C., Hunter, D. and Warne, Y. (1988) *Skills for Adolescence: An Analysis of Project Material, Training and Implementation*. Canterbury: Christ Church College.

Tones, K., Tilford, S. and Robinson, Y. (1990) *Health Education: Effectiveness and Efficiency*. London: Chapman & Hall.

Ware, S.R. (1989) *An Evaluation of Skills for Adolescence in Hertfordshire Schools*. Hertford: Hertfordshire County Council.

Wright, J.D. and Pearl, L. (1986) Knowledge and experience of young people of drug abuse 1969–84. *British Medical Journal*, 292.

CHAPTER 14

The guidance tutoring approach to pastoral care

LYN THEILE AND COL McCOWAN

Background

Since the mid-1970s Australian education has experienced surges of interest and activity in the non-academic or non-traditional subject area. Each of these surges has had a particular focus, and these could be said (in chronological order) to include: career education, transit education, life skills, pastoral care, community links, industry links, behaviour management, at-risk students and social justice. Each has been characterized by

- a rush and grab for activities to be located in hastily arranged programmes; and
- a reward system of promotions and other incentives for those who led these 'quick-fix' fashionable topics in their schools.

Having been through the process of trying to provide some sound foundation and sense of direction for career education and transition education, we found it difficult to stand by and watch the proliferation of programmes, often consisting of a jumble of fragmented, superficial and unrelated activities, which purported to satisfy the 'core' needs of students. (Of course, there were some schools that did pursue the issues with purpose and dignity.) In the early 1980s we set about the task of attempting to provide meaning, purpose and direction for schools seeking to address non-academic subjects. The initial work was based on the material John Miller produced for the Further Education Unit in the UK (Miller, 1982) and resulted in the publication of *Guidance Tutoring: The Guidance Counselling Role of Teachers in Secondary Schools and Colleges* (Theile and McCowan, 1986). Because this was a background and stimulus document and not a list of additional entertainment-style activities, it did not have as much impact as we envisaged. Since then, we have added training programmes and example programme materials, all of which have been received enthusiastically. These will be detailed later.

Some of the basic premises for the initial work in 1984 can be represented best by the two following quotations:

All schools I have visited in Queensland have been 'thinking schools' devoting much energy to curriculum reshaping and development. The majority have also been 'caring' schools, in which concern for the personal development of the youngsters has been obvious.

Few, however, appear to have made the leap to become 'thinking/ caring' schools, in which the two functions illuminate and support each other irresistibly – so that curriculum pattern and activity deliberately encompass students' personal development as part of everyday learning strategies and pastoral care (uncomfortable phrase) explores and reinforces learning opportunities. Intimate knowledge of students is the strongest of levers in removing learning barriers. (Cooksey, 1984)

Much of the current pastoral care activity in schools is based on a separation of caring and teaching (the pastoral–academic split). In this framework teachers are divided into 'teaching' teachers (mainly orientated towards their subjects) and 'caring' teachers (mainly orientated towards their pupils); and even the individual teacher is split between sometimes 'caring' (during pastoral care time) and sometimes 'teaching' (during subject time).

The challenge of schools now is to integrate these two notions and resist the temptation to concentrate on the caring aspects at the expense of the teaching–learning activities of the school or vice versa ... the teacher who cares is the teacher who teaches effectively in the same way that the doctor who cares is the one who treats his or her patient effectively. (Hamilton, 1985)

Key concepts of guidance tutoring

The key concepts which constitute this approach to pastoral care are:

Link to learning   Schools are about student learning.

The aims of schooling generally focus on both *the student as a learner* (communication; competency; knowledge; application) and *the student as a person* (development; values/attitude; relationships; becoming a mature adult).

To enhance student learning we must simultaneously focus on *cognitive development* (achievement; mastery) and *affective development* (self-worth; motivation).

These must be seen as being complementary rather than in competition (e.g. recognizing that a temporary rejection by peers may affect a student's capacity to learn).

All of the above takes place in a rapidly changing social context.

Affective development Affective development must take account of *adolescent development tasks* (e.g. independence; autonomy; intimacy) and *critical incidents in schools* (transition; induction; experience; selection), which determine:

Issues (what)	*Approaches* (how)	*Timing* (when)
needs	promote self-reliance	year rivals
themes	individuals	terms
		crises

Support and intention Successfully linking and promoting cognitive and affective development can be assisted by *access to a reasonable adult* (a point of continuing contact) and *intentional skills development* (staff development and student programming).

As Bronfenbrenner (1981, p. 38) puts it: 'In order to develop normally, a child needs the enduring irrational involvement of one or more adults, or someone has to be crazy about the kid.'

These concepts inform the one approach. The term 'guidance tutoring' was chosen in place of terms such as 'pastoral care' because the latter, for us, tended to conjure up notions of shepherds, mindless sheep and dependency (cf. Dooley, 1980).

Some definitions

'Guidance' denotes a range of enabling activities which help students to overcome potential blocks to learning while becoming increasingly self-reliant. 'Tutoring' is the taking of responsibility for a student's general education by a competent and trusted teacher.

Guidance tutoring is thus the provision of 'first line' support and guidance by teachers or students on issues or concerns affecting their development or achievements. The major aims of guidance tutoring are to enhance student learning and to promote self-reliance.

The underpinning assumption is that teachers working directly with young people are involved in the process of guidance and counselling as well as teaching and administration. One aim of guidance tutoring is to explore an approach to pastoral care that borrows appropriate concepts from guidance and counselling without suggesting that teachers become counsellors. The emphasis on these concepts should not imply that teaching and administrative tasks of teachers are not valid and important. They are, however, not addressed directly in the materials.

The guidance tutoring approach

The essential elements of the guidance tutoring approach are:

- a structure which allows a teacher to become a point of continuing contact for a specific number of students and links the academic and affective components of education;

- a programme which deals intentionally with critical incidents and adolescent developmental tasks as students move through the school;
- a policy of whole-school staff support and development, which is provided through networking and a continuing process of evaluation and inservice;
- a school that is committed to the goals of the guidance tutoring approach to pastoral care and backs up this commitment by allocating time and personnel, and establishing support structures for staff.

For this approach to be effective it needs to operate at four levels:

1. As a whole-school approach to teaching and working with students.
2. As a provision of support and guidance by individual teachers for individual students on issues affecting development and achievement.
3. As a continuous thread of regular, structured, skill-based tutorial sessions.
4. As a provision of staff support where issues of increased complexity or intensity are dealt with by appropriately trained personnel with designated responsibilities.

The first, second and fourth levels are dealt with in *Guidance Tutoring* (Theile and McCowan, 1986). For level 3, a framework has been devised within which the tutorial sessions can be presented in a coherent manner and follow a developmental sequence. However, teachers often do not have the time to rearrange their existing materials and activities using this framework, nor do they retain the fundamental approaches to these activities of self-reliance and enhanced learning. In 1986 we began to produce a suggested set of materials exemplifying the approaches and framework critical to *Guidance Tutoring*.

The 40-week *Guidance Tutoring* school year is divided into four programme stages: Induction, Experience, Selection and Transition. In essence they parallel the 'critical incidents' created by the organization of the secondary school (Hamblin, 1978). Students who fail to negotiate these 'critical incidents' are at risk either of disaffiliating from the school or of developing 'blockages' to learning. The stages, although of equal importance in the total scheme, receive different emphasis depending on year level and time of year.

Within each stage six themes are developed, in an attempt to deal, in a coherent way, with issues created by the critical incidents as well as addressing the key adolescent developmental tasks of independence, autonomy and intimacy. In this way the programme is focused on the main *Guidance Tutoring* issues operating in each year level. The six themes are: care and support; interpersonal skills; group skills; learning to learn; future planning; and health and personal safety. As with the stages, all themes are held to have equal importance but are given different emphasis at certain times of the year. For example, in Year 8 (the first year of the secondary school), time is devoted to interpersonal skill development and learning to learn during the induction stage. The emphasis here is on developing interpersonal skills as the students go through the processes of getting to know each other. Similarly, learning to learn is given prominence at this point with a view to settling the students into their role in the school and setting up good homework and study routines.

Implementation

British personnel working on a similar project reported in *Pastoral Care in Education* (NAPCE, 1985) that the greatest obstacle to the introduction of new concepts into teaching was the lack of skills training for teachers to help them use a wide variety of techniques with confidence. Consequently, three-day skill development workshops were offered for school personnel across Queensland. Most of those who attended were year co-ordinators, although administrators and class-room teachers also took part. The workshops included rationale, skills development, modelling activities and behaviours, implementation and establishing support structures. Over 1000 personnel opted to undertake the workshops in 1989, 1990 and 1991. The aim was to train these people to be future workshop leaders and adopt the role of key personnel back in their schools.

In taking account of the latest theories about change, the approach adopted was to identify all the existing relevant activities in the school and slowly modify or add to them in accordance with the guidance tutoring approach. Participants were not encouraged to make wholesale changes to existing school programmes. Rather, they were encouraged to take every opportunity to assist their schools to undertake tasks such as needs analysis, skill development of teachers, and the provision of helpful resources, using the concepts, approaches and skills applic-able within the *Guidance Tutoring* approach, but without necessarily identifying them as such. That is, the concepts were to be treated as more important than the labels attached to them. Accordingly, no schools have labelled their approach under the heading 'guidance tutoring', but discernible features of this approach are beginning to be seen and to flourish in many schools.

The follow-up three-hour 'summer series' of workshops have been a great success, both meeting the articulated needs of experienced personnel on highly specific issues and providing advanced skills development.

Finally, it must be stressed that this scheme depends upon all teachers in a school adopting a consistent and coherent approach to their teaching responsibilities, particularly in the affective areas as well as in their general attitude to all teaching and learning.

References

Bronfenbrenner, U. (1981) Children and families: 1984? *Society*, 18, 38–41.

Cooksey, G. (1984) *Felix Incommunicato*. Brisbane: unpublished consultancy report to the Queensland Government.

Dooley, S. (1980) The relationship between the concepts of 'pastoral care' and 'authority'. In Best, R., Jarvis, C. and Ribbins, P. (eds) *Perspectives on Pastoral Care*. London: Heinemann.

Hamblin, D.H. (1978) *The Teacher and Pastoral Care*. Oxford: Blackwell.

Hamilton, P. (1987) The role of the educational psychologist in pastoral care provision. *School Psychology International*, 8(2, 3), 153–8.

Miller, J. (1982) *Tutoring*. London: FEU Curriculum Review and Development Unit.

NAPCE (National Association for Pastoral Care in Education) (1985) Initial training for the pastoral aspect of the teacher's role. *Pastoral Care in Education*, 3(1), 73–7.

Theile, L. and McCowan, C. (1986) *Guidance Tutoring: The Guidance and Counselling Role of Teacher in Secondary Schools and Colleges*. Spring Hill, Queensland: Department of Education.

CHAPTER 15

Caring, upbringing and teaching

The Danish class form teacher system[1]

NIELS REINSHOLM, NIELS KRYGER, LEJF MOOS
AND KIRSTEN REISBY

During the past hundred years, the Danish class form teacher system has developed into one of the cornerstones of Danish education. Despite the fact that until 1993 the system had only found minimal expression in educational legislation and professional agreements, there is wide political and popular support for it in Denmark.

It is the system according to which the same teacher follows a class, or form, over a period of years, in some cases throughout the entire ten-year period of compulsory schooling. The class form teacher will usually be the teacher of Danish, and will normally take several other subjects as well, as the aim is that she should take as many lessons as possible for her class.

One aspect of the class form teacher tradition is that pupils, parents, colleagues, the authorities and society in general expect the class form teacher to assume functions relating to caring and upbringing in co-operation with the parents. This article attempts to describe how these expectations, and the class form teachers' own understanding of what their job entails, are under development at the present moment, as they are adapted to new conditions of life in society and the new conceptions of what 'the good life' is.

The Danish school system: a short introduction

The Danish school system consists of the Folkeskole (state, or public, school) and a number of private schools, founded on the basis of particular religious, educational or political beliefs. The Folkeskole is free, whereas private schools are financed by a combination of enrolment fees and state subsidies.

The Folkeskole is a nine-year all-through comprehensive school: schooling begins with a one-year optional kindergarten class, followed by grades 1-9, topped by an optional 10th grade. Pupils attend non-streamed classes from the start, at the age of six, to the end of the 9th grade. Educational legislation does, however, permit the setting of pupils (using two levels) in German, English and Mathematics at the 8th and 9th grades, and in Physics/Chemistry at the 9th grade, though only a minority of schools avail themselves of this possibility. From the 9th (and 10th) grades pupils can continue on to the sixth-form college ('Gymnasium'), and to various other kinds of further education at this level. In the present Education Act (1975) regulating the Folkeskole, great emphasis is placed on the general education of pupils and on their upbringing as citizens of a democratic society. This concern must inform the teaching of individual subjects. In other words, the school must attempt to tackle the academic and social development of the pupils as two sides of the same process.

Teacher education in Denmark

Teacher education takes place at 18 colleges of education ('Seminarium') geographically spread throughout the country, and takes an 'all-through' approach. This means that the course aims to train students to teach the whole Folkeskole age range, and formally to qualify them to teach all the subjects offered. A general course, covering a number of compulsory general subjects, is combined with a specialized course concentrating on two main subjects and an education special area, chosen by the student and providing the subject of a dissertation. The specialized course equips students with the competence to carry out specialized tasks, including specialist subject teaching and the further development of subject areas within the curriculum. However, in practice it is up to the headteacher to decide which subject(s) will be taught by newly qualified teachers appointed to a school.

The subjects in the general course are called 'class form teacher subjects'. It is the study of these, together with an obligatory study of the functions of the class form teacher, which prepares the student later to act as a class form teacher.

The class form teacher tradition, in the past and today

The Danish class form teacher tradition is roughly 100 years old. The system arose in the larger towns, especially Copenhagen, when increasing industralization made it difficult for families to bring up their children as before, not least because the direct transfer of norms and the social apprenticeship offered by participation in the production processes of rural culture no longer took place automatically. The school had to fill the gap, and the practice gradually developed of giving one teacher in the class a special function: that of playing a caring role in the upbringing of the children as well as teaching them and giving general guidance.

The emphasis given to this role has led to ways of organizing the work of the class form teacher to enable him or her to carry out the relevant functions. For example, one very important aspect of the class form teacher tradition is the continuity of the relationship between teacher and class. This is made possible by the 'all-through' approach to teacher education and allows the class form teacher to follow the same class throughout its entire career at the school. Since the all-through comprehensive school became a reality with the Education Acts of 1958 and 1975, it has been possible to preserve a class as a social unit from the 1st to the 9th grades.

Our research was aimed at investigating to what extent this potential was utilized in practice. We discovered two patterns: in the first the class form teacher follows the class all the way from the 1st to the 9th grades; in the second, a change of class form teacher occurs after the 5th, 6th or 7th grades.

In 95 per cent of cases the class form teacher takes the class for Danish, and is therefore the teacher responsible for the weekly 'own lesson', a period set aside to enable the pupils and their teacher to discuss matters relevant to the daily life of the class and other things not covered by subject lessons.

One reason for the change of class form teacher in the middle school is the question of academic competence: some class form teachers do not feel competent to continue with the teaching of Danish up to the level of the school leaving examination. Another reason is the apparently paradoxical one that schools and class form teachers attempt to combine the ideal of continuity with the notion that pupils at the age of puberty may benefit from the chance to forge a relationship with a new class form teacher. This is because it can be difficult to change the style and intensity of the caring function adopted by the teacher in the lower grades to another, more emancipatory type of caring function required by older pupils in the later grades.

The programme of educational development for the Folkeskole

In recent years much attention has been paid to the class form teacher function. This was most clearly demonstrated when in 1987 the Danish Parliament passed legislation relating to 'A Programme of Development for the Folkeskole' and assigned funds in the region of 400 million Danish kroner for the implementation of this programme in 1987–91 (Folketinget, 1986–7). Point 3 of this programme of development reads as follows:

> The class form teacher is to be offered better conditions for the task of co-ordinating the academic and social aspects of work with the class and the individual pupil, including better opportunities for co-operation with other teachers involved with the class and for contact with parents.

That part of the developmental activity which had to do with the function of the class form teacher was called 'the extended class form teacher function'. Between 1987 and 1991, about 500 development projects were approved and carried out under this heading in the Folkeskole, involving some 1500 class form teachers in all. Evaluating these activities provided the basis for this chapter.

The task of the class form teacher in the school of today

Our research made it possible for us to pinpoint the functions that Danish class form teachers feel are in most need of development. We made our investigations by means of: a questionnaire involving *c.* 1000 class form teachers; interviews covering 15 development projects; and classroom observation and re-interviewing in respect of four development projects (from level 2).

Our experience led us to group class form teachers' concerns under five headings: the daily life of the class; the individual pupil; co-operation with parents; co-operation with colleagues; and the culture of the school.

The daily life of the class

One of the central tasks of the class form teacher is to ensure the best possible learning environment for the pupils in the class. The long-term aim is that pupils should develop independence and take responsibility for their own learning processes, and indeed for their own lives. In terms of day-to-day practice this involves the teacher working on two interconnected levels: making the content of teaching meaningful to the pupils, and helping them establish good relationships with each other and with their teacher. The second task is especially demanding and important in view of the widely different backgrounds children bring with them to school. It requires the class form teacher to respect and understand the different forms of culture and life style represented by individual pupils.

Another requirement is the establishment of a common basis of experience and common norms as the foundation of the class's social life. In this it is important to respect the subjective peculiarities of the individual pupil, while seeking to transcend them. The wish and the requirement that pupils participate in decisions relating to the class as a social unit and to teaching activities are factors that have a direct influence on the learning processes of the individual.

This work can take place in various settings: in the class and in the class's 'own lesson', in groups of pupils, in the class council and in the manifold processes of teaching. The class's 'own lesson' gives an admirable opportunity of practising these long-term aspects of general education, but it is important to stress that they should not be confined to the 'own lesson'.

The reason that so much attention is paid to this process, based on dialogue, in the Danish school is because class form teachers know from experience that democratic practices cannot be learned without the training and support of an adult, who at the same time can help pupils obtain an insight into the general rules governing democratic procedures.

The individual pupil

Many class form teacher development projects have concerned the care of the individual pupil. Class form teachers have been given time and resources to try to solve a wide range of pressing personal and social problems and devote more caring attention to individual pupils and also to their families.

In some cases the tasks undertaken by class form teachers have closely resembled therapy, which naturally raises the question of whether class form teachers should take on problems which in general they do not have the training to solve. Be that as it may, there is a tendency for class form teachers to tackle such problems on the prompting of their own conscience, simply because no one else is prepared to support the children – or the families – who are in difficulties. Any other course of action would be inhuman, because there are certain supportive functions society is not able to provide. 'If I don't do it, who will?', as one of the class form teachers put it in an interview.

Some class form teachers are aware that this type of help is extrinsic to what goes on in the classroom, and they attempt to maintain in principle the position that the caring work of the school should take place not primarily on a one-to-one basis, but in the classroom, between the teacher and the pupils as a group. A very special aspect of the work of the Danish class form teachers is perhaps this search for an intrinsic connection between the functions of caring and teaching.

Such problems notwithstanding, the developmental projects have shown that it is often valuable for class form teachers to deal with pupils at the level of individual conversations. Different types of conversation are needed: the informal chat, conversations initiated by the pupils, and those planned by the teacher.

The basic model for all types of conversation must be that of a dialogue based on certain ethical principles: the expectation that those involved say what is right and true, and in a comprehensible manner. A realistic understanding of the conditions for comunication, however, must include the fact that conversations between teachers and pupils can rarely take place on an equal footing, or in a setting totally free of power structures. The teacher cannot entirely avoid being an instrument of power and authority, and should therefore regard her or his communicative task in a strategic light, seeing it as part of the long-term process of the general education of the pupil. The best protection against a distortion of the conversational structure is, therefore, to make the authority aspect visible.

Co-operation with parents

The Danish Education Act of 1975 states that the school shall carry out its task in co-operation with the parents. Since the passing of this law, co-operation between schools and parents has been intensified, and there are high hopes of continued positive development.

The class form teacher is the interface between the school and the parents, and many efforts are being made to find the best ways of realizing school–home co-operation, including a definition of those areas best suited to such co-operation and the finding of a realistic level of activity.

Class form teachers today often work hard to establish a parental group in which the parents know each other, the class form teacher and, possibly, other teachers attached to the class. The guiding idea is that increased personal knowledge of others reduces the risk of forming 'enemy stereotypes' and provides a good basis on which to meet, if problems arise to which solutions cannot easily be found. In this connection, many class form teachers take part in informal gatherings in the evening, and in day or weekend trips with the pupils and their parents, solely with the purpose of bringing people closer together. Other types of meeting, the aim of which is, directly or indirectly, to treat questions relating to upbringing or to the teaching situation in a more specific manner, are also used in this co-operative work with parents. An example would be game-like activities dealing with questions of upbringing or teaching, which can form the basis of further discussion relating to these areas.

Naturally, school–home co-operation also involves conversations with individual parents concerning the general development and progress of their child at school. There is an increasing tendency for children to be involved in these conversations and for the main topic of the conversation to be agreed on in advance.

Co-operation with colleagues

In all classes, other teachers are involved apart from the class form teacher. In the first years of school, in accordance with the 'few teachers' principle, there is a tendency for class form teachers to have only one or two other teachers as their co-operative partners. This means that as few teachers as possible are attached to the class, within the limits of what is professionally justifiable, on the grounds that a close emotional relationship between teachers and pupils is important at this stage. It is becoming more usual in these early grades for two teachers, normally one of each gender, to share the tasks and function of the class form teacher.

In the later grades, more teachers gradually become involved as new subjects enter the curriculum. The number can vary a great deal, depending on whether the school uses a specifically subject-teacher approach, that is, a tendency to draw in other teachers on purely academic grounds, or a team-teaching approach, which involves attaching as few teachers as possible to a given class, while modifying the specifically academic demands made on teachers in relation to the various subjects.

A number of class form teachers, however – no matter whether they are working within a subject-teacher or a team-teaching system – have complained that the lack of professional expertise in co-operation between colleagues is becoming a pressing problem. Co-operative ability is demanded in several areas: between colleagues in relation to individual pupils or the class as a whole, between teachers and parents, and between teachers in relation to the planning of teaching activities as a whole, with an eye to the fact that the actual teaching is normally done by individual teachers on their own. This situation is referred to in the slogan, 'Do away with the teacher in private practice'; that is concentrate instead on the idea of a group of teachers taking the responsibility for the school life and educative activities of the class.

In this connection, a number of class form teachers have expressed the need for, inter-collegiate leadership: the class form teacher as leader of a team. However, few class form teachers have put this into practice, possibly because the idea of acting as a leader for colleagues is an almost insurmountable hurdle for many teachers.

The culture of the school

In our research experience, some of the schools we have visited have acknowledged that the work of the individual teacher should be seen as part of the organizational culture of their school. By organizational culture is meant the traditional pattern of myths, norm and routine procedures typical of the organization, which have been passed on from generation to generation, and within which certain types of explanation and action are accepted as natural and self-evident.

Yet it remains the case that the culture of the Danish Folkeskole is orientated towards individuals operating on their own, though with a commonly accepted distribution of responsibilities within the institution. The headteacher, the class form teacher and the other teachers in the class carry out their various tasks in relative independence of each other. The individual teacher is, for good or ill, free to carry out her or his duties without much intervention from colleagues or the school leadership.

Some class form teachers, however, see a movement towards a more collective type of school culture as both logical and necessary. For these teachers the ideal is that teachers and the school leadership should work together to formulate a common professional platform as the basis for co-operation with pupils, parents and politicians; that is, there should be a unified approach to the development of the school. There has been little progress towards such a model because the majority of teachers and school leaders have yet to recognize the need for, and accept, a development of this nature.

Towards a professional concept of the class form teacher

During the past decade, the task of the class form teacher has become increasingly difficult and complex in line with teaching in general. But there are demands made of the class form teacher which require a new set of qualifications if they are to be adequately met.

The children we meet in school are children of their time. They come from families with only one or few children. School does not hold the same immediate attraction for the pupils, and some choose to take a back seat. How can they be encouraged to be more involved? At the same time, schooling has become vital for the pupils because of increased competition for places further up the educational system, especially for the attractive, longer courses of higher education. In this situation it is more than ever necessary to find a way to motivate children to learn, through providing suitable course content and relevant goals.

Of course, conversations with individual pupils themselves can suggest the way, but there remains a need, as yet only partially satisfied, for inter-collegiate discussion on how the various subjects may contribute to this complex question of content and goals. It is the subjects, as bearers of the communal cultural memory, that can throw light on the questions that concern children.

The problem may possibly be expressed in this way: teachers must accept that the school has lost its monopoly hold on the transmission of knowledge, and must instead get on with the job of sorting and structuring the massive input of knowledge children receive through the electronic media. This new task demands organization, collegiate leadership and the tools necessary to tackle it in a professional manner.

At the same time, greater co-operation between teaching colleagues is necessary to improve classroom practice. In some of the best development projects we have seen, teachers established a system of inter-collegiate supervision as the best way of being to each other 'the friend who will tell you the truth'. They offered professional criticism of each other's teaching on the basis of a previous, voluntary agreement about what was to be supervised.

This could all be summarized under the heading of 'collective efforts to improve professional competence'. We see such efforts as the most important contribution to developing the Danish class form teacher tradition. Improved competence is the precondition for success in achieving through nurture and instruction the unified social and academic development of children.

1. This chapter is based on the findings of Projekt Klasselæren (1989-92). For related literature see References.

References

Folketinget (1986-7) Folketingsbeslutning om et udviklingsprogram for Folkeskolen og skolen som lokalt kulturcenter af 26. maj 1987 (Resolution of the Danish Parliament (26.5.1987) relating to a Programme of Development for the Folkeskole and the School as a Local Cultural Centre).

Harrit, O., Kryger, N., Moos, L., Reinsholm, N. and Reisby, K. (1990) *Klasselærere*. Projekt Klasselæreren (The Class Form Teacher Project), Interim Report 1. Copenhagen: Royal Danish College of Educational Studies.

Harrit, O., Kryger, N., Moos, L., Reinsholm, N. and Reisby, K. (1991) *Klasselærere - midt i skolen*. Projekt Klasselæreren, Interim Report 2. Copenhagen: Royal Danish College of Educational Studies.

Harrit, O., Kryger, N., Moos, L., Reinsholm, N. and Reisby, K.
(1992) *Klasselærere: Tradition og fornyelse*. Projekt Klasselæreren,
Copenhagen: Danish College of Educational Studies.
Harrit, O., Kryger, N., Moos, L., Reinsholm, N. and Reisby, K.
(1992) Form teachers: tradition and renewal. In Norgaard, E. (ed.):
School Improvement, Development and Innovation. Copenhagen:
Royal Danish College of Educational Studies.

PART III

Training and support

CHAPTER 16

Caring for the care-givers

BILL MANN

Introduction

Modern industrialized societies have relatively few formal structures within which young people may learn their culture, and the totality of knowledge and experience it encompasses, while at the same time preparing themselves for future life roles of worker, parent, voter, consumer, and so on. More and more, schools are seen as the only vehicle available for this transfer of knowledge, skills and attitudes. The role of teachers as professional helpers thus becomes critical in ensuring the successful transition of our youth into adulthood.

In describing the demands placed on people such as teachers, Lawrence Brammer (1988, p. 25) concludes that:

> To avoid obsolescence, professional helpers must keep up with the rapid changes in the concepts and methods of helping. All helpers, however, need renewal experiences to counter the draining effects of continuously demanding contact with people. Teachers, for example, are vulnerable to the 'burnout' effect unless they plan systematically for renewal experiences to regain their enthusiasm, energy and effectiveness. Some of the indicators of such needed renewal are increasing irritability, low energy levels, cynicism about people, indifference to the suffering of others, loss of self-confidence, and general malaise. While the helping process has some built in renewal potential, most helpers find that they must seek their renewal outside of their helping relationship.

This raises an important issue: how does the education system provide for teachers those conditions, incentives, and renewal experiences that enhance their self-esteem, build their morale, and ensure they maintain a high level of motivation and commitment to their profession?

The Western Australian scene

Recent years have seen three major reforms occur in the Western Australian education system. The first two, McGaw (1984) and Beazley (1984), related to curriculum, assessment and certification structures in secondary schools. Their recommendations resulted in rapid change being imposed on school systems. The third, *Better Schools in Western Australia* (WA Ministry of Education 1987), followed a functional review, at the state government's initiative, of the Education Department of Western Australia. Major structural changes, including the transformation from a Department of Education to a Ministry of Education, have left schools in a state of considerable uncertainty. These changes still have a considerable way to go before their full impact is felt at the school level.

Many classroom practitioners have struggled to come to grips with these changes. There is little doubt that the majority of teachers are not philosophically opposed to the reforms. Indeed, many teachers have long advocated the freeing up of the upper school curriculum, a closer match between the lower school curriculum and the needs, abilities and aspirations of students, and the decentralization of the education system to allow schools greater powers in determining their future. Unfortunately the pace of change has been so rapid that many teachers have been swamped by the flood of ministerial decrees poured upon them.

Furthermore, the concept that 'state schools are great schools' has received a severe battering in the media. Questions related to maintenance of standards (academic, social and moral) in schools, competence of teachers, and confidence in the education system have encouraged a drift from the public to the private sector. Such public debate is guaranteed to undermine the morale of an already embattled teaching body.

Teacher morale is a critical factor in establishing a quality education. Unless teachers are motivated to perform at or near their potential in their duties to their students, it is likely that students will leave their classrooms having learnt a little less than they would have done under better circumstances. The business of motivating teachers and enhancing their self-esteem has been and will continue to be a determining factor in the quality of education.

Teacher motivation and job enrichment

Motivational theories draw attention to the provision of both extrinsic rewards (pay, better working conditions, etc.) and intrinsic rewards (recognition, achievement, etc.). Despite early management theories that saw the former as the major motivational force for worker participation at high efficiency levels, more recent research has shown that organizations must pay close attention to the provision of intrinsic rewards if workers are to be motivated to achieve their full potential.

Owens (1987) saw job enrichment as the means by which intrinsic rewards can be built into a worker's daily routines. Luthans and Reif (in Owens (1987, p. 119)) define job enrichment as being 'concerned with designing jobs that include a greater variety of work content; require a higher level of knowledge and skill; give the worker more autonomy and responsibility for planning, directing and controlling his own performance; and provide the opportunity for personal growth and meaningful work experience'.

Batcheler (1981) takes this concept into the educational sphere. He suggests three major areas administrators could address if they wish to increase teacher motivation:

(a) Staff control over work (goal setting)

Teachers are more likely to be committed to the goals and philosophy of a school if they have had input into their development and thus feel they have some ownership of them. Concurrently, motivational forces would be further enhanced if administrators were able to develop strong links between individual teachers' goals and those of the school. Batcheler notes also the importance of ensuring that 'dissatisfiers' are minimized or eliminated, allowing motivating factors uninhibited application. However, he points out that administrators should not simply be seen as developing a structure that enables staff control over work. Rather, administrators must be seen to be leaders, actively involved with teachers, and providing regular feedback on initiatives undertaken by teachers.

(b) Staff participation in decision-making

Participative decision-making is becoming an increasingly important component in schools' organizational structures. Chase (in Batcheler (1981, p. 50)) found that 'teachers who report opportunity to participate regularly and actively in making policies are much more likely to be enthusiastic about their school systems than those who reported limited opportunity to participate'.

Batcheler sees it as important that administrators recognize that staff do not wish to be involved in making decisions regarding the totality of experiences that a school encompasses. Often teachers will be happy to apply decisions made without their consultation. The key to participative decision-making was to identify those areas of the school's operation where teachers had the level of involvement, the degree of expertise and the positions of responsibility to enable such decision-making to be realistic and applicable.

(c) Inservice training to increase the professional competence of staff

Increasing professionalism among teachers is an important motivational force in encouraging them to reach their full potential. Whether through inservice programmes that update professional knowledge and competence, or through programmes that induct teachers into modern educational philosophy and practice, participating teachers can develop and extend their professionalism, leading to changes in classroom and school management.

Batcheler (1981, p. 52) concludes that 'the opportunity for all to experience self-fulfilment in their teaching job ought to be provided'. By providing such opportunities, teachers who previously might not have been motivated to high levels of achievement, recognition and responsibility will strive for these goals. He sees administrators as those in schools charged with this motivational task.

Towards effective schools

In describing how schools become effective, Middleton *et al.* (1986, p. 123) quote the State Board of Education in listing five characteristics for effective schools:

* democratic and participatory governance, with the capacity for the school to control resources and to be supported by consultancy and grants;
* school policies which direct resources around priorities, emphasizing high achievement for all students in a caring and supportive environment;
* curriculum-orientated leadership in the school;
* a focus on the use of evaluation and planning to bring about improvement;
* a curriculum which is collaboratively designed and implemented.

All these require a committed, professional and motivated teaching body who engage regularly in curriculum planning, participative decision-making and competency enhancement. They also require an administrative team that seeks, by a variety of means, to motivate teachers to reach their full potential in their professional duties, and to undertake the tasks that develop the above characteristics.

Certainly the current educational climate demands that teachers demonstrate a commitment to their profession. Such a commitment will come when motivational factors focused on intrinsic rewards of achievement, recognition and responsibility are clearly present in schools. It is no longer an adequate response to problems of motivation and morale to undertake a review of the environmental conditions and remuneration for teachers. Motivation theory recognizes this. Those responsible for our schools must ensure that teachers are rewarded for their achievements in ways that engage them more fully in their profession; that is, in ways that will continue to build their motivation and morale.

Local applications

As has been stated earlier in this chapter, there is considerable disquiet among teachers and administrators in Western Australian schools, with considerable uncertainty about education's future direction. What was previously a stable structure with clear lines of communication and authority has become a much more diffuse organizational framework in the establishment of the Ministry of Education. Additionally the previously accepted (not necessarily acceptable) curriculum has undergone dramatic change in secondary schools, and seems to be under considerable pressure (through ministerial decrees) to continue to adapt to changing emphases brought about by political and social perceptions of good educational practice. Finally, major public criticism of the public education system, coupled with demands for increased accountability, a raising of standards and an increased commitment in the teaching body, is generating a lowering of morale among teachers. In summary, the education system and its workers are under considerable stress.

I want to argue that the solution lies at least in part in the application of the theories of motivation, organizational behaviour and job enrichment outlined above. For example:

(a) *Changing organizational structures.* Devolution of responsibility from a central office to schools (through district offices) is designed to allow those responsible for implementing policy some say in both determining policy and applying it to best local advantage – clearly a strong motivational factor. Promoting (by merit) those teachers who clearly demonstrate outstanding leadership and pedagogic skills ensures that the best candidates are placed in promotional positions – a strong motivational force.

(b) *Changing the curriculum.* A unit curriculum that allows students to choose appropriate pathways, through lower school, that best suit their interests and abilities is empowering for them and the school community since inappropriate course placement (due to lack of suitable alternatives) often leads to student discontent, disruption and alienation. This provides a strong motivational force for teachers (through students). A similar situation obtains for upper school courses and upper school students.

(c) *Encouraging collaboration at the school–community interface.* Allowing the school more freedom in adapting both its structure and its curriculum to the local environment is useful, but to then allow the community to have some input into the school's policy development (though school-based decision-making groups) can become a very powerful force in engaging community support for the school.

Unfortunately, the reality of the situation does not match its theoretical prognosis. School administrators, teachers and district office personnel have had considerable difficulty coming to grips with issues of devolution and communication. Promotion (whether by merit or otherwise) has ceased to be a realistic ambition for many teachers in a system with relatively fewer positions to which teachers might aspire.

The unit curriculum has for many schools become the 'crowded' and/or 'confused' curriculum, presenting problems of timetabling, student choices and changing directions due to shifts in central office policy.

The development of a 'school plan' – that document central to long-term school planning at the local level – has been too difficult for administrators with little time and few of the skills necessary for such an undertaking. To incorporate concurrently community views in such an exercise has proved an impossible task for all but a few schools.

So where does that leave teachers and administrators in schools in Western Australia? Certainly the Ministry of Education has appeared to have done its homework in establishing structures more likely to enhance participant motivation. Sadly, few participants have the prerequisite skills, access to training facilities, or the time successfully to implement these structures. It is probably time for the education system to step back from itself and critically examine its current state, diagnosing strengths and weaknesses. Such a programme for action would restore confidence among teachers and the wider community in our education system, enabling the catalysts for motivation to work to the advantage of students in schools.

Pastoral care for teachers

The motivation of teachers cannot be maximized unless our institutional plans and procedures take account of the personal, social, emotional and professional needs which the teachers themselves identify. This was well illustrated during a recent staff development day in a Perth metropolitan high school where a discussion of pastoral care for teachers generated the following points:

1. *School administration needs to be effective.* There was a strong perception (expressed verbally and on paper) that the administration of the school had fallen short of expectations. It was considered to be lacking in knowledge of staff, motivational skill, energy and leadership. The general argument was that if the administration did its job diligently, the school would run more efficiently and staff would be happier.

2. *The importance of time organization.* There is too much to do and too little time. Partly because of the advent of the unit curriculum and *Better Schools*, teaching staff spend more time on non-classroom tasks. There were many suggestions for improved time management ranging from clerical assistance for all departments to having a regular classroom in which to teach.

3. *The need for recognition.* There is a very great need for recognition of the work being done by staff, both in and out of the classroom. This need includes recognition at all levels, from peers, through administration, to District Office and the Ministry.

4. *The physical environment of the school.* Frustration and anger build up because simple physical problems are not dealt with promptly. It is a source of great irritation to teach in a room which does not have enough tables or chairs, where the chairs do not match or fit, where the heaters do not work, or where the toilets stink.

5. *Isolation of staff.* Small departments and new staff often feel

isolated. Faced with shrinking resources and declining enrolments there is a tendency for a 'grab for numbers' causing staff to 'close ranks' and retreat within their faculty boundaries.

6. *Support structures for staff.* Much concern was expressed about support structures, both formal and informal, within the school. At the moment support is given in an *ad hoc* way. Teacher development is not being systematically addressed, either personally or professionally, at any level.

The staff concluded that morale was generally low and individual members were feeling lost and unable to do their jobs efficiently because of the pressures they were under. However, some very positive responses came during discussion of suggestions for support structures. These included:

*   The development of a more dynamic leadership role for the administration, built around the key-words of *co-ordination*, *co-operation* and *organization*.
*   Acceptance of teacher *recognition* as imperative.
*   The tightening up of the organization of school structures in regard to discipline and attendance.
*   Proper attention to the maintenance of the building.
*   The need for staff to be supportive of each other and of other subject departments. This may involve discussion groups or simply being available to talk to each other.
*   The need for someone to co-ordinate the staff support structures. (Policy documents place this function in the hands of the Staff Association.)

Three recommendations for immediate action followed:

1. Prompt, positive steps to be taken by administration staff to provide more dynamic leadership in the areas of:
    (i) their authoritative role in the school.
    (ii) their action in response to teacher and student needs (including acknowledgement of achievement and counselling of staff not meeting professional expectations).
2. A co-ordinator of teacher development to be appointed.
3. Prompt action to be taken to implement as many of the workable suggestions put forward by staff as is feasible.

The above provides a good example of one school's expressed concerns regarding pastoral care for teachers. It clearly addresses issues of teacher morale, motivation and job satisfaction. It is important that other schools take a planned approach to teacher pastoral care, and professional development. The concept of the self-determining school demands an empowered team of teachers.

A planned approach to teacher pastoral care and professional development

From the teacher's perspective, the rapid and *ad hoc* imposition of new curriculum and management structures on schools during the 1980s, often without regard for the consequences, has given teachers little opportunity to adapt systematically to these changes. Symptoms of this approach are many and varied in our schools. One is obvious, however: the many teachers now seeking career pathways outside their chosen profession, or else retiring early.

It is of critical importance, therefore, that schools now address issues of teacher pastoral care and development in a planned, systematic way. Such planning must take account of:

* the school's ethos and *modus operandi*;
* the system's expectations for curriculum and school management;
* the current and ongoing needs of the students, and community perceptions of the nature and role of education;
* the current skill base of the staff, and their needs for support and professional development;
* the need for this programme to be proactive in its approach, anticipating future needs and trends, rather than reactive, simply responding to external pressures imposed on the school;
* the need for participative decision-making by the school staff to determine the priorities of the programme;
* the particular needs of new and beginning teachers, and their induction into the school.

Such an approach would go a long way towards eliminating teacher concerns about their professional responsibilities and their ability to take up these responsibilities, while at the same time decreasing stress, and enhancing self-esteem and motivating forces. An essential element of any programme is the evaluation of its merits and its weaknesses. This rarely happens with teacher induction programmes, which often proceed year after year to a tried but never tested formula. New and beginning teachers are rarely given the opportunity to reflect critically on their induction, to suggest alternative strategies or to be involved in the following year's induction. This evaluation must indicate;

* an examination of the programme's outcomes;
* an examination of the effectiveness of the programme in relation to its objectives;
* a review of the processes involved and their relationship to the outcomes;
* an examination of the attitudinal and behavioural changes of the participants both during and after the programmes.

The result of the evaluation should be made available to all participants and the rest of the school staff. It should form the basis of development for further such programmes.

Summary

The provision of in-school support structures that build teachers' self-esteem and professional competencies is a critical component of any school's management structure. Such has always been the case, but recent changes to education in Western Australia, coupled with decreasing community support for the public education system, have increased the importance of staff development programmes. Effective schools demand effective teachers, competent in tackling the academic and pastoral needs of their students.

Just how schools access programmes that facilitate staff development and meet the pastoral needs of teachers has not been addressed in this chapter. Whether from within the school's established staff and resources, or by engaging the help of external facilitators, schools must determine the current and ongoing pastoral and professional needs of their teachers, and set in place programmes to meet these needs.

Caring for the care-givers in our schools remains an essential part of every school's daily *modus operandi*. Schools which take up this challenge reap the rewards of an empowered, motivated and professionally competent teaching staff. Those schools which ignore this demand do so at the peril of their clientele.

References

Batcheler, M. (1981) Motivating staff: a problem for the school administrator. *Journal of Educational Administration* 19(1), 44–54.

Beazley, K. (chair of committee) (1984) *Education in Western Australia: Report of the Committee of Inquiry into Education in Western Australia*. Perth: Education Department of Western Australia.

Brammer, L.M. (1988) *The Helping Relationship*, 4th edn. Englewood Cliffs, NJ: Prentice-Hall.

McGaw, B. (1984) (chair of committee) *Assessment in the Upper Secondary School in Western Australia: Report of the Ministerial Working Party on School Certification and Tertiary Admissions Procedures*. Perth: Education Department of Western Australia.

Middleton, M. *et al.* (1986) *Making the Future: The Role of Secondary Education in Australia*. Canberra: Commonwealth Schools Commission.

Owens, R.G. (1987) *Organisational Behaviour in Education*, 3rd edn. Englewood Cliffs, NJ: Prentice-Hall.

Western Australian Ministry of Education (1987) *Better Schools in Western Australia*. Perth: WA Ministry of Education.

CHAPTER 17

Teacher training in pastoral care

The Singapore perspective

ESTHER TAN

Pastoral care Singapore style

Although the term 'pastoral care' is a relatively new one in Singapore schools, the concept of care in schools is not new at all. In fact, for many decades care and concern for the welfare of pupils have always been given due recognition in Singapore schools. Some schools have set up pupil welfare programmes to meet both expressed and identified needs of pupils; in other schools, selected teachers double up as student counsellors to identify and help pupils in need. However, in the past the preoccupation with attaining excellent examination results has tended to eclipse the guidance and welfare aspect of education.

Since care and concern in schools is not a new concept in Singapore, what is new about pastoral care? Three characteristics distinguish current practice from the pupil welfare programmes of the past:

The first of these is *the shift from a reactive to a proactive approach*. Pastoral care is developmental, a caring programme designed to facilitate the total development of the pupil, not just to remediate in times of need and crisis. Thus pastoral care is not something reserved for badly behaved pupils or the underprivileged. It is for all pupils, regardless of their age, ethnic background and stage of development.

The second important feature is *the use of the group approach* in the delivery of pastoral care in schools. Because of its developmental nature, pastoral care is best delivered through a series of planned group guidance activities whereby pupils attain learning and growing in a conducive, tension-free atmosphere. Under the guidance of their pastoral care tutor and in the security of a caring school community, the pupils learn and grow together through fun and participation.

The third characteristic in the current practice is the adoption of the *whole-school approach*. In the past, pupil welfare programmes in schools usually involved only a handful of teachers who would work with a selected group of pupils known to have learning difficulties or behavioural problems. In the current practice of pastoral care, the preference is to involve the whole school staff in a concerted effort to plan and implement a developmental programme which enhances the quality of school life and facilitates the growth of all pupils. The ultimate goal is to ensure that all pupils in the school community feel wanted and valued as individuals, and are given opportunities to develop their potential in all areas of their development, regardless of their age, abilities, social and cultural background.

This new approach has been introduced into 54 secondary schools in Singapore since 1988 through a pilot scheme. Many other schools, some primary, have also embarked on pastoral care programmes on their own initiative. Since the success of any pastoral care programme depends on the quality of the care-givers, these developments pose a new challenge to the Institute of Education (the country's only teacher training institution): that of providing comprehensive and adequate training to equip thousands of teachers for their pastoral care role in schools.

The challenge for teacher education

This sudden and sharp increase in the demand for trained pastoral care-givers brought with it two basic questions: what kind of pastoral care-givers do we need in the schools? And what are they expected to do?

Looking at the guidance scenes in other countries and learning from their experience, it seemed that Singapore had two options. One would be to give in-depth training to a selected group of teachers to equip them as guidance counsellors in schools. This trend of specialization in the provision of care can be observed in countries such as the USA and Canada where schools have full-time counsellors whose main responsibility is to give educational guidance and personal counselling to the pupils. These school counsellors are further assisted by visiting school social workers, school psychologists and school psychiatrists who provide specialized care to pupils facing more serious problems (Ontario Ministry of Education, 1985; Tennyson et al., 1989; Thomas, 1989).

The second option would be to adopt a generic approach in providing care for the pupils, as in the case of many British schools. It has been observed that in the British pastoral care system, all form tutors are frontline care-givers charged with facilitating the overall development of the pupils placed under their care. This is often done through the implementation of a pastoral curriculum and programmes of Personal and Social Education (Hamblin, 1978, 1986; Lang and Marland, 1985). The responsibilities of these tutors are many: conducting group guidance activities, offering individual counselling to pupils, collaborating with colleagues and working with parents. To discharge such a wide range of responsibilities, these teachers need a repertoire of guidance knowledge and counselling techniques in addition to teaching skills.

To learn from the experiences of the USA and the UK, what would be a viable model of providing care in Singapore schools? It is obvious that Singapore cannot afford the luxury of a high level of specialization in the provision of care for the development and welfare of pupils. Since currently there is still an acute shortage of classroom teachers, it will be some time before we can afford to have full-time counsellors in schools. On the other hand, adopting a generic approach in providing care has its limitations. It is neither possible nor realistic to expect classroom teachers to be experts in everything: teaching, pastoral care, counselling and career guidance.

After much deliberation, it was felt that a feasible approach would be to introduce a two-tier guidance system in the schools, providing generic care for all pupils and specialized services for those who need them. Accordingly, we have a system in which the first level of intervention provides developmental guidance as well as some form of career guidance to facilitate the total development of the pupils, and is the responsibility of the generalists who are classroom teachers doubling up as pastoral care-givers. The second-line care-givers are year co-ordinators or heads of level; these are the key personnel who will provide counselling as well as crisis intervention to pupils in need. In addition, these 'specialists' will also take on the leadership in planning, implementing and evaluating pastoral care programmes in their respective schools.

In view of the constraint of manpower in Singapore schools, it is unrealistic to have full-time school counsellors. Thus while frontline care-givers carry a full teaching load in addition to their pastoral duties, the second-line care-givers are given a lighter teaching load to allow them time to carry out their 'specialist' responsibilities (d'Rozario and Chia, 1988; Lang, 1988). Working side by side, these two groups of teachers perform different but complementary functions. They also require different skills and differential training, as summed up in Table 17.1.

Table 17.1. Functions and required skills of pastoral care-givers

Type of intervention	Major concerns	Training needed
Developmental guidance	Enhancing pupils' self-concept; developing study skills; social and communication skills; civic/moral education	Life skills training Knowledge and skills in group guidance
Career guidance	Career self-awareness; career exploration; career decision-making; job-hunting skills	Principles and practice of careers guidance
Individual counselling and crisis intervention	Short-term counselling for learning and personal problems	Counselling skills
	Remedial help in time of need	Networking with community resources

The training programme

A decision having been taken on the type of pastoral care-givers needed, the immediate task facing the Institute of Education was to train a great number of tutors (the generalists) and a much smaller group of teacher counsellors (specialists) to provide the two-tier intervention described above.

To face this new challenge, in 1988 the Institute introduced a specially designed part-time inservice training programme known as the Specialist Diploma Programme in Pastoral Care, Counselling and Career Guidance. Keeping in mind the wide range of training needs of our teachers, this Specialist Diploma Programme was designed to provide basic training for the frontline care-givers as well as in-depth training for the smaller group of key teachers who take the lead in the planning, implementation and evaluation of pastoral care in the schools.

The structure of this Specialist Diploma Programme is modular: eight modules of 30 hours each, adding up to a total of 240 hours of course work plus about 100 hours of practical work in the schools. The modules are arranged in sequential order at three levels.

Level One training

Level One consists of foundation courses to meet the general needs of classroom teachers who are preparing to be front-line care-givers (generalists) in the pastoral provision of their schools. These courses are intended to provide them with the basic knowledge and skills in pastoral care, counselling and career guidance to help them make optimum use of their contact time with pupils under their care.

Module 1 Introduction to pastoral care and career guidance in schools
An overview of the nature, scope and function of pastoral care and career guidance in schools. The course emphasizes the proactive aspect of pastoral care and encourages teachers to examine critically their pastoral care role in schools.

Module 2 Basic skills in tutoring and group guidance
This course examines the place of group guidance in pastoral care and introduces the teachers to theories of group process as well as a whole range of group guidance techniques.

Module 3 Basic skills in pastoral casework
This course focuses on the remedial aspect of pastoral care. It aims at enhancing understanding of mental health and maladjustment. The teachers are introduced to a variety of counselling methods which illustrate affective, cognitive and behavioural approaches in pupil counselling.

While providing basic training for the frontline care-givers in the schools, these foundation courses also form the prerequisites for teachers who wish to proceed to higher levels of training.

Level Two training

Level Two courses are designed to provide both breadth and depth in the training of specialists who are expected to provide leadership in planning and implementing pastoral care and career guidance in the schools. Thus in addition to more in-depth training in guidance and counselling, the teachers are also taught managerial skills, programme development skills as well as assessment and evaluation skills.

Module 4 Planning and implementing career guidance in schools
Aimed at equipping the teachers with both knowledge and skills in careers guidance, this course examines theories of career development and introduces the teachers to a variety of approaches in career counselling.

Module 5 Developing and implementing a pastoral curriculum
Provides training for pastoral leaders who are entrusted with the responsibility of leading a pastoral team on how to plan and implement pastoral care programmes in schools.

Module 6 Assessment and evaluation in pastoral care and career guidance
Focuses on the role of assessment and evaluation in pastoral care and career guidance, introducing the teachers to a variety of assessment methods and examining issues in programme evaluation.

Level Three training

Level Three courses are intended to give pastoral leaders advanced and in-depth training in counselling. These courses also have a special focus on research and the development of pastoral programmes.

Module 7 Advanced skills in pastoral groupwork and casework
This course probes deeper into the realms of group guidance and individual counselling. It aims at further sharpening the teachers' counselling skills and thus prepares them for supervisory roles.

Module 8 Research and development in pastoral care, counselling and career guidance
Examines research issues and surveys current practices and new developments in pastoral care in Singapore and other countries.

While frontline pastoral care-givers are expected to complete at least the three basic courses at level one, pastoral leaders in schools are encouraged to proceed on to the more advanced levels of training. Upon successful completion of all eight courses in the training programme, course participants will be awarded a Specialist Diploma in Pastoral Care, Counselling and Career Guidance.

Innovative approaches to training

In order to meet the challenge of training a great number of pastoral care-givers to function at different levels within a short period of time, the Institute of Education experimented with two non-traditional approaches alongside conventional inservice training.

Since pastoral care and career guidance in the Singapore context adopts a whole-school approach, we were convinced that the most effective way to prepare frontline care-givers would be to conduct school-based inservice courses for staff of the pilot schools. So instead of the teachers coming to the Institute to attend classes, lecturers from the Institute go to the school to conduct weekly training sessions, for the whole teaching staff. Such an approach has three advantages. Firstly, this is one way to train many generalists within a short period of time. Thus in two years (1988–90) more than 1500 teachers from the 54 pilot schools underwent basic training. Secondly, this approach allows teachers from the same school to get together to share experiences and engage in problem-solving relevant to their particular school. Thirdly, such involvement of the total teaching staff is an effective way of creating a caring environment and a school ethos that is conducive to the implementation of pastoral care and career guidance.

In addition to school-based inservice courses, we also conduct what are known as campus-based, school-focused inservice courses. This means schools can send a specified number staff (usually about 30 from each school) to form a cohort but the training is to be conducted on campus. Such an approach allows 60 to 120 teachers from two to three schools to undergo training at one time. The format of training includes mass lectures for the whole cohort to be followed by workshops in smaller groups led by a team of lecturers. In the workshops the grouping of teachers is by school so that discussion can be school-focused. We have found that this is a good way to cover several schools at one time. On average about 90 teachers complete their Module 1 training within a three-month term.

To cater to the needs of the non-pilot schools that wish to send only a handful of key teachers to be trained, we also continue with the traditional format of campus-based training courses for which enrolment is open to all teachers from both primary and secondary schools. Thus a class of 30 often comprises teachers from 15 to 20 schools. The advantage of such an approach is that it allows teachers from many different schools to interact and share professional views as well as to discuss practical problems, in this way obtaining mutual support and mutual help. Such open-enrolment courses are very popular, and each term there is often a demand for as many as ten classes at various levels of training, each class containing 20 to 40 teachers.

Regardless of the format of training, course work comprises lectures followed by group discussion and workshop activities. As the emphasis in training is on experiential learning, there is much opportunity for hands-on activities such as micro-counselling sessions. Two approaches are used in the training and supervision of counselling skills. The first is through videotaping of role-play sessions which are later replayed in class for critique and feedback by course lecturers and fellow participants. The second is by audio-taping of actual interview sessions conducted in schools which are then listened to in class in small groups for critique and feedback. Initially rather shy about having their taped sessions heard in class, most of the teachers eventually overcome their shyness and are able to benefit from these practical sessions.

Running these three training approaches simultaneously allows the Institute of Education to train 'generalist' pastoral care-givers at the rate of approximately 200 per term and 800 to 1000 per year. As the pastoral leaders require longer and more in-depth training, our plan is to produce about 30 to 40 'specialists' per year to function as pastoral leaders in the schools.

General feedback on the training programme

To evaluate the effectiveness of the courses and to ascertain how much teachers are able to put into practice what they have learnt, the participants are followed up three to six months after completion of their training. This is usually done through a survey using either the questionnaire or the interview method.

One such follow-up study was conducted in December 1988 with a random sample of 100 teachers from 10 secondary schools who had completed Module 1 training. As shown in Table 17.2, the results of this follow-up study revealed that at least 75 per cent of the respondents were able to apply the knowledge gained to understand their pupils better. They had also put their newly acquired group guidance and counselling skills to good use. When asked if they had the opportunity to develop a pastoral curriculum for use in their schools, about 50 per cent answered in the affirmative. More than half of the teachers had opportunities to share their knowledge with their colleagues. Lastly, 80 per cent of the teachers indicated that they had benefited from the training and would strongly recommend the course to their fellow teachers.

Another method of obtaining feedback is through informal meetings with principals and key teachers to obtain their views on the effectiveness of the training programme as measured by the level of functioning of the trained teachers. One such meeting was held at the Institute in October 1988. On the whole feedback from the principals present was both positive and encouraging. They felt that their teachers had

Table 17.2. Feedback on training (*N* = 100)

Comments	Response	
	Yes (%)	No (%)
I have used the knowledge learnt to understand my pupils better	75	25
I have applied the group guidance skills gained in tutoring my pupils	82	18
I have put the counselling skills learned to good use	62	38
I have been involved in the development of a pastoral curriculum	48	52
I will strongly recommend this course to my colleagues	80	20

benefited from the training. They also spoke enthusiastically in favour of the school-based approach, pointing out that it has the advantage of involving practically the whole teaching staff of the school, including the principal, and is therefore an effective way of promoting an environment conducive to a whole-school approach to implementing pastoral care in schools.

Comparing the effectiveness of the three approaches

To compare the effectiveness of the three different approaches in inservice training, a survey was conducted in March 1990 to obtain the views of participants.

In a questionnaire, they were asked to indicate on a five-point scale the extent to which they were satisfied or dissatisfied with various aspects of the training they had received. It is interesting to note that with the exception of one area, participants from the school-based courses consistently rated various aspects of the course higher than participants who had undergone the other two types of training. Their responses are computed and presented in Table 17.3.

Although essentially the course content was almost identical for all three types of courses, school-based training courses are usually preceded by a 'needs assessment meeting' between the school personnel and the course lecturer from the Institute to discuss specific needs of the school. Subsequently, the proposed syllabus would be adjusted. This probably explains why on the whole school-based course participants found the course content more relevant to their training needs. They also rated high the extent to which they had gained new knowledge from the training and were the most satisfied when asked to rate the adequacy of the training they had received in preparing them for their role as pastoral care-givers in schools.

In terms of lecturer–participant interaction, class involvement of the

Table 17.3. Feedback on the three formats of inservice training

Area of concern	School-based (N = 80) Mean	Institute-based (N = 54) Mean	Open enrolment (N = 90) Mean
Relevance of content	4.44	4.41	4.20
Organization of course	4.44	4.22	4.03
Lecturer–participant interaction	4.64	4.56	4.58
Ease/spontaneity	4.63	4.74	4.62
Participant–participant interaction	4.57	4.43	4.29
Gain in knowledge	4.28	4.13	3.94
Enjoyment	4.40	4.13	4.07
Motivation	3.84	3.57	3.86
Conviction	4.29	4.07	4.20
Satisfaction	4.28	4.04	4.02
Adequacy of training	4.18	3.74	3.69
Overall mean	4.36	4.19	4.14

participants and the degree to which they were at ease with each other, again school-based courses were the most favoured. As one participant put it: 'We already knew each other well and therefore felt free to interact.' Such free and active participation probably explained why this group were the most satisfied with the format of training. They were also the group that had enjoyed the course the most.

In response to the statement 'The course has convinced me of the relevance and importance of PCCG in schools', participants of school-based courses gave the highest rating. Considering that many of them had not been motivated in the beginning, being asked to attend the course rather than signing up on their own accord, this speaks much of the power and influence of the school-based approach in motivating and persuading the teachers of the need for and relevance of pastoral care, a necessary step in bringing about a whole-school approach in the implementation of pastoral care.

The one area that was rated in favour of the open enrolment approach pertained to the extent to which the training had stimulated and encouraged the participants to seek further training in the area. This was probably because the participants in these classes were motivated in the first place: they had signed up for the course voluntarily, whereas in the case of school-based training courses all staff members were asked to undergo the training regardless whether they subscribed to the concept of pastoral care or not.

When asked to identify the strengths and weaknesses of the various approaches, the participants made some interesting observations. As expected, the most frequently cited reason for their preferring the school-based approach to the other approaches was the convenience. As the classes were held in their own school, they did not have to travel: 'More time, less stress'. Second, familiarity with the classroom environment and fellow participants resulted in freer and more spontaneous interaction.

As for the disadvantages of the school-based approach, four were identified. The most obvious limitation was that they did not have the opportunity to interact with teachers from other schools for fresh ideas. As one participant put it, 'sharing of ideas was limited as we all come from a similar background and share similar ideas'. One teacher observed that as participants were all from the same school, 'sensitive issues could not be discussed openly in class'.

With regard to the open enrolment approach, about 40 per cent of the respondents were happy that such an approach gave them opportunities to meet teachers from other schools and to find out what was happening in the field. They were also appreciative of the fact that because of the open enrolment format, they had the autonomy to decide whether to attend or not. They could also choose to sign up at a time convenient to them. Another interesting observation was that since the participants enrolled for the course of their own accord, they were usually keen and motivated which 'made the learning fun'.

In terms of the disadvantages of the open enrolment approach, one area of concern was that the diverse needs of the participants made it difficult for the course lecturer to address the needs of all schools represented. Also, some participants felt inhibited and were reluctant to speak up in class. A few teachers lamented the fact that, because they signed up of their own accord, they did not receive much support from their principals and sometimes did not get the chance to practise what they had learnt in class. However, to judge from the responses, it was obvious that the advantages cited far outweighed the disadvantages.

Participants in the campus-based school-focused courses appeared to be at a disadvantage as they seemed to experience the dissatisfactions of both the school-based groups and the open enrolment groups. Like the former, they were asked to attend rather than being allowed to sign up voluntarily. To make matters worse, they had to travel to the Institute and some complained about transport problems. However, when one looked at the brighter side of things, such an approach also had its advantages. As pointed out by some teachers, because they 'shared the same problem and had the same vision', they could work well as a team. A few observed that the change of environment had done them some good as colleagues were more relaxed in a different environment. Some found this experience 'refreshing' and were delighted that they 'got to know each other better through attending the course'. All in all, the responses from all three groups of participants reflected a general satisfaction with the training.

Problems related to training

Although our training courses have been met with much enthusiastic response from the schools and the teachers, as in any new endeavour we also have our share of teething problems.

The first of these is related to the motivation of the teachers. While we have had the benefit of having many enthusiastic and highly motivated teachers participating in the training courses, there is still a minority of teachers who are sent to the courses rather than enrolling of their own accord. The result is a lukewarm attitude and half-hearted participation in the lectures and workshops. This problem seems to occur more often in the school-based inservice courses, where the whole teaching staff of the school are expected to participate in the training, regardless of whether they subscribe to the idea of pastoral care and career guidance or not. This is especially true in cases where the principal of a school is keen to implement pastoral care programmes and have the school staff trained but the latter do not share the same enthusiasm.

The second problem is related to the resistance to change found among a number of teachers and some principals. Sometimes keen teachers who have completed a training course return to their schools inspired and eager to try out new ideas learned, but, unfortunately, support from their colleagues and principals is not forthcoming. When their efforts to introduce changes and new programmes are thwarted by resistance from their colleagues, these teachers finally give up in disappointment and frustration.

From these experiences we have come to realize that if we want the training to be successful, it is imperative to involve the principals and administrators in the schools from the very beginning and convince them of the need for and the relevance of the inservice training. Being leaders in the schools, they are the people who set the pace and provide the necessary support for the teachers in the implementation phase.

Conclusion

The inservice training programmes I have described arose from a strong desire to meet a growing demand in teacher education in pastoral care in Singapore. They also reflect the concerted efforts of a team of teacher educators in search of better and more effective methods of preparing teachers as pastoral care-givers in schools. In the two years of experimentation, we have succeeded in some areas. We have also failed in other aspects. What is important, however, is that we have learnt valuable lessons in the process. Such a comforting thought is enough to urge us on.

References

d'Rozario, V. and Chia, L. (1988) Pastoral care in British schools: applications for Singapore. *Singapore Journal of Education*, special issues edn.

Hamblin, D. (1978) *The Teacher and Pastoral Care*. Oxford: Blackwell.

Hamblin, D. (1986) *The Teacher and Counselling*, 5th edn. Oxford: Blackwell.

Lang, P. (1988) Pastoral care: unique or universal? *Singapore Journal of Education*, 9(1), 19–27.

Lang, P. and Marland, M. (eds) (1985) *New Directions in Pastoral Care*. Oxford: Blackwell.

Ontario Ministry of Education (1985) *After 8? A Guide for Grade 8 Students and Their Parents*.

Tennyson, W.W., Miller, G.D., Skovholt, T.G. and Williams, R.C. (1989) Secondary school counselors: What do they do? What is important? *School Counselor*, 36, 253–9.

Thomas, M.D. (1989) The role of the secondary school counselor. *School Counselor*, 36, 249–52.

CHAPTER 18

Training needs in an international context

RON BEST AND PETER LANG

Introduction

There are a number of good reasons why attention should be focused upon the training and support needs of teachers whose roles include, to a greater or lesser extent, some responsibility for the delivery of the affective dimension of education. This is so whether the responsibility is ascribed (as in those systems of schooling where pastoral care and personal and social education are required of teachers in official statements of contractual obligation) or merely acquired (as in systems where such duties are taken on board as a commonsense part of the daily work of any teacher).

First, teachers need to be trained. Although it is sometimes argued that 'good teachers are born and not made', if this is true at all, it is only true at the margins. Some teachers do seem to have outstanding qualities of personality or charisma, or seem to have natural 'gifts' for recognizing a pupil's needs, or for winning pupils' co-operation, but even such 'gifted' individuals require some kind of training to be able to put these qualities to good use in classrooms.

In any case, some kind of training is implicit in the mission of education. As Peters (1966) argued in the 1960s, teaching is not an activity which can be engaged in by accident, or in passing. It is an *intentional* activity, and that means that those who decide that teaching should take place must be committed to the *planned* provision of learning experiences. It is not enough to want something to happen: steps must be taken to ensure that it does, and where teaching and caring are concerned this surely must include planning to equip teachers with the skills necessary to convert commitment into practice.

Second, there has been too little attention given to the preparation of teachers for the affective dimension of their roles, either because it is held to be unimportant, or because it is assumed to be delivered through the transmission of curricular knowledge. The introduction to a recent document providing guidelines for tutors and tutorial work in Spanish schools (CEVE, 1990) puts it this way:

Education properly understood must have two aspects: instructive and formative. Through the first, the student progressively acquires culture, mastery of knowledge and science. With the second, he develops as a person integrating attitudes, values and aspirations until he reaches a personal maturity which enables him to integrate in society as an individual person, free and responsible ... [T]here is a lot of emphasis on the first role, the instructional aspect ... on evaluation, marking, assessment.... However, the formative aspect frequently receives secondary value and it is assumed that by emphasizing the first you achieve the second, but this is not always true. Teachers usually give less emphasis to the formative and guidance role of the school, which is a mistake.

Third, precisely because education has for so long, in the minds of so many, been equated with the transmission of a body of knowledge organized into an (academic) curriculum, it is to this end that training has most often been directed. It is part of the commonsense wisdom of societies that teachers are expected to have a greater command of the facts and concepts of school knowledge than the 'ordinary' person. 'Fancy a teacher not knowing that!' is a common enough exclamation when a member of the profession is found wanting in knowledge of some piece of trivia. So a good deal of teacher training has always been devoted to the mastery of teaching subjects.

Teachers are often expected to be knowledgeable also about the methods by which that knowledge can be transmitted to others. Practical technique is often valued above theoretical knowledge, and it is now commonplace for training courses to be criticized for giving insufficient attention to the development of pedagogical skills. In some cases this represents a significant change in attitude. In Italy, for instance, secondary school teachers are not usually required to have undergone any training in pedagogical skills, and in England many graduate teachers have in fact received very little such training. Whether the inference is justified that such teachers are poor educators is, of course, another matter.

Finally, there is a general expectation that teachers will have the skills and presence necessary to exercise control over the behaviour of a class of children. In the extreme, teachers may be held accountable for misbehaviour or indiscipline outside and after schooling. In the UK certainly, and in all likelihood elsewhere, juvenile delinquency, sport-related 'hooliganism', drug abuse and sexual precocity have all at one time or another been attributed by the popular press to a supposed decline in teachers' skill in controlling their pupils. Most people would expect skills development in this area also to feature prominently in teacher training.

According to Hargreaves (1972), the predominant perspective among teachers also stresses these dimensions of instruction and discipline. He argues that teachers see their roles in these terms, and that students are labelled as 'good', 'bad', 'under-' or 'over-achiever' according to the degree to which they 'please the teacher' on these two criteria. We think this is a common and fairly realistic perspective in most cultures, and it is reasonable to expect the cognitive and the behavioural domains to dominate training.

The *affective* domain, with its involvement in the personal, social and moral aspects of self, receives much less consideration.

As the chapters in this book demonstrate, at the level of general principles there is much common ground between the countries and systems they represent. However, there are significant differences within and between cultures in regard to the shape and style that pastoral care takes, and in regard to the way the teacher's role is perceived.

The degree to which the contribution which schools make to the affective, personal, social and moral development of children is felt to require the skills of a specialist is one dimension along which systems vary. For example, if this area is handled at all in France, it is by specialists based and working outside the school. In the UK, primary school teachers tend to accept pastoral work as integral to their roles as class teachers whereas in secondary schools, where the basic role of form tutor may be filled, without remuneration, by any teacher, the specialist middle-management roles of head of year/house/section draw an extra allowance. In Denmark, the class teacher as generalist is the main medium for personal and social education, and this is attributed explicitly to the quality of training:

> With the exception of vocational guidance in the 7th to 10th class, the extra functions of the class teacher carry no extra remuneration or benefits, being seen as a normal part of the teacher's job.... the majority of class teachers accept the socio-pedagogical aspect of their work, perceiving it as equally important as specific subject teaching. As a result of the breadth and depth of teacher training in Denmark, most teachers will at some point assume the functions of class teacher. (Denmark Ministry of Education, 1988, p. 8)

What counts as 'personal', 'social' and 'moral' in the development of the child also varies from one system to another. In some cases, considerable emphasis is given to the significance for the person, of the connection between schooling and the development of human capital through careers guidance and education (see Chapter 8). In others (e.g. Chapter 11) a particular concern with the religious or spiritual dimension of the self shapes the pastoral curriculum in distinctive ways. In yet others, a social welfare perspective emphasizes the moral right of the individual for support through schooling and school-related social services (see Chapters 9 and 10). Finally, the role of counselling skills and theories in reactive casework and proactive coping strategies is more readily accepted in some cultures than others (see Chapters 5 and 6).

All these contributors and the systems they describe recognize that an 'education' limited to the purely cognitive would be unacceptably narrow. There is evidence here of the growing recognition among teachers of the importance also of the affective domain. The question we wish to raise in this chapter is the degree to which teacher training recognizes the importance for the development of effective teachers of the bodies of concepts, facts, skills, attitudes and values necessary for meeting the welfare needs of pupils and for promoting appropriately their personal and social development.

A picture of inadequacy

In the last fifteen years or so, a number of published reports have commented on the inadequacies of pastoral care and personal and social education in schools. Explicitly or implicitly, these reflect upon the quality of training teachers receive for pastoral roles.

In 1980 a NSW (Australia) Department of Education Committee of Enquiry into Pupil Behaviour and Discipline in Schools established a direct connection between the attitude adopted by schools towards pupils (and, indeed parents) and pupil behaviour (Committee of Enquiry, 1980, p. 11):

> Our visits [to schools] also confirmed that the most frequent behaviour problems were those often associated with schools rather than with the home. . . . it would seem that in most schools, teachers and pupils alike work hard and have solid achievements to show for their efforts. These schools are orderly communities where thought and time are given to promoting the well-being of individual pupils.

In this context, pastoral care and personal and social development programmes designed to promote self-esteem, motivation to study and social skills played an important part (ibid.):

> It was our impression that under adverse circumstances the staff of these [new, large and under-resourced] schools had devised programs to assist pupils who have difficulty with the school situation. One school we visited, had established a program that emphasized the value of praise to motivate studies and others conducted successful pastoral care programs. Many of these schools served as the 'focus' for their local community and provided a range of services not always found in other schools.

The report goes on to observe (p. 15) that a

> lack of self-esteem can foster feelings of worthlessness and failure and the idea that there is no benefit in schooling. This with boredom can soon lead to disruptive and inattentive behaviour. Courses to promote the self-esteem of both boys and girls have become relatively common in secondary schools through personal development, non-sexist education and living skills programs. These programs appear to be reasonably successful although at times they suffer from a lack of resources and appropriately trained staff.

The report records a general dissatisfaction with pre-service training expressed by many beginning teachers (pp. 40–41):

> The common elements of their criticisms were: insufficient teaching practice, lack of instruction in the basic principles of classroom

management and lack of preparation for dealing with discipline problems.... The staff of some schools we visited also argued that pre-service teacher education programs did not equip beginning teachers with the skills required to identify and interpret the needs of the individual child. They believed that this was a particular problem when the child had a class or cultural background that differed from the teacher's background.

The connection between a teacher's ability to empathize across cultures and to control behaviour is interesting, as is the importance for good discipline, of the teacher's awareness of individual needs. That these and other skills necessary for sound pastoral work were judged to be neglected in initial training led the Committee to include the following in its recommendations (pp. 77–8): that

2. a thorough and comprehensive programme of in-service training for teachers involved in personal and social development programs be established to develop skills in such areas as relationships with others, fostering pupil self-esteem, and developing pupils' communication and decision-making skills ...

16. in-service courses covering various aspects of counselling be made available at the state and regional level ...

Four years later, comparable conclusions were reached by a survey undertaken in the UK on behalf of the National Association for Pastoral Care in Education (NAPCE) (Maher and Best, 1985). Questionnaire responses from teachers in 18 schools, interview data and questionnaire responses from lecturers in 12 training institutions, and written responses from representatives of ten local education authorities (LEAs) painted a depressing picture where training and support for pastoral roles was concerned.

Of the 91 schoolteacher respondents (other than headteachers) only six commented on their initial training in positive terms. The remainder considered that 'their initial training contained either a negligible amount of work on pastoral care topics or nothing at all' (Maher and Best, 1985, p. 53). This was confirmed by the colleges survey, where few courses were identified as having a visible concern with pastoral care or personal and social education. In the one-year Post-Graduate Certificate in Education (PGCE) courses, typically as little as half a day was devoted to these topics. Only two colleges said they took account of pastoral work in assessing students on teaching practice. In summary (Maher and Best, 1985, p. 54):

The vast majority of our teacher sample could not recall any training that was relevant to their pastoral role in school; those who could, for the most part found the experience of little practical value.

Inservice training opportunities were more favourably described. Over half the teacher respondents claimed to have been on INSET courses to do with pastoral care, and these were generally felt to have been of value. However, availability of courses of differing levels and duration varied enormously from one geographical area to another, and provision generally did not provide a systematic pattern of opportunities for teachers at various levels of the pastoral structure.

Two reports from Her Majesty's Inspectors (HMI) suggest that training is still inadequate.

A 1986-7 survey of PSE courses in 21 secondary schools in England and Wales (DES, 1988) found the quality of such courses to be very patchy. A significant proportion of the schools gave inadequate attention to planning, timetabling, resourcing, co-ordinating and evaluating the programmes they provided. There was a lack of balance between the personal, social and vocational elements of many courses, and all too often the staff allocated to teach these programmes were reluctant to be involved in this part of the curriculum. Both the teaching and co-ordination of these courses appeared to have suffered because of inadequacies in training opportunities. As HMI (1988, pp. 10-11) concluded:

> virtually all degree courses leading to a teaching qualification can provide teachers interested in PSE with some relevant knowledge, understanding and skills. Nevertheless, it did appear that neither initial training nor long courses which were concerned specifically with PSE had been readily available or accessible to teachers in the survey.... It was clear that many teachers, particularly those with co-ordinating responsibilities, would have benefited from opportunities to consider, with others on a course, the nature of PSE and its place in the curriculum.

Much the same was said in the light of a 1987-8 survey of pastoral care in 27 secondary schools (DES, 1989). Teachers appeared to be ill-prepared to meet the demands of either pastoral casework with individuals or the delivery of a pastoral curriculum, and there was little evidence of this deficiency being made good through INSET (DES, 1989, p. 40):

> It was clear that there was a widespread need for training in various areas including counselling, interviewing and group work skills and record keeping. However, it was a matter of some concern that opportunities for teachers to receive in-service training relevant to pastoral care responsibilities were limited.

Nor was the training available adequate for those who co-ordinate teams of form tutors and PSE teachers (ibid., pp. 39-40):

> It was unusual to find any teachers with pastoral management responsibilities who had received a major relevant element of initial teacher training.... Formal qualifications can only be acquired at a later stage, when teachers have gained some professional experience. Only a small minority of teachers [in the survey] had such qualifications. Degree qualifications, other training and professional experience helped in many cases to prepare staff in general terms to exercise pastoral reponsibilities. However, the rarity of relevant formal qualifications must be a matter requiring review.

These reports, and their equivalents in other countries give cause for concern, but they should not be seen as entirely negative. They are, themselves, evidence of an increased awareness of the broader roles that teachers play, and of the importance of being adequately trained to fill them. The question is: how might better training be provided?

Better training

Reports like those considered above provide important pointers to deficiencies in training in at least a significant number of education systems. An understandable response is to provide programmes of inservice training to make good some of these deficiencies. This was a conclusion reached by the authorities in both the UK and New South Wales reports. However, it is possible to argue that this is not necessarily the most sensible way to proceed.

For one thing, on the principle that 'prevention is better than cure', priority ought perhaps to be given to initial training to ensure that at least the future generations of teachers are better equipped than those in the past. As noted above, in some cases teachers do not receive any training over and above their degree, so an emphasis on initial training would not be misplaced. Moreover, it is arguable that the purpose of inservice training should be to extend the professional through post-experience training, building upon the firm foundations laid by initial training, rather than to serve an exclusively 'remedial' purpose.

Third, since the identification of deficiencies is possible only against some template of the ideal training, it might be better to begin with an analysis of what it is that we are asking teachers to do under the headings of 'pastoral care', 'PSE' and the like, and then begin to determine what sort of training they need. Such an analysis might then distinguish between the knowledge and skills required by every teacher – the pastoral 'generalist' – and those required by specialist counsellors, middle-managers and co-ordinators, and between those skills which are better acquired before beginning teaching and those which are more usefully developed in the light of some years of professional experience.

Even the notion that certain aspects of training are appropriate only to one or the other, and that such training must therefore be provided separately is simplistic. In the UK, the Open University's 'IT/INSET' scheme some years ago provided one model of the way in which the inservice training of teachers and the initial training of students might be brought together, and in the University of East Anglia, experiments in bringing inservice MA and initial PGCE students together for work on pastoral topics has met with some success (Whittaker, 1986).

There have been a number of attempts to produce an objectives-based scheme of training for pastoral roles. The NAPCE policy statement on initial training for pastoral roles explicitly chooses to focus on goals rather than making specific prescriptions for training (NAPCE, 1985, p. 74). The training goals are identified by focusing upon the role of the form tutor, since this is the pastoral role in which most beginning teachers will find themselves soon after they enter the profession. The role is then analysed (NAPCE, 1985, pp. 74–5) according to:

(i) Goals: what the role is created to achieve

(ii) Structure: how the role relates to other roles

(iii) Tasks: what is to be done by the role-holder

(iv) Skills: expertise which the role-holder needs to engage

(v) Resources: materials and technology required to achieve the goals.

Training goals are thus identified (ibid., p. 76) as:

(i) an appreciation of (and commitment to) the goals

(ii) an understanding of the structure and its use

(iii) a recognition of the nature of the tasks

(iv) a training in the skills

(v) a knowledge of the resources required.

From there on, the planning of a training course is no different from that of any other course designed according to what is usually known as the 'objectives model' of curriculum planning: determining appropriate learning experiences which will lead to the desired goals, deciding who is to provide them, by what teaching methods, and using what locations and resources.

A later NAPCE statement concentrated upon inservice needs using a comparable model (NAPCE, 1986). Beginning with the conventional hierarchy of pastoral roles in British comprehensive schools – form tutor, head of house/year/division, deputy head (pastoral) – the reader was provided with a detailed set of goals for programmes designed to provide the knowledge, skills and understandings requisite for each level.

Both these statements are of value, yet from an international perspective they share a fundamental flaw. By beginning with analyses of the requirements of conventional roles, those roles, and the structures within which they are located, are taken for granted. As the chapters in this book make abundantly clear, the structures of institutionalized roles by which pastoral care and PSE may be provided vary greatly both within and across education systems in different parts of the world. The NAPCE prescriptions for the UK might require substantial adaptation to make them fit in other places. They may not even fit too well in a UK system significantly altered by changes in funding, the prospect of 'opting-out' into the grant-maintained sector and the advent of a National Curriculum with its associated testing procedures.

It might be better to begin with an analysis of what pastoral care and PSE are. In this way, the related questions of, on the one hand, the knowledge and skills necessary for task performance and, on the other, the structure of roles appropriate for the allocation of those tasks, might both be addressed without pre-emption by current custom and practice.

A model

One such model has been developed and refined over many years (Best *et al.*, 1983; Best and Ribbins, 1983; Lang and Ribbins, 1985; Best, 1988b, 1989) and has now been specifically applied to training (Best, 1990). According to this model, the broad area of a school's work with which this book is concerned – loosely identified as 'pastoral care and PSE' – may be broken down into four major functions. Each function is designed in terms of the needs of the child in one of three roles: child, pupil and citizen in the community of the school.

Pastoral casework is largely reactive, providing at times of anxiety, distress or unhappiness, the counselling, guidance and moral support individual children may reasonably expect in their dependent relationship with the teacher. The *pastoral curriculum* is proactive and comprises intentional learning experiences designed to provide pupils with the coping strategies and personal/social skills necessary to minimize 'critical incidents' (Hamblin, 1978) as well as developmental programmes designed to promote their personal, social and moral development. The third dimension – that which has to do with the creation and maintenance of an orderly social environment – is most often identified with discipline, but is rather better conceived as *promoting the school as a community* within which the child may grow and flourish as a citizen. Since a set of shared rules and a system of sanctions is a necessary part of any effective community, the connection with discipline is not inappropriate (Best, 1988a), but we wish to stress also the positive promotion of well-being which comes from opportunities to engage in corporate activities, to share a common sense of purpose and a feeling of belonging, and to accept mutual responsibility for one another.

How an education system organizes itself to provide casework, curriculum and community/control may vary. At the risk of labouring the point, the conventional roles may not be the most effective division of labour for this purpose. Indeed, the degree to which 'generalists' rather than 'specialists' can deliver these is open to debate. In any event, some management, co-ordination or leadership is going to be necessary. Therefore, a fourth dimension – that of *pastoral management* – needs to be added to the model. An important part of this management function will be the organization of training and support for all those who provide pastoral care.

From this model, it is possible to infer the kinds of concepts, skills, facts and attitudes that staff require to perform effectively on each dimension.

Pastoral casework will require interpersonal skills of all kinds in order to get to know children and establish the conditions for trust between teacher and pupil. Many of the skills associated with counselling are relevant here, including the skills of listening, questioning, reflecting back and affirming, by which the teacher may help the child come to a clearer understanding of her or his own feelings, needs and attitudes.

The pastoral curriculum will require all the skills needed for teaching conventional subjects, but there are others necessitated by the distinctive character of personal and social education. Competence is necessary in setting up and controlling group activities including role-play, socio-drama and other simulations, as is skill in facilitating the exploration and discussion of personal experiences, and in handling issues of a moral, political and ethical nature. In this context, teachers need what Button (1974) has described as a 'repertoire of techniques' in the developmental group work which an effective pastoral curriculum requires.

Since behavioural problems are frequently associated with personal, social and emotional problems, all the skills of casework will be required where pastoral work focuses upon discipline. In addition, teachers need to be skilful in defusing highly charged situations, and in negotiating the resolution of confrontations in ways which are face-saving for all parties. More importantly, they need to understand the importance of analysing behavioural patterns in order to identify causes and 'triggers' of such situations (Watkins and Wagner, 1987), and in managing activities which build a sense of corporate identity and community membership.

Effective pastoral management requires skills of a different order. Whereas the activities involved in casework, curriculum and control/community are aimed at meeting the needs of the children directly, the function of pastoral management is to facilitate that work by meeting the needs of the staff. This demands knowledge and skills in team-building and co-ordination, resource management, curriculum planning, monitoring, appraisal and evaluation, in communicating and recording information, and in negotiation with staff at all levels.

The range of skills involved in effective provision for the affective realm of human development – including the activities generally described by terms like 'pastoral care', 'personal', 'social', 'moral' and 'health education' – is clearly very wide. Many of these skills may also be important for the other work which teachers do, but for pastoral work they are crucial. This is not to say that all these skills are needed to the same extent by all teachers. As already noted, that is dependent upon the division of labour set up by the system in question. What is certain is that, in any system, a useful start may be made by asking, first, to whom might responsibilities for the provision of casework, curriculum and control/community be given; and, second, which knowledge, skills and understandings are needed by everyone, and which only by those specializing in particular tasks.

Esther Tan (see Chapter 17 above) describes how such an approach has been employed effectively in Singapore. Backed by a commitment to institutionalize pastoral care on the UK model, and it having been determined that existing and anticipated staffing levels made a concentration of training on large numbers of specialist school counsellors unviable, a two-tier system of training was initiated. A modular course was then designed to meet the training needs of both the first-level 'generalists' and second-level 'specialists'. The first four modules, which every teacher is encouraged to take, are characterized by some exciting innovations in teaching methods. It is not our purpose to describe these in detail, but we may note that the use made of art, music and drama in training teachers for work in basic guidance is novel and effective (d'Rozario *et al.*, 1992).

Training in context

We have spoken thus far of training somewhat in isolation from two things with which it ought to be closely linked. The first is the *appraisal of staff* in the context of the evaluation of the programmes they teach. Many teachers are apprehensive when appraisal is mentioned. Fearing a critical verdict from superiors who are thought to have at best only a partial understanding of the circumstances and events with which class teachers have to contend, appraisal is seen by many as something to be avoided. Yet it is difficult to see how, once the teacher is in post, staff development which is not related to appraisal of some sort is defensible. For without some assessment of present performance, there are no rational grounds for seeking to improve expertise.

This is a microcosm of the relationship between curriculum evaluation and curriculum development. As noted earlier, calls for the provision of initial and inservice training are frequently the result of enquiries into the suitability and effectiveness of teachers' work. The HMI reports in the UK are cases in point. There are good grounds, therefore, for pastoral training to be founded not only on the kind of analysis of the purposes of affective education described earlier, but also on systematic and on-going evaluation of current provision (Clemett and Pearce, 1986).

The second is what might be termed *pastoral support for staff.* In some quarters, the question: 'Who cares for the carers?' has become something of a cliché (see, for example, Dunham, 1987; Stibbs, 1987). It expresses a perceived mismatch between the declared (and sometimes real) commitment of the educational decision-makers to caring for the pupils, and their perceived treatment of the staff who are supposed to provide this care. Teachers recognize the demands on them to provide moral support and positive motivation to their pupils, yet feel that they receive in their turn little by way of positive appreciation or feedback from their senior colleagues.

Related to this is the stress which teachers experience in their working lives and the disaffection to which this can lead. This is well documented in more than one of the countries dealt with in this book (see, for example, Galloway *et al.*, 1987; Freeman, 1987; Booth and Coulby, 1987). All teaching is potentially stressful, but perhaps pastoral work is particularly so. Working with children who are distressed, disturbed or otherwise in trouble is bound to be stressful. So, too, is teaching a PSE programme which confronts head-on issues of great sensitivity (e.g. sexual relationships). Where there are no arrangements to alleviate this stress, 'burn-out' or break-down is the likely outcome (Vernon, 1987).

In many cases, the best sort of support that can be given to teachers under stress is training: training that provides insight, knowledge, understanding and skills which equip the teacher much better to perform the tasks required of her or him.

Yet technical training alone does not go far enough. Advice on how to teach more effectively is not going to cut much ice with the teacher who is unhappy and isolated socially within the staff, whose domestic life is in turmoil, or who is on the edge of a nervous breakdown. As Lodge *et al.* (1992, p. 10) point out, in addition to professional needs, teachers need

- feelings of belonging to a group which values one for oneself
- opportunities to give and receive love and affection
- opportunities to 'grow' emotionally and psychologically
- opportunities to 'let off steam', express deeply held feelings, beliefs and fears
- [to be] forgiven for unacceptable actions.

If the concern for others as *persons* rather than role-incumbents is to be more than mere rhetoric, then personal support of one kind or another is needed as well. Sometimes this is provided as moral support from self-help groups. Sometimes it comes from informal social groups outside of formal school time. Sometimes it is provided by senior colleagues in a counsellor role. All too often, it isn't provided at all.

Conclusion

Throughout this chapter we have been at pains to recognize the wide variations to be found in the way the affective dimension of schooling is understood and delivered in different cultures. The discussion has been limited by our partial and uneven knowledge of the education systems of other countries, and it might be argued that such generalizations as have been ventured here are built on shaky ground. In spite of this, we have argued that there are some general principles which can be applied in contemplating appropriate training for teachers in caring roles.

In the final analysis, well-conceived structures and programmes for the related activities of pastoral care, PSE and affective education will be no more effective than the teachers who fill the posts and deliver the caring. Adequate training – both initial and inservice – has a crucial part to play in this, though there is enormous scope for variations in emphasis, organization and delivery. Clearly, the acquisition of appropriate knowledge and skills is very important, but this alone is unlikely to be achieved if the teachers themselves have not arrived at an appreciation of the importance of the affective domain in human development; if they have not grasped the reasons why they might be expected to involve themselves in pastoral work or the justifications that might be offered for their participation in programmes of guidance or personal and social education.

Whatever form training takes, it must promote the values of caring, mutual concern, justice and respect for persons (whether adults or children, colleagues or parents). It must also promote teachers' self-awareness, and their capacity to empathize with their pupils, through reflection upon their own experiences as learners. It must promote critical reflection and self-evaluation without which no teacher can be truly professional. Unless teachers are brought to the point where they embrace such values, their application to the task is likely to be half-hearted and misconceived.

But teachers are human too. As well as training and self-awareness, they need moral and emotional support. Just as an excessive pre-occupation with the cognitive domain produces a narrow (and narrowing) curriculum for the pupil, so a preoccupation with technical skills may deny teachers the support they need as persons.

As the Singapore example shows, much can be achieved by imaginative and innovative approaches to training and support. But this is only one model. There is good practice elsewhere also if we care to look. Clearly, we have as much to learn from one another here as we do in any other aspect of education.

References

Best, R. (1988a) Care or Control: are we getting it right? *Pastoral Care in Education*, 6(2), 2–9.

Best, R. (1988b) Monitoring and evaluating pastoral care. In SEAS: *The Pupil's Growth – Our Major Concern*, Proceedings of the third biennial seminar of the Singapore Educational Administration Society, Singapore.

Best, R. (1989) Pastoral care: some reflections and a re-statement. *Pastoral Care in Education*, 7(4), 7–13.

Best, R. (1990) Pastoral care in schools: some implications for training. *Australian Journal of Teacher Education*, 15(1), 18–23.

Best, R. and Ribbins, P. (1983) Rethinking the pastoral–academic split. *Pastoral Care in Education*, 1(1), 11–18.

Best, R., Ribbins, P., Jarvis, C. and Oddy, D. (1983) *Education and Care*. London: Heinemann.

Booth, T. and Coulby, D. (eds) (1987) *Producing and Reducing Disaffection*. Milton Keynes: Open University Press.

Button, L. (1974) *Developmental Group Work with Adolescents*. London: Hodder & Stoughton.

CEVE (1990) *Orientación y Tutoría*. Madrid: CEVE Estudios a Distancia.

Clemett, A.J. and Pearce, J.S. (1986) *The Evaluation of Pastoral Care*. Oxford: Blackwell.

Committee of Enquiry into Pupil Behaviour and Discipline in Schools (1980) *Self-Discipline and Pastoral Care*. Sydney: NSW Department of Education.

Denmark Ministry of Education (1988) *The Folkeskole: Primary and Lower Secondary Education in Denmark*. Copenhagen: Ministry of Education.

DES (1988) *A Survey of Personal and Social Education Courses in some Secondary Schools*. London: Department of Education and Science.

DES (1989) *Pastoral Care in Secondary Schools: An Inspection of some Aspects of Pastoral Care in 1987-8*. London: Department of Education and Science.

d'Rozario, V., Khoo, A. and Soong, C. (1992) Using creative arts in the training of pastoral care-givers in Singapore. *Pastoral Care in Education*, 10(1), 43-9.

Dunham, J. (1987) Caring for the pastoral carers. *Pastoral Care in Education*, 5(1).

Freeman, A. (1987) Pastoral care and teacher stress. *Pastoral Care in Education*, 5(1), 22-8.

Galloway, D., Panckhurst, F., Boswell, C. and Green, K. (1987) Sources of stress for class teachers in New Zealand primary schools. *Pastoral Care in Education*, 5(1), 28-36.

Hamblin, D.H. (1978) *The Teacher and Pastoral Care*. Oxford: Blackwell.

Hargreaves, D.H. (1972) *Interpersonal Relations and Education*. London: Routledge.

Lang, P.L.F. and Ribbins, P. (1985) Pastoral Care in Education. In *International Encyclopedia of Education*. Oxford: Pergamon.

Lodge, C., McLaughlin, C. and Best, R. (1992) Organizing pastoral support for teachers: some comments and a model. *Pastoral Care in Education*, 10(2), 7-12.

Maher, P. and Best, R. (1985) Preparation and support for pastoral care: a survey of current provision. In Lang, P. and Marland, M. (eds), *New Directions in Pastoral Care*. Oxford: Blackwell/NAPCE.

NAPCE (1985) Initial training for the pastoral aspect of the teacher's role. *Pastoral Care in Education*, 3(1), 73-7.

NAPCE (1986) *Inservice Training for the Pastoral Aspect of the Teacher's Role*. Oxford: Blackwell.

Peters, R.S. (1966) *Ethics and Education*. London: Allen & Unwin.

Stibbs, J. (1987) Staff care and development. *Pastoral Care in Education* 5(1).

Vernon, M. (1987) A burnt-out case. In Booth, T. and Coulby, D. (eds), *Producing and Reducing Disaffection*. Milton Keynes: Open University Press.

Watkins, C. and Wagner, P. (1987) *School Discipline: A Whole-School Approach*. Oxford: Blackwell.

Whittaker, R. (1986) Combining in-service and initial training in pastoral care. *Pastoral Care in Education*, 4(1), 47-51.

Index

Name index

Subject index